A CITIZENS' EUROPE

In Search of a New Order

edited by

Allan Rosas and Esko Antola

SAGE Publications

London • Thousand Oaks • New Delhi

First published 1995

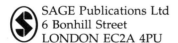 SAGE Publications Ltd
6 Bonhill Street
LONDON EC2A 4PU

SAGE Publications Inc
2455 Teller Road
Thousand Oaks, California 91320

SAGE Publications India Pvt Ltd
32, M–Block Market
Greater Kailash – I
New Delhi 110 048

British Library Cataloguing in Publication data

A catalogue record for this book is
available from the British Library.

ISBN 0 8039 7560 0
ISBN 0 8039 7561 9 pbk

Library of Congress catalog card number 95-67020

Printed in Great Britain at the University Press, Cambridge

CONTENTS

ACKNOWLEDGEMENTS

This book originated in a research project on 'A Citizens' Europe: Democracy and Participation', which was sponsored by the Academy of Finland. A planning meeting for the book was held in Turku/Åbo in December 1993. Dr Nanette Neuwahl was instrumental in the planning process and in bringing together an eminent group of authors. A workshop with the authors was organized in Turku/Åbo in July 1994, when the Turku archipelago was at its very best.

Many individuals at the Department of Law and the Institute for Human Rights of Åbo Akademi University have lent a helping hand throughout this project. Johanna Bondas and Raija Hanski deserve special thanks for their full commitment to making this project come true. George Maude was kind enough to help in checking the language and style of some of the chapters.

Last but not least, we are very grateful to the authors for devoting their precious time to this enterprise, and to Sage Publications for producing the final volume.

Allan Rosas and Esko Antola

Turku/Åbo, December 1994

CONTRIBUTORS

Esko Antola is Associate Professor in the Department of Political Science of the University of Turku and Director of the Institute for European Affairs, Turku, Finland. Together with Allan Rosas, he is coordinator of the project on 'A Citizens' Europe: Democracy and Participation', sponsored by the Academy of Finland.

Andrew Evans is a Research Fellow in the Department of Economics at the European University Institute in Florence and a Visiting Professor of Law at the University of Umeå (Sweden). He has previously taught at the Universities of Dundee and Liverpool.

Kay Hailbronner holds the chair of European law and public international law at the University of Konstanz. He is the director of the Research Centre for the International and European Law of Aliens.

Erik Lundberg is a doctoral student at Åbo Akademi University. He is a research fellow with the project on 'A Citizens' Europe: Democracy and Participation', sponsored by the Academy of Finland.

Epaminondas A. Marias is an adjunct Assistant Professor at Vesalius College, Free University of Brussels. He is the Director of the Institute of Continuing Training of the National Centre of Public Administration in Athens.

Karlheinz Neunreither is an honorary professor at Heidelberg University and presently chairman of the International Political Science Associations' Research Committee on European Integration. He is a Director General with the European Parliament and responsible for parliamentary committees and legislative coordination.

Nanette A. Neuwahl is lecturer in law at the University of Leicester. She holds degrees from the University of Leiden and the European University Institute (PhD) in Florence. Her research centres on issues of European integration, especially where questions of competence and powers and the relationships between different legal orders are concerned.

Siofra O'Leary is visiting fellow at the University of Cadiz, where she is in charge of a project on 'Subsidiarity and the Regions in the EC', sponsored by the Spanish Ministry for Education and Science. She obtained her doctorate in law from the European University Institute in Florence on the subject on European citizenship.

Hans Ulrich Jessurun d'Oliveira is professor at the European University Institute in Florence (1987–1994) and at the University of Amsterdam. He teaches and writes on jurisprudence, comparative law, private international law, European law and migration law.

Allan Rosas is Armfelt Professor of Law and Director of the Institute for Human Rights of Åbo Akademi University. He is coordinator of the project on 'A Citizens' Europe: Democracy and Participation', sponsored by the Academy of Finland.

Teija Tiilikainen is a doctoral student at Åbo Akademi University. She is also a research fellow with the project on 'A Citizens' Europe: Democracy and Participation', sponsored by the Academy of Finland. She is chairperson of the Finnish International Studies Association and Editor-in-Chief of *Politiikka,* a Finnish journal of political science.

ABBREVIATIONS

ACP	Asian, Caribbean and Pacific States
Bull. EC	Bulletin of the European Communities
CCPR	International Covenant on Civil and Political Rights
CDE	Cahiers de Droit Européen
CFSP	Common Foreign and Security Policy
CIREA	Centre for Information, Discussion and Exchange on Asylum
CIREFI	Centre for Information, Discussion and Exchange on the Crossing of Borders and Immigration
CMLR	Common Market Law Reports
CML Rev.	Common Market Law Review
COM	Commission
CSCE	Conference on Security and Cooperation in Europe
EC	European Community
ECHR	Convention for the Protection of Fundamental Freedoms and Human Rights
ECJ	Court of Justice of the European Communities
ECR	European Court Reports
ECSC	European Coal and Steel Community
EEA	European Economic Area
EEC	European Economic Community
EFTA	European Free Trade Association
EJIL	European Journal of International Law
EL Rev.	European Law Review
EP	European Parliament
ETS	European Treaty Series
EU	European Union
Eu GRZ	Europäische Grundrechte Zeitschrift
EURATOM	European Atomic Energy Community
GATT	General Agreement on Tariffs and Trade
ICLQ	International and Comparative Law Quarterly
IHRR	International Human Rights Reports
ILM	International Law Materials
ILRM	Irish Law Reports Monthly
IO	International Organization
JCMS	Journal of Common Market Law Studies
JO	Journal Officiel
LIEI	Legal Issues of European Integration

MLR	Modern Law Review
MNS	Migration News Sheet
NILR	Netherlands International Law Review
NJW	Neue Juristische Wochenschrift
NYIL	Netherlands Yearbook of International Law
OEEC	Organization for European Economic Cooperation
OJ	Official Journal
PE	Parlement Européen
RdC	Recueil des Cours d l'Académie de Droit International de la Haye
RDI	Revue de Droit International, de Sciences Diplomatiques et Politiques
RMC	Revue du marché commun et de l'union européenne
RUDH	Revue Universelle des Droits de l'Homme
SEA	Single European Act
SEC	Document of the Secretariat-General of the Commission
TEU	Treaty on European Union
UDHR	Universal Declaration of Human Rights
YEL	Yearbook of European Law
ZRP	Zeitschrift für Rechtspolitik

1 CITIZENS AND THE EXERCISE OF POWER IN THE EUROPEAN UNION: TOWARDS A NEW SOCIAL CONTRACT?

Karlheinz Neunreither

1 THE IDENTITY CRISIS OF THE EUROPEAN UNION AND THE DESPERATE SEARCH FOR THE CITIZEN

The campaign for European elections in June 1994 confirmed a trend which had been emerging for about two years: all major political groupings have discovered citizens and put them as a major emblem or trademark on the political commodities they have to sell. A 'Europe of the citizens' has become the common slogan for almost all political competitors. If one turns the front page of the various pamphlets and reads beyond the introductory chapter, the citizen is usually quickly forgotten and one is confronted with the traditional party programme or electoral platform. In programmes following an integrationist approach you may find proposals concerning the strengthening of representative democracy, usually by giving more powers to the European Parliament. On the other hand, subsidiarity is evoked as a potentially powerful principle to bring the exercise of power closer to the citizen and to limit centralizing tendencies.

The smoothness of the coming into force of the Single European Act (SEA) and the substantial success it had both inside and outside the Community—including a completely new appraisal from the then still existing Soviet bloc—made many observers forget the fact that the basic question of the political finality of the European Community was still not resolved. The Maastricht Treaty, prepared behind closed doors in a diplomatic conference, did not lead to further clarification. The first major shock came when the United Kingdom opted out of the Social Chapter, drawing a clear limit to how far the British government was inclined to go. The ensuing ratification debates in all Member States revealed a remarkable situation: the governments had negotiated a substantial leap forward towards a European polity, while major parts

---

The views expressed in this chapter are strictly personal.

of the population were unprepared to follow them along this path. The difference in most countries—like Denmark or France or Germany—between a very substantial consensus of political parties in Parliament on the results of the Maastricht negotiations on the one hand and, on the other, the extremely hesitant support of the population—oscillating around 50 per cent in most cases—showed that both governments and major political parties had misjudged the issue at stake. Among other things, they had played down the political significance of European integration and argued mainly in terms of economic benefits to be had from closer cooperation.

Citizens were made to believe, all through the past three—or even four—decades of European integration, that they could stay what they were without having to change, and still gain additional benefits from a new kind of cooperation called integration. Above all, a possible loss of identity—perceived as national identity—was never discussed by the mainstream approach and it was left up to those political parties who were opposed to integration to raise this issue for quite different reasons.

To some extent citizens were told: you *can* have your cake and eat it. Perhaps this was justified in an initial phase, but in any case it was a dangerous approach because it was based on the belief that decisions taken in common were beneficial to your own country. Member governments in the late 1960s and during the 1970s were caught in this trap and, as a result, EC common decision-making deteriorated into bargaining and the counting of immediate benefits. Rather strange package deals were elaborated in order that everybody could go home and tell their public that they had gained something and certainly not lost out. Mrs Thatcher was perhaps a champion of this tactic, but even in the early 1970s in Germany the slogan was coined that Germany should not be Europe's 'paymaster', an argument still put forward today. Hard-nosed bargaining not only minimized the possibilities for problem-solving, which of course would also have to include compromises, but also discouraged citizens from a more direct and political involvement.

If one bears in mind the indifference with which citizens were treated during many years of the EC's evolution, one is bemused by the enthusiasm of the new approach. Above all, citizens are given many qualities: when they cross a border, they are travelling citizens; when they take up a job, they are working citizens; when they buy a piece of soap or a jar of jam, they are consuming citizens. All aspects of life are segmented and given the quality of citizen activities. It is then easy to prove to these segmented citizens how they benefit from the existence of the European Union: due to consumer protection, they can identify the contents of the soap or of the jam and expiry dates must be clearly visible; if they book travel through an agency, minimum safeguards are guaranteed, and so on. Though this may be very useful, it leaves out the basic quality of citizens: that they are political beings. Citizens in the European Union's approach are the object of caretaking policy-making, not its subject.

The strange situation we find ourselves in is that political structures are in place which not only discuss and decide upon policy issues but on the evolution of the overall polity itself. Of course, this reflects the situation of the polities of the Member States but is somewhat sharpened and highlighted in the European Union as a relatively new polity in the making. It may be difficult to decide whether the chicken or the egg came first, but in the European Union there is no doubt that political—and, of course, economic—structures were created first and in their paternalistic approach they were kind enough to care about the people who were supposed to benefit from this enterprise, that is, the individuals who make up the various populations.

In order to demonstrate how strange this situation is, we may go back more than 200 years in history and look at what Jean-Jacques Rousseau put forward in his famous essay on the Social Contract in 1762, at a time when citizens were confronted with an existing political authority which additionally claimed to be completely independent and founded on divine authority. Basically, each human being was born into an already existing political system the fundamentals of which could not be changed; the sovereign was the sovereign and the subjects were the subjects. Rousseau then developed the paradigm that all men are born free and that they give up their freedom only to achieve very precise goals, above all to secure peace, which they cannot do individually. The exercise of power is therefore very closely linked to the consent of the citizens.[1]

Unfortunately, Rousseau's heuristic scheme became blurred quickly, especially during the French Revolution. The original rights of the citizen were soon replaced by the general will of the people and in the nineteenth century we see the evolution of the theory of popular

---

[1] Rousseau, *Du Contrat Social ou Principes du Droit Politique* (1762). Rousseau also uses the term 'pacte social' describing a contract between individuals to establish a common political entity, a sort of government or state. There should be no confusion with contemporary terms like 'social policy', 'Social Chapter' in the Treaty on European Union, or sometimes 'social pact'. These terms cover only limited policy areas concerning living and working conditions and related questions. Rousseau's objective which radicalizes the conclusions of earlier authors including Thomas Hobbes (*De Cive*, 1642) and John Locke (*Two Treatises of Government*, 1690) would nowadays rather be called *Gesellschaftsvertrag* (societal contract).

3

sovereignty and its embodiment in parliament. With the ensuing evolution of representative democracy not much more than lip service was paid to the permanent and active role of individual citizens. It is 'the people' which has taken over as the ultimate source of legitimacy in all our constitutions and individual citizens are only asked to cast their vote because, to put it cynically, progress has not yet provided us with a formula whereby the people can vote without having recourse to a whole series of old-fashioned individuals.

If we look back from our situation at the end of the twentieth century to Jean-Jacques Rousseau, we have to conclude that not too much has changed from the point of view of citizens. They are still born into an existing polity where the distribution of political power has already been determined. Of course, they are now told that the exercise of public power ultimately relies on the people and that they as individuals are part of the people and can exercise influence by casting their vote, among other things. But still the hen was there before the egg.

Now the strange thing about European Union is that we are confronted with a political system in the making. Astonishingly, we are already here and yet the polity is being born before our eyes. A new centre of political power is emerging which obviously, as the debates during the past years have shown, badly needs citizens' consent. Following traditions which have evolved over the past 150 years, the consent of citizens is likely to be organized from above, that is by creating structures which provide ways of finding a legitimacy through the citizen.

The question is then whether this approach is the only feasible one in the rather unique historical situation in which we find ourselves, or whether we should not dare to ask the much more radical question Jean-Jacques Rousseau asked two centuries ago, that is: if we are the citizens of Europe, then might we not be willing, for well-defined purposes, to associate and possibly conclude a contract to the purpose of exercising public power with one another?

Perhaps it might be useful to leave this question as it stands with all its radical and utopian finality. Let us first have a look at the various phases of the European Union's evolution and its different approaches towards the problem of the citizen before we come back to the interesting question of a possible new Social Contract.

For our purposes, it might be useful to divide the European Union's development into three stages, the first stage being characterized by a marked absence of popular participation or, if you want, by a grand technocratic design. In the second stage, we find a growing concern in an increasing number of Union activities for the people actually affected by them. During this period, two approaches should be considered as quite separate, the first one being the endeavour to arrive at concrete results through EC regulations which would interest citizens, and the second one being a growing awareness on the part of political leaders that a minimum of political identity would be needed if the European Union were to progress. The first approach led to what we might call the 'segmented citizen', the second one to the 'indirect citizen'. Currently, we are in a period where these two approaches are still dominant and are likely to prevail for a number of years. Nevertheless, as the European Union both deepens and widens, new elements emerge; that is why it might be useful to explore possibilities for a more direct and dynamic involvement of citizens in the construction of Europe. This will be done in the final part of this chapter.

2   THE FIRST EUROPE: EUROPEAN INTEGRATION WITHOUT THE CITIZENS—A PATERNALISTIC APPROACH

The naming of the first phase of European integration, the 'European Coal and Steel Community' (ECSC), was significant in this context: no political or bureaucratic institution could be further away from the citizen than one dealing with regulations on the production and distribution, including prices, of steel and coal and their derivatives. Production and distribution of these basic commodities were, by the way, in the hands, in as far as they were not directly nationalized, of large-scale enterprises and of cartels. This meant that market decisions in this economic sector were (and still are) taken by a relatively small number of actors, both in the private sector and in public administrations.

It may be argued that it would be unfair to generalize on the basis of the extreme limitation in scope of the first Community of Six. As a matter of fact, it was supposed to be only one pillar of three, the two others being a more general political Community and a defence Community. We know that a veto—in practical terms—from the French National Assembly destroyed all hopes for the establishment of the two other pillars.[2]

---

[2] There are two obvious historical analogies. The first one is the creation of GATT (General Agreement on Tariffs and Trade) after the Second World War, which was supposed to be embodied in or counterbalanced by a wider economic and financial organization, a kind of economic United Nations, which never came into force. The result was that only the somewhat technical instrument for the application of economic decision-making was established. (In these circumstances, it has to be said that the GATT's balance sheet has been largely positive.) The second analogy, of a completely different kind, is the

5

Even if we give the founders of the Community credit for their political intentions, it might be argued that the end product which saw the light of day and was presented to an astonished public as a major event, as a new dimension making traditional international relations suddenly look very old and obsolete, was rather technocratic. As a matter of fact, the centre of decision-making of the ECSC was a new body which cannot be easily classified. The High Authority, as the name indicates, was supposed not just to be an administrative or second-grade executive body. The dialectical opposition to the Council of Europe as a competing model becomes obvious in all the details of this institutional design: the objective was to create an institution with real powers within a given area of competence, as opposed to the wide but, as a matter of fact, unlimited competence of the Council of Europe to discuss each and every issue. This was beginning to frustrate a number of participants due to the lack of any follow-up. The gamble taken by Jean Monnet was very simple: the more you limit the competence to areas which might be economically and politically important but less sensitive both for the public at large and for political parties, the more you were likely to get real powers for a body of more or less independent decision-makers. Jean Monnet won his gamble and we see, in the five years of existence of the ECSC before the creation of the Common Market, the gradual establishment of the new Community system. The centre of the institutions and the major innovation is without doubt the High Authority, with its high degree of independence. It is true that its members were nominated by the six governments and that major decisions had to be submitted to the Council of Ministers, but in Jean Monnet's vision eminent individuals from the member countries would only serve one term in the High Authority and from the beginning could not speculate on their renomination, which would have increased their independence. The same should have been the case, by the way, for senior officials, i.e. Director-Generals and Directors, who were offered attractive salaries in

---

three-pillar structure of the Treaty on European Union (TEU). The similarities of the external structure should not hide a fundamental difference: in the early 1950s, the three pillars were supposed to have the same rules of decision-making and identical institutions, in other words, if you were to use our present vocabulary, they were to operate according to the Community method. Maastricht is, from an architectural point of view, rather unbalanced, compared to this; on the one hand, we find a very strong Community pillar, in the middle a somewhat mixed CFSP (Common Foreign and Security Policy) one and, on the other hand, a rather weak intergovernmental one for justice and home affairs. We can only speculate what would have happened in the French National Assembly had a much more intergovernmental structure been presented to it forty years ago instead of the markedly 'Community' one.

order that they would be willing to serve for a number of years in the new institutions and give up the obligations they might have in Paris or other more attractive centres for the rather provincial life of Luxembourg. Additional independence by temporary secondment, as opposed to professional dependence in a lifelong career, was the intention. This recalled somewhat the discussions earlier this century at the beginning of professional parliamentarism when a political class emerged which defined their main profession as 'representatives of the people', including increasingly similar, connected positions in a party political hierarchy.

It is not my purpose here to analyse the career profiles of the members of the High Authority and their successors in the EC Commission, nor that of the senior civil servants who were recruited to spend part of their lifetime in the service of the Community. It may only be remarked that the overall trend towards professionalism in the sense of sticking to the job prevailed more and more and that the original model looks rather outdated.

If the independence of the High Authority was the main objective, then it does not seem indispensable to include a Parliamentary Assembly in the institutional set-up. As a matter of fact, the Common Assembly—as it was called as a reminder that it should be the assembly of all three Communities, should the other two ever come into existence—was composed of members designated from the national parliaments and was given a number of scrutiny powers and a rather weak role in regulation in the form of parliamentary opinions. In addition to the classic prerogative of oversight in budgetary or audit matters, its right to sack the High Authority like a parliamentary government was the most political element. These parliamentary prerogatives limited to some extent, it is true, the powers of the High Authority. But, on the other hand, the existence of a parliamentary body within the ECSC structure enhanced its political role, and the similarities to parliamentary government in particular introduced the first elements of legitimacy for the new executive which were not directly linked to that of member governments. In the mind of the founding fathers it seems that the gain in political stature outweighed the possible limitations in the exercise of power. In this perspective, the introduction of a parliamentary body becomes rather instrumental. It seems, as a matter of fact, that Monnet hesitated for a long time about whether a parliamentary body should be introduced or not, and that serious lobbying took place to convince him of its possible benefits for his overall plan.

In any case, the rather weak role of the Common Assembly indicates that it was only seen as having an ancillary function. One must also not forget that the Council of Europe Assembly already existed and had plans to play a role we would now call of a 'mother of Parliaments', that is, that all parliamentary assemblies having competence within limited sub-regional organizations should be directly linked to the Council of Europe Assembly. The Council of Europe Assembly would be the chest and all the others would be the drawers encased by it. Obviously it was impossible to abandon this formula and create new sub-regional organizations without parliamentary representation. Since the new power elite of the Six did not like the Strasbourg plans, a new Assembly was set up which, by the way, moved its secretariat as a consequence away from Strasbourg and placed it in Luxembourg, the seat of the High Authority. It was only due to the lack of a hemicycle in Luxembourg that plenary sessions continued to be held in Strasbourg.

If parliamentary participation in the ECSC was, to some extent, circumstantial, the decision-making and deliberative system of the new Community took into account some peculiarities of the two fields of activities it was to cover, namely their mixture of public and private ownership. This included a peculiar form of *Mitbestimmung* in Germany as a result of a historical compromise between the trade unions and the Christian-Democratic government which guaranteed continued private ownership of large parts of the German coal and steel industry. The creation of a Consultative Committee, composed mainly of represen-tatives of producers and workers as an advisory body, reflected this situation. Another element was the insistence of the ECSC on improving working conditions, security in the mines, treatment of professional diseases and on organizing a programme of housing for miners and steel workers. Here we are confronted with the first actual practical expression of an overall concept which included social responsibility, conceded an advisory role to representatives of those directly concerned, but left the decision-making to a very limited corps of professional actors. This may be characterized as a paternalistic approach. Another question is whether we might also call it corporate.[3] If a corporate approach means that professional organizations and comparable interest group representations are given a direct and important function in the exercise of power, and this clearly over and above the involvement in preliminary steps of decision-making which is common to all our political systems, then one should be rather hesitant to use this label both for the intentions of the founding fathers of the Community and for its actual evolution. It is true that the

---

[3] See Wallace, 'Deepening and Widening: Problems of Legitimacy for the EC', in García (ed.), *European Identity and the Search for Legitimacy* (1993), pp. 95–105.

evolution of the Community system has become so complex, and the interlinkage of numerous actors at various levels in different activities and roles so difficult to analyse, that classic categories and notions now seem inadequate.

We could leave the institutional structure and the first years of activity of the ECSC to the historians if the pattern which was outlined then had not held true for the next decades of EEC evolution. In fact, the EEC Treaty basically confirmed the approach taken a few years earlier. Due to the wide scope of competence of the new Community, the role of the executive, that is the EEC Commission, had to be changed. The new Treaty was thus much more evolutionary by setting only an overall framework filling out the first chapters, but leaving the rest of the programme largely open and to be defined in the course of events. If we read the EEC Treaty today, or at least the relevant parts, it is astonishing to see what is *not* in it. Basically it outlines, and very clearly so, a number of principles and gives more exact rules for the gradual establishment of a customs union. But even the chapter on agriculture limits itself to a number of principles and what has since become the Common Agricultural Policy was negotiated separately.

We can leave aside the EURATOM Treaty in this context, which is, by the way, unfortunate because EURATOM could have been a perfect example of policy-making in an area obviously vital for the future and where economic interests were not yet vested in a traditional way. To some extent it was quite the opposite of the situation that pertained in respect of the ECSC. We cannot discuss here why EURATOM failed so dramatically, giving way to the pressure of a few powerful, emerging economic players and the strategic interests that were linked to some of them. Instead of being able to work out far-reaching plans for energy policy through to the next millenium, EURATOM soon dragged its feet and was put in the not very comfortable position of being asked to compromise between conflicting and controversial interests. The failure of EURATOM made the European Economic Community the predominant actor in European integration during the following decades.

3   THE SECOND EUROPE: FROM A FUNCTIONALIST TO AN INDIRECT CITIZEN

Within the European Economic Community, which was soon given the utilitarian label of 'The Common Market', we can discern two separate lines of approach as far as its relations with citizens were concerned: the first might be called a functionalist approach, in as far as individuals were perceived as exercising a number of functions which, in one way or another, might be affected by EC intervention or agenda setting. This approach abandons individuals because it divides them up into segmented parts and tries to find ways to influence each of the different parts of their existence. This functionalist citizen might also be called a 'segmented citizen'.

Another approach, which is quite distinct, is one which appeals to the human being as a whole and endeavours to establish lines of contact on questions such as political identity including national, regional, cultural, linguistic and other elements. Here the highly complex area of the self-consciousness of the citizen is approached directly and not via channels of rather secondary importance, like the maximum amount of the cigarette allowance when passing customs, or access to a European-wide insurance system for a new car. As a result, we find ourselves in an altogether different ball game. The search for state symbols was the first clear sign of this new approach: from the burgundy-red European passport to the adoption of the former Council of Europe flag of the twelve stars for EC purposes and the desperate search for a European anthem, there is a constant, perhaps not very prominent, but certainly growing, concern to strengthen elements of citizenship which are classically linked to nation-states. With the Treaty on European Union (TEU) and its chapter on European citizenship, this evolution has been formalized to a certain point. Here, quite evidently, it is not the market citizen which is the objective, but the political citizen as such. The main characteristic in this second approach, for the time being at least, is that political European citizens are not given their own rights as the new sovereign of the European Union by a sort of constituent act. Rather, this new quality is introduced in a somewhat timid way, via his or her former, still existing, quality of being a citizen of one of the Member States. Consequently, after 'the market citizen', if we can speak of a new 'political citizen', even in an embryonic state, this citizen must be qualified as an *indirect* citizen or as a *derived* one.

To take a closer look at the first approach concerning the functionalist or the segmented citizen, it might be useful to remind ourselves of our main focus point, Jean-Jacques Rousseau's distinction between *citoyen* and *bourgeois*.[4] If the citizen is defined as a political being—whether a sovereign or not—then evidently all other approaches to the notion of citizenship, in the areas of economy, social affairs, culture and others, are excluded. Unfortunately, Rousseau's rigidity was abandoned long ago and if we look at contemporary literature on the

---

[4] See 'Du Contrat Social', in *Petits Chefs D'Oeuvre de J.J. Rousseau* (1848), p. 162.

citizen, extremely wide and diversified areas of human existence are covered.[5]

If fundamental criteria are abandoned, it is not easy to replace them with new ones. If, for example, a fundamental economic right, such as the right of establishment, is considered to be a major activity of the European Union in favour of the citizen, why should we not also include a more liberal handling of imports of tax-free goods purchased at external airports? The various possible items of functional citizenship have nothing more in common than commodities you put in your purchasing trolley in a supermarket—with the only exception that the citizenship commodities offered by the European Union are supposedly free, while in the supermarket at least you know you have to pay before you leave.

The widening and lowering of the notion of the citizen reflects of course the erosion of the classic nation-state. When Georg Wilhelm Friedrich Hegel in 1823 could still describe the state as the highest possible conception of the spirit and the goal of individual citizens was to be raised from mere individual existence towards this higher category,[6] then we find on the elevated abstract level of a classical philosopher more or less the paradigm of what you might call the nation-state of the nineteenth century. We are told that this nation-state does not exist any more as a unit and that, following a long-lasting erosion, for the time being it is being replaced by highly complex network systems, or rather non-systems, where, behind the institutional façade of decision-making, increasingly complicated negotiations are going on between a steadily growing number of participants.

Compared to the classic relationship between the citizen and the almighty nation-state—here we include the quite opposite theoretical approaches of Rousseau and Hegel—contemporary designs for citizenship look rather colourless. The former kind of state which marked its presence in all areas of daily life, including the uniform of the postman delivering the mail, is retreating from many areas. Not only does the postman nowadays very often deliver the mail in jeans, but the state is even selling its monopolies just like the postal service or railways, and, perhaps, tomorrow its army. As a result, the 'citizen' is left in the desert of individualization, with very few landmarks left for possible group identification. The laws of physics demand that a vacuum cannot be maintained, but that it must be filled: in our case it has been filled first of all from the outside by means of commodities.

---

[5] See for many others, Meehan, *Citizenship and the European Community* (1993).

[6] Hegel, *Philosophie der Weltgeschichte* (1930).

'Citizens' become not only consumers, but gain a principal means of self-identification through the products they acquire (*Warenfetischismus*). In addition, television, more than any other media, sets the new citizens' limits for experiencing the outside world and influences their social behaviour. Since this commercialized supply only satisfies a small section of the demands of the individual for self-identification, which was classically done in groups with other human beings, substantial deficits remain. Fear of the future becomes one of the major characteristics, especially of the younger generation; first, as far as their own individual future is concerned, and secondly, in the form of a rather diffuse fear about the future of mankind. It is on this basis that a new dialogue between the public power and the very irritated citizens of Europe could find a starting-point.

In the familiar environment of a nation-state with all its possible linguistic, historical and cultural identifications, including its daily confirmation by national television and major newspapers which give primary importance to events on the national scene, citizens are nevertheless able to develop and maintain an overall network of orientation. This network is largely dependent on intermediate structures, which transmit the permanent stream of input necessary for their self-identification. In the European Union this intermediate structure does not exist and consequently citizens are directly confronted with the decision-making power.[7] In a national political system, if citizens do not agree with a decision or with a general line of policy-making, usually they do not question the system itself but will criticize those in power and decide for an opposition party next time. So both agreement and disagreement with political decisions—with the rare exception of fundamental opposition of the anarchical, religious or ideological kind—expresses itself within the system itself and may even stabilize it. In the European Union this classic interplay between citizen reaction and public power does not take place. If unpopular decisions are taken, very often the intermediate structures, like the media or political parties—and the governments of the Member States as well—shy away from responsibility and blame the decision on the anonymous monster of the 'Brussels bureaucracy'. If citizens do not agree with a decision, they have no means of opposition within the system, whether immediately or in the medium term through elections, because their participation in European elections does not imply a possible change of policy orientation.

---

[7] On the relation between European institutions and European civilization see Duverger, *Europe des Hommes* (1994).

As a consequence, the general evolution in the role of the citizen in Western industrialized states which we have witnessed over the past decades has been accelerated in a dangerous way by the European Union entering the game as an important political actor. Of the two approaches followed so far (the functionalist approach of trying to some extent to appease citizens by giving them a number of specific benefits from market integration, or the second approach leading to political but indirect citizens with rather weak forms of political self-identification either through symbols or through modest means of political participation), neither will be sufficient to overcome the present defects of the system.

4   THE THIRD EUROPE: THE UTOPIAN DIALOGUE BETWEEN THE EUROPEAN UNION AND ITS CITIZENS

The Maastricht Treaty represents a major leap forward in the ambitions of the European Union to constitute itself as a powerful decision-making centre. The debates about this Treaty showed that large parts of the populations of the twelve Member States were not prepared to follow their political elites. In addition to the need to keep the citizens much better informed, which would involve a major change to the predominant utilitarian paradigm, the political system itself will have to be strengthened considerably if the major decisions foreseen for economic and monetary union and in external policy are to be taken in an acceptable way. The question this chapter raises is whether the approaches followed so far will be sufficient, or whether a major change will be needed in order to arrive at a coherent and well-balanced system of decision-making, maintaining and possibly strengthening the traditions of democratic government.

It is vital that a thorough reflection on these questions takes place during the preliminary phase of the forthcoming intergovernmental conference on the revision of the TEU. Both the SEA revisions and the TEU were negotiated with the prime objective of defining areas and goals of decision-making and of adapting, at least to some extent, the institutional mechanisms involved. Questions reaching beyond the institutional were only taken up in a limited way: in the SEA, practically not at all; in the TEU, only with regard to the chapter on European citizenship, and the provisions on subsidiarity and transparency.

It is not my objective here to speculate about the possible contribution of the notion of subsidiarity[8] towards a more effective Europe of the citizen. Certainly the reversal of the trend towards centralization is highly popular. It is generally assumed that it is more democratic, and perhaps even more efficient, to keep large areas of public policy on a regional or even local level. On the other hand, this may lead—as the Swiss example shows—to a rather parochial view of the world. In Germany, for example, the European elections of June 1994 in some *Länder* were held on the same day as local elections. Here it was noticeable that questions such as the improvement of existing bicycle lanes on urban roads were debated much more widely than those concerning the future of Europe, including such pressing political problems as those concerning the Bosnian conflict.

The question then it seems is how European policy, in free competition with national, regional and local policy issues, can gain in profile in the minds of the citizens. Obviously, much more information is needed on the activity of the European Union and various reports and studies commissioned by the Union institutions suggest a number of improvements.

But whatever the European institutions, despite their budgetary constraints, could do to improve their information services in the twelve Member States, in the four new ones and in the associated members in Europe, in providing brochures, discussion centres, seminars, films, invitations to groups to visit Strasbourg or Brussels, and Jean Monnet chairs at universities, though certainly useful, this is vastly insufficient to get the much-needed dialogue with citizens up and running. One of the main stumbling blocks is the hesitancy of existing intermediate structures like political parties to accept the idea that the citizen can participate directly in a dialogue on complex issues. In fact, one of the main functions of political institutions and, above all, parliaments and political parties is the reduction of complexity. Many political or legislative issues are understood in all their details only by a limited number of experts. Even ministers need careful preparation highlighting the political issues at stake in order to enable them to assume their responsibilities. This is much more the case in parliament, where you may of course have parliamentary experts in permanent committees, but where the main function is nevertheless to bring out into the open a few possibly controversial points on a limited number of elements in the proposed legislation. Further reduction is then done by the press and even more so by radio or by the news on television, where the

---

[8] For my own appraisal, see *Government and Opposition: Subsidiarity as a Guiding Principle for European Community Activities* (1993), Vol. 28, No. 2.

extremely complex legislative act may be summarized in only a few sentences. But this complexity reduction mechanism generally makes possible the identification of citizens with the system as a result, even if they do not agree with the solution envisaged. In the EU, on the other hand, the danger is much greater that, in the absence of intermediate structures integrated in the system, citizens, confronted directly with a decision, not only criticize it on its own merits, but shy away from the system itself. Complexity reduction within a national political system tends to promote citizen involvement, while within the European Union it is likely to be the opposite.

We may assume that the rather low involvement of citizens in Union decision-making results less from a higher degree of complexity than from the lack of intermediate structures within the system. The complexity of Union policy decisions is not much greater than in the Member States. In fact, it is practically the same policy areas that are the object of regulation in both cases. Of course, it is more complex to find a formula in a highly regulated area of policy-making, like agriculture, for a Community of twelve based on different traditional national systems of subsidies and other interventions, which has also to take into account variations of temperature, of the structure of agricultural employment, and so on. The new quality of a political scale certainly plays a role. But, if you look at information on Union decision-making in this controversial area, it has mostly presented, and very often in negative terms, the bureaucratic aspects of the highly detailed regulations. The public at large was thus confronted over the years with the substantial failings of a regulative system, without having been informed about similar shortcomings which existed for many years in their own countries. Everybody has heard negative comments in the media on the imports of bananas or the destruction of apples and it is much easier to provoke a controversial discussion on the Union agriculture than on the national system of subsidies where the details are generally less well known and where irritating facts are much less often reported in the press.

The main question we have to ask ourselves is whether the present intermediate structures, all organized more or less on national lines (with only few exceptions), do not fundamentally underestimate the interest of citizens in having a free flow of information which is within their capacity to react to. One sees how political parties still organize their contacts with their own rank and file members, very often in periodic gatherings, in small circles similar to organizational forms deriving from the nineteenth century where people met at the local bar, and one can raise questions about how political parties will react to the new demands of the age of information. In fact, if you want to get an impression of what will happen in ten or twenty years, it is not to the politicians you have to turn but to the information specialists. For them, there is no doubt that telecommunications systems of all kinds, and above all interactive ones, will dramatically develop over the next decade or two. It will be one of the most rapidly growing industries with about 60 million people forecast to be employed in telecommunications by the end of this century, that is in a few years' time.

Already, we can see the first effects of this dramatic new revolution on the structure of our society itself. It is no longer the hierarchical society which is the model but a new horizontal one, where each participant has a chance to become an actor on the basis of a high level of information available to all.[9] 'Knowledge is power' was the slogan of the Renaissance. It seems that this slogan will soon attain a much more dramatic significance than ever before. What are then the likely elements of the new information society and its possible repercussions for a dialogue between the Union decision-makers and the future citizens of Europe?

If we agree to the assumption that in a relatively short time interested citizens will be in a position to have direct access to basic knowledge in policy relevant areas, this could mean the beginning of a new era of relationship between the citizen and his or her government. For the first time in history, beyond the limitations of city boundaries where in classical Athens the citizens could discuss matters known to them in the market place, or in Geneva's local government, which was in Rousseau's mind, citizens would be able to participate actively in policy matters of a large territory.

Such participation would need a number of prerequisites. If our citizen is interested in what the Europeans should do in common against the foreseeable danger of the further depletion of the ozone layer he or she would at present probably have major difficulties in getting unbiased information unless he or she is linked to a professional data base. Even the positions of the major political parties are not easily available. You have to write to party headquarters in order to get brochures and then it is not easy to compare the information you get from various sources. Why should it not be possible as a public service and free of charge to provide summaries of scientific data on such a question as mentioned above? This might be done by an outside and 'independent' source. A second step would then be to ask political parties to give summaries of their position on the question so you could

---

[9] Dusan Sidjanski in his *L'avenir federaliste de l'Europe* (1992) analyses the relationship between European integration and political innovation (p. 189).

easily find out what the major differences are and if possible what the costs are for proposed solutions. In addition, interest groups could be asked to put in—and they could even pay for this—their own opinion, let us say from the automobile industry or from ecology movements. If our citizen is especially interested in what the European Union is doing about this, the Commission could put in a summary of proposed action. The European Parliament could summarize what it has done and what its own contribution would be. Information could also be made available on the discussion of the same subject in Member States: what have the national parliaments to say, how does this discussion and its importance vary from one country or from one region to another?

Of course, no citizen can be pushed to use information of this kind. It is foreseeable that all over the European Union after some time hundreds of thousands of citizens would use such a system in order to be able to participate in a discussion on the basis of more or less common knowledge. Political debates would not just be nourished by one or other newspaper article or television documentary. Gradually, more and more people interested in such topics would find it wise and economical to have a look at their data base and possibly get a print out of relevant points before discussing it with friends or going to a political meeting.

The more the citizens would be informed, the more the present claim of their representatives to be 'experts' on complex questions would be challenged. A member of Parliament going to a meeting of, let us say, a hundred participants, would discover that fifteen or twenty would discuss on a much higher level of knowledge than ever before. This would in turn influence his or her own preparation for such rallies and as a matter of fact the whole interplay between intermediate structures and the citizen would change.

If we look at television we see more and more discussions and talkshows. Very often these are boring and imitations of cheap American productions, but some of them are quite interesting and fit into the new trend of 'infotaining'. In German television, for example, there is a series called *Pro und Contra*, where a major subject of general interest is presented, one speaker presents arguments in favour, another against. A few experts participate also. The invited public and TV viewers (by telephone) can cast votes before and after the transmission and it is interesting to see which arguments are more convincing. Transmissions like this might be a model for much more elaborate political dialogues.

Of course, there is no question of replacing parliamentary democracy, which is deeply rooted in our traditions, by computer games. It would be horrifying to envisage replacing the social network and possibilities of group identification which still exist in our political systems by procedures which might tend to lead to further atomization of our populations. The final goal should be the 'interactive citizen', that is, one who on the basis of modern information possibilities is able and motivated to participate in a dialogue both with other citizens and with those exercising public power.[10]

The objective would not be to get an immediate final response from the citizen on numerous questions; the danger of populist proposals and decisions would be enormous. The new dimension would consist in the entering of the citizen into public discussion together with political parties, with the media, with interest groups and other information networks, and this on an equal footing which does not presently exist.

Such an outlook may seem very utopian. But what are the alternatives? The classic role of political parties has been decreasing over the past decades in our national systems, and progress towards European political parties has been minimal. As recent events in Italy have shown, the danger of the taking over of public power by important players from outside classic structures is imminent in our political systems, and will become more important with the process of concentration which is going on in the transnational media. Our political systems are changing substantially and, as we have already noted, the European Union acts as a catalyst in this respect. The basic option is either to invest in the capacities of the citizen to participate in a new dialogue or to envisage a much more elitist solution in reserving major political decisions on the large European scale to a small elite, while transforming the role of political parties and of the media, in order to provide a smoke-screen of legitimacy. It is very doubtful if the second solution, if it were envisaged, would produce acceptable long-term results. The lessons of the debate about Maastricht should not be forgotten so easily. For the time being we are at a crossroads and we have to make up our mind which direction we should take.

---

[10] See on this subject Habermas, *Citizenship and National Identity: Some Reflections on the Future of Europe.* Praxis International, Vol. 12 (1).

2 THE PROBLEM OF DEMOCRACY IN THE EUROPEAN UNION

Teija Tiilikainen

1 LEGITIMATION OF POLITICAL POWER IN EUROPE

The democratic deficit is usually approached as an institutional problem of the European Union. Thus, its origin is found in the constitutive treaties conceding a majority of powers to the non-representative organs of the Union and leaving only secondary functions to the people's representation. Institutional reforms in favour of the European Parliament have proved colossally difficult to achieve because of the clearly federalist quality they have necessarily had. In this deadlocked situation new ways of getting over the shortfall of democracy are being sought. The principles of subsidiarity and regionality confirmed by the Maastricht Treaty have already been celebrated as the saving features of European democracy.

In this chapter I will try to go behind the institutional problems by studying the democratic deficit as a problem of the legitimizing of political power in Europe. Democracy here represents the least disputed rule of all the general governmental principles in the European Union. Yet it is precisely democracy that has run up a lot of organizational difficulties.

Although democracy stands as the point of departure for this analysis, it will not constitute its sole object. The European Union will be seen as an effort to build a new European government, the true character of which is of special importance here. First I will focus on the controversial nature of the European Union itself. I shall argue that the lack of agreement as to what constitutes the essential character of the Union means that democracy is being decisively contested by alternative principles of political power. The principles that interest me in this particular connection are those of national sovereignty and bureaucratic governance. In the first part of this chapter I shall cast light on these rival conceptions and on the way they justify the threat to democracy in the European Union. Democracy is in this part defined in very general terms with reference to the kind of practices of power normally acknowledged as democratic.

In the second part of the chapter I will take the present obstacles to a democratic European Union for granted and will try to work out proposals for change in this situation. This type of analysis purports to take into account the elements of historical particularity vested in the Union and to discuss its governmental structures from these premises. The idea of democracy will, for instance, be analysed in order to find out to what extent the efforts to apply it in the Union context are bound to the meaning democracy has as a principle of power in a sovereign state. The decisive issue to be aired is the governmental nature of the European Union from a broad historical perspective and its relation to the sovereign nation-state in particular. If we have reason to argue that the conditions for democracy in the European Union are not comparable to those of a sovereign state, then we should perhaps reassess the instruments of democracy in the European context. I believe that this is, indeed, the case and that I will find support and specification for this argument from the first part of my work dealing with the contested essence of the Union.

If the traditional means to democracy prove to be insufficient the big question of the day is whether we already have alternative means available in the European Union which could meet, or could be developed to meet, the demands for its specific model of democratic government. Here, the principles of subsidiarity and regionality and the phenomenon of Union citizenship will be addressed. The final critical question is whether there are still further means of democracy in the Union repertoire, which have not yet proved their illegitimacy in the course of its history.

2   DEMOCRACY AND THE EUROPEAN COMMUNITY

The principle of democracy has played a significant role in the plans for European unification in the twentieth century. Its meaning has, however, varied according to the specific political traditions it has been derived from. Among the resistance groups of the Second World War the idea of a common Europe matured as a means of democracy in particular. This idea of a unification of the European people through a democratic government had its origins in nineteenth century, mainly French and Italian, republican and socialist doctrines.[1] In our century these reactive aspirations were pushed forward in EC politics above all

---

[1] Duroselle, *L'Idée d'Europe dans l'histoire* (1958), p. 214.

by Alberto Spinelli and by various groups close to him.[2]

More extensive support has, however, been won by the idea of a Europe in which democracy appears as one of the key values to be protected. This idea connects the conception of a united Europe to the broad liberal tradition which puts the emphasis in unification upon individuals' rights and liberties. As an idea of Europe, this tradition also has its roots in the Romantic era and, in particular, in the liberal-nationalist movements of Southern and Central Europe.[3]

The aims of integration have, indeed, varied considerably with respect to their economic and political emphases since the nineteenth century and the birth of modern political thinking. Since then there has, however, never been any doubt about democracy being the constitutive element of a common European government.[4] The division of opinions that has had most practical importance in Union history concerns instead the principle of state sovereignty, its legitimacy and 'natural' context in Europe.

The legitimacy of state sovereignty forms a watershed as far as the question of European government is concerned. This watershed is an expression of the general division of Western political culture which took place in the Reformation. The first dividing question is whether political power in Europe should have a centralized structure. This is thus a question of the sovereignty principle itself. The legitimacy of the principle is greatest in those parts of Europe which have a firm collectivist political heritage as in the pure Catholic cultures and in the Lutheran states in the North. The centralism is, however, more flexible and less nationalist in the first case. The Catholic cultures have traditionally tended to include in their idea of sovereignty the whole of Christian Europe, while the more nationalistically oriented Lutheran cultures have treated sovereignty as a quality of their nation-states only.[5]

---

[2] Lipgens (ed.), *Documents on the History of European Integration*, vol. 1. *Continental Plans for European Union 1939–45* (1985, 1st edn), p. 27 et seq.; later phases, e.g., Pryce (ed.), *The Dynamic of European Union* (1989); and Lodge (ed.), *European Union: The European Community in Search of a Future* (1986).

[3] Heater, *The Idea of European Unity* (1988), p. 113.

[4] The commitment to democracy is included in the preamble to the Maastricht Treaty: 'the contracting parties ... *confirming their attachment to the principles of liberty, democracy and respect for human rights and fundamental freedoms and of the rule of law ...*' (emphasis added).

[5] The structure of nationalism can be regarded as an example of this decisive cultural difference. The nationalist movements of Catholic Europe treated national unification as just one necessary phase in a broader European unification, while, for example, German nationalism was based upon the idea of the nation as the highest political form. Mazzini and Hegel can be mentioned as the leading figures of these opposing traditions.

The other dividing question concerning the focal political conceptions in Europe does not deal with the structure of power but with its essence. This time Europe is divided along more different lines than in the first case. Cultures with strong individualist elements tend to find the essence of political power in rules of a constitutional type. These rules are seen as constituting and limiting political power and as having as their major task a proclamation of individual rights and liberties that are treated as constitutive of the whole system. Here, it is the semi-Catholic and Calvinist cultures that share the demand for constitutionality in the question of European government even if the structures they propose for it are quite the opposite.[6] In Lutheran Europe the essence of political power has, due to its self-legitimated character, been more connected with physical power than with rules. This does not mean that politics there entirely lacks the constitutionalist dimension, but that issues of security and defence tend to be treated as the core of political power.

The previous discussion purported to indicate that even if the main political traditions of Europe have much in common they still differ from each other in many essential questions. This has made itself apparent in the construction of the European Community. Even if democracy has been highly valued by everybody as a governmental principle, its closer application at the European level has encountered much disagreement. In the following passage I will try to make clear how the alternative principles of political power have, in fact, benefited from this situation. Bureaucratic rule is the less deep-rooted of the two principles working against governmental democracy in the European Community. With its roots deep in EC history, bureaucracy has, however, become a typical characteristic of the organization. The qualities of bureaucratic governmental structures which are most in conflict with democracy are its closed processes and organization that favours narrow expertise at the expense of general citizen participation. The immediate origin of the bureaucratic nature of EC government can be found in the constitutive treaties.

---

[6] The emphasis between individualist and collectivist heritage varies in Catholic cultures. Catholicism has been able to reconcile these elements since the Counter-Reformation (Skinner, *The Foundations of Modern Political Thought* (1978), vols 1–2). Constitutionality has been a key element in the integration policy of the Christian Democrat parties in Europe (Cardozo and Corbett, 'The Crocodile Initiative', in Lodge, *European Union*, pp. 15–46, p. 40). The Court of Justice of the European Communities (ECJ) has made a considerable contribution to the development of certain parts of Community law in a constitutional direction (Weiler, 'Journey to an Unknown Destination: A Retrospective and Prospective of the European Court of Justice in the Arena of Political Integration', 31 JCMS (1993), 417–446 ; Burley and Mattli, 'Europe before the Court', 47 IO (1993), 41–76).

22

If the first obstacle to democracy has its origin in the closer form of the unification plan, the second originates in the general legitimacy of this plan. The other idea that is analysed as an obstacle to democracy in Europe reflects deeper cultural differences than the idea of bureaucracy. The age-long conflict between a Europe of sovereign states and a united Europe has also, in this particular case, prevented the realization of the original integration plan. National sovereignty has pulled the use of power into a state-centricist direction and hindered the development of a clear and rational system of democracy at the European level.

My intention is to open the discussion on the characteristics of Union government by analysing the conceptual origins of the constitutive treaties. The modern origins of European unification are of special importance with respect to the present forms of Union government and its heavy bureaucratic elements. These origins will be perceived in terms of two focal forces of change which were activated during the first decades of this century. The element that constitutes the conservative force will be studied subsequently. That element is the vitality of the European nation-state and its impact on the forms of European government.

3 FEDERALISTS, LIBERALS AND THE UNIFICATION OF EUROPE

The present form of European integration can be seen to be a result of two different pressures for change, which strengthened during the first decades of this century. The two World Wars functioned as stimuli for these plans whose common base was the achievement of a more or less permanent peace in Europe. It has to be admitted that to approach the miscellaneous field of political thinking in terms of two traditions implies a heavy simplification and appears feasible only if the grounds are clear enough. In this case the basis for this rough categorization is constituted by one focal quality vested in the European government that is now being constructed. The European government can be seen to be adopting either a centralizing or a decentralizing role with respect to the existing national governments. In the first case it is a question of some type of federalist elements that are dominant and in the second case the aspirations could be described as liberal and internationalist. Any other governmental qualities are not meant to be caught by this division.

The first of these forces of change has been working in a federalist direction and could thus be connected with those historical traditions of unification which have been present in European politics throughout the centuries in varying shapes and intensity. A federal Europe has appeared to be the natural conception of Europe in Catholic cultures which have had grave difficulties with nationalist ideas of the northern extreme type. The federalist forces that had been decisively nourished by the two World Wars had been looking for their moment to turn Western Europe into a federal state under a common federal government.[7] There have been at least three important federalist efforts to change European political structures since the late 1920s. They have all proceeded quite close to the objective, but have at last failed in the final straight.[8] So, the Treaty of Paris and the Treaties of Rome were nurtured in an intensely federalist spirit engendered by the Hague Congress of 1948 and by the project to establish European political union in the early 1950s. The essence of federalism then was the formation of a European federal government that would be comprised of elements like constitutional and legal supremacy *vis-à-vis* European states combined with a European representation.[9]

The other force pushing the European state system towards a structural change was based upon typical liberal ideas. The liberal internationalist doctrine of free trade as a means of peace in the world extends itself at least to figures like Jeremy Bentham and Immanuel Kant in the eighteenth century. A theory that took a European perspective in particular was drafted by the Frenchman Comte de Saint-Simon at the same time as the first measures were being taken to break down customs barriers between certain European states. While federalists advocated a centralist protection of European values, liberals stood for a movement *from* sovereignty towards common rules and institutions in a more universal sense, evincing a greater respect for

---

[7] Heater, *European Unity*, pp. 116–155. The federalist projects were numerous during the inter-war period and in the 1940s and 1950s. The main area of this activity was in southern Europe, in France and Italy, but Great Britain was also an unparalleled source of federalism in these times.

[8] The first effort was closely connected with the French Foreign Minister Aristide Briand who offered the representatives of other European governments a concrete proposal for the creation of a federal union in the year 1929 (Heater, *European Unity*, p. 130). The two other efforts were connected with the Hague Congress of the year 1948 and with the project to establish a European Political Community in the years 1952–1954 (Gerbet, 'In Search of Political Union', in Pryce (ed.), *Dynamic of European Union*, pp. 35–48; and Cardozo, 'The Project for a Political Community', in Pryce (ed.), *Dynamic of European Union*, pp. 49–77).

[9] The institutional emphasis tends, of course, to vary in the different federalist plans according to their origin. While the Spinellian left-wing federalists have demanded the supremacy of a European popular assembly, the Christian Democrats, for instance, have underlined the necessity of a European constitution which would include the protection of civil rights and liberties (Lipgens, *Documents*, vol. 1).

individual reason and capacities.

Liberal ideas, in their more extreme form, have their basis in medieval humanism, which was politicized through Protestant, and, in particular, through Calvinist doctrines.[10] They have thus had a great impact upon the concept of Europe in countries like Britain and Holland in the first place, but also to some extent in the Nordic countries. The goals of the liberal and federalist plans were different and remained so, but in the heavy longing for change that followed the antagonisms of the 1930s and 1940s the two plans became effectively intermingled into the Communities of Europe.

The Treaty of Paris and the Treaties of Rome can thus be seen to represent a combination of these historical thought structures. Certain individuals in key positions, above all Jean Monnet and Paul-Henri Spaak, were the immediate sources of the final unification plan. The European Communities reflected their ideas as far as both the structure of the organization and issues of substance were concerned.[11] The general compromise worked out by these figures, and supported by other key political figures around them, was based upon the incorporation of federalist *goals* and liberal *means* of European unification. The European Communities that were born, including their government, also bear, of course, the trace of other more contextual political factors. These are the factors reflecting the demands and interpretations associated with the particular situations behind the birth of the treaties.

I suppose, however, that this compromise between the two historical political conceptions carries with it something essential to the problems connected with the creation of a democratic government in Europe. The federalist conception of a democratic Europe has been essentially connected with the democratic qualities of federal government. The federalist long-term democratization project has concerned the legislative role of the European Parliament and its election by direct elections. Another project with the same purpose has been that enshrined in the concept of Union citizenship and the establishment of political rights on this basis. The liberal internationalist conception of

---

[10] A historical analysis of the concept of right can be found, e.g., in Tuck, *Natural Rights Theories, their Origin and Development* (1979).

[11] The fact that integration started with coal and steel is thus no coincidence. Jean Monnet had worked as a key actor in the French Commissariat Général du Plan de Modernisation et d'Équipement that had given special attention to the coal and steel industries (Diebold, *The Schuman Plan: A Study in Economic Cooperation 1950–1959* (1959), p. 17). The bringing in of atomic energy was also based upon Monnet's personal conceptions and connections (Küsters, 'The Treaties of Rome', in Pryce (ed.), *Dynamic of European Union*, pp. 78–104).

a democratic Europe has in many ways implied a negation of the federal model. Its essence has been in the linkage of states through a variety of channels which would in most cases be of a non-governmental nature.[12] Seen from this point of view, the plurality of political processes and open political debate have thus appeared the best guarantees for democracy in Europe.[13]

The problem resulting from this compromise seems to be that the present European Union has a governmental structure that is clearly federalist in its outline, but whose internal structure and division of power reflects liberal pragmatist aspirations. This combination has been apt to nourish the bureaucratic qualities of the present Union government, thus making any large-scale improvements in a democratic direction impossible. The main governmental organization was born out of the pressure of a conflict between federalist and liberal ideas. The High Authority, like its counterpart in the EEC, the Commission, represented Monnet's conception of an international institution that would contribute to the conciliation of international interests.[14] This type of organ was planned for the needs of the Franco-German coal and steel pool and it seems that its suitability for further integration was not given any significant consideration by the founding fathers.[15] A legislative European Parliament that would also possess some financial powers was not a part of the same plan, either. The idea of a federal type of directly elected parliament was incorporated in the unification plan only at the end of the 1950s. The Common Assembly of the EEC bears clear evidence of the ultra-federalist Union project that had failed just a few years earlier. The European Coal and Steel Community (ECSC) had already established an assembly consisting of parliamentarians from the Member States and including a weak idea of parliamentary control over the High Authority. A directly elected 'European Parliament'[16] with traditional parliamentary powers was an obviously

---

[12] Holsti, *The Dividing Discipline* (1985), p. 27.

[13] The whole functionalist school of integration is based upon the focal liberal premises. See, e.g., Mitrany, *The Functional Theory of Politics* (1975).

[14] For the 'identity crisis' of Monnet and his reasoning concerning the compromise, see Monnet, *Memoires* (1976), p. 341; and Burgess, *Federalism and European Union: Political Ideas, Influences and Strategies in the European Community 1972–1987* (1989), pp. 43–60. In general, Monnet was of the opinion that human nature was weak and that cooperation was achievable only by means of common rules and institutions (Burgess, *Federalism*, p. 46).

[15] Diebold, *The Schuman Plan*, pp. 47–76.

[16] The Assembly of the Coal and Steel Community, which functioned also as the assembly of the EEC, adopted this new significant name in the year 1962 (Nugent, *The Government and Politics of the European Community* (1989), p. 110).

loose part in the further organizational context and with respect to the narrow economic profile of unification.

The present Union government could be subjected to a variety of criticisms emanating from this decisive distance between the two constitutive plans. My general theme here is the problem of democracy, because it stands as one of the most fateful issues with respect to the final result of the twentieth-century effort of European unification. It is time to return to the fact that most Union powers are exercised by agencies which represent narrow expertise and which are not elected by the people. The origin of these bodies and the acceptance they have gained during the history of the European Union can be explained through the liberalist plan of which they constitute an immediate part. The first element of the Union to be studied in this respect is the emphasis put on its juridical character and the implications this emphasis has had upon its power structure. The juridical emphasis of unification has benefited the Court of Justice of the European Communities (ECJ) as well as the Commission, which appears as a conglomeration of activities of the most undemocratic sort.

4   THE CHALLENGE OF BUREAUCRACY

The juridical emphasis of the twentieth-century integration project is treated here as a particular feature of the liberal plan. It bears most of all evidence of the strength of the French impact in the initial phases. Jean Monnet and his French partners did not quite share the peace-plan outlook typical of British liberalism. According to the *laissez-faire* spirit of that plan, the processes of international cooperation should be mixed with a minimum of governmental powers. The form of powers that was most accepted was one of a conciliatory nature connected with the settlement of disputes.[17] Due to the impact of the Catholic tradition and the long history of monarchical powers, the value of governmental powers has been higher in French political culture.[18] This feature

---

[17] The father of this traditional liberal peace-plan is Jeremy Bentham and his work *A Plan for an Universal and Perpetual Peace* (written in 1789 as a part of his work *Principles of International Law*). The same opposition to supranational or federal powers can be found in Mitrany, *Functional Theory of Politics*, pp. 105–132. For later liberal views on European integration see Lipgens, *Documents*, vol. 1; and for the British attitude towards the Coal and Steel Union see Diebold, *The Schuman Plan*, p. 48.

[18] Tiilikainen, 'Where Finland Meets Europe: Getting to the Roots of Finnish Europeanism' (unpublished, 1994). This paper discusses the outlines of European political thinking with the purpose of clarifying some main geo-cultural differences.

reflected itself clearly in the concept of gradual integration adopted by Frenchmen. The essence of integration was seen as consisting of supranational juridical powers which would gradually weaken the national context. According to this conception, it was not in the first place liberties, the direction of which had to be changed or extended, but regulative rules which were the basis of political life.[19]

From the beginning, and in spite of its narrow substance, the European Community was thus vested with a unique juridical machinery. The machinery was based upon the roles of the High Authority and the ECJ and upon the particular qualities of Community law.[20] This initial model of unification laid down the outlines for EURATOM and the EEC and emphasized the nature of the later EC as a juridical project in the first place. This emphasis, combined with the initial approach to integration through sectoral policies, contributed to the rise of bureaucratic structures of power in the EC. These structures were certainly not an intended element of the original plans, but their maintenance and strengthening can be seen to have resulted from the conflict between the two constitutive plans for unification.

The fact is that while the French plan was later accepted in northern Europe (meaning by this both the original and later northern members) too, as the basis for progressive integration, the idea of a gradual transfer of powers to the *federal* organization has not been endorsed. The establishment of direct elections in the European Parliament took twenty years and the provisions for a uniform procedure have not yet been fulfilled. Parliament has not achieved real and effective legislative powers in spite of various efforts in this direction. The weak idea of the parliamentary control of the Commission present in the constitutive treaties has lost its relevance rather than been strengthened. The bureaucratic appearance of the European Union has been constantly reinforced due to the fact that new policy areas have been included in its powers.

Liberally oriented internationalists have not been willing to increase democracy in Europe through supranational means, but have

---

[19] Monnet, *Memoires,* e.g., p. 371 and p. 460. For French arguments in favour of integration see Haas, *The Uniting of Europe: Political, Social and Economic Forces 1950–1957* (1958), pp. 114–127.

[20] The particularity of Community law has been decisively strengthened by the policy of the ECJ (e.g., Case 26/62, *N.V. Algemene Transport—en Expeditie Onderneming Van Gend & Loos* v *Nederlandse Administratie der belanstingen (Netherlands Inland Revenue Administration),* [1963] ECR 1; and Case 6/64, *Flaminio Costa* v *ENEL,* [1964] ECR 585). The key elements of the strong position of law, like the provision of direct applicability, were, however, already present in the constitutive treaties.

been loyal to their original view of a democratic Europe that could be achieved through a plurality of processes.[21] The northern members have traditionally been keen on developing alternative institutional structures in Europe like the Organization for European Economic Cooperation (OEEC) earlier and the Conference on Security and Cooperation in Europe (CSCE) and the European Economic Area (EEA) more recently.[22] But the long process of integration has corresponding- ly created more and more self-sufficient actors and institutions in the Union which regard a development of this kind as a threat to their own position and which, therefore, push the Union in a federalist direction.

5   THE CHALLENGE OF NATIONAL SOVEREIGNTY

The problem of democracy in the European Union cannot, however, be entirely captured without touching the issue of national sovereignty. Sovereignty will be analysed here as a separate issue, while its role will be conceived as a more or less conservative force guarding the integrity of the Westphalian system and acting in opposition to European unification in its original sense. The two World Wars, which inspired a spirit of unification in the European heartland, led to a strengthened feeling of national sovereignty on the rim. It was the high value put on national sovereignty in northern Europe that watered down the all- European efforts of unification immediately following the war.[23] Sovereignty got a decisive grip on the European Community through Charles de Gaulle's policy in the 1960s. De Gaulle's concept of unification was equal with a political rule which would be based upon national sovereignty and which would have its essence in external

---

[21] This concept of a democratic Europe goes back to Bentham and its great twentieth century proponent was Woodrow Wilson (Holsti, *The Dividing Discipline*, p. 27). The liberal conception of European democracy has been visibly emphasized, e.g., in connection with the Schuman declaration (Nicoll and Salmon, *Understanding European Communities* (1990)) and in connection with the Single European Act (Moravcsik, 'Negotiating the Single European Act: National Interests and Conventional Statecraft in the European Community', 45 IO (1991), 19–56).

[22] In the general EC rhetoric this phenomenon has been described as priority given to the enlargement of the EC by the northern members and to the deepening of the Community by the southern members. For recent differences in national policies see, e.g., Holland, *European Community Integration* (1993), p. 158.

[23] The best example of these hampered efforts is the Council of Europe, which ended up as a pure intergovernmental organization (with its parliamentary organ as a debate forum) in spite of the intensity of federal aspirations connected with its birth (Gerbet, 'In Search of Political Union').

unity. Neither the idea of a federalist government nor the concept of a fragmented fusion of states' activities appeared acceptable to him. De Gaulle instead contributed to the powerful activation of a new meaning of European unity inside the European Community.[24]

This new meaning of unity clearly bears with it the heritage of Protestant Europe as well as a trace of a Cold War that left Europe divided between hostile superpowers. This kind of 'unification' of European powers has its motives in global power politics more than in any peace-plan. The unification of foreign policies that has taken place since the 1970s has, due to its intergovernmental structure in particular, been an indication of the legitimacy of this 'Europe of the Sovereignties'. This tradition has brought into European integration a new dimension which was not present in the original logic. This dimension has, above all, implied that the unification project has been drawn into an intergovernmental direction at the same time as new policy areas have been brought under Community powers.[25] Contrary to the original integration plans, which purported to weaken national sovereignty in favour of European peace and welfare, this intergovernmental model implied rather a reinforcement of national sovereignty for the sake of the external strength of Europe. De Gaulle saw in this form of cooperation between the European states a possibility of uniting the European forces under French leadership. For the smaller European states external unity has appeared to be a valuable source of political and economic security.

With intergovernmental cooperation as the political framework, democratic processes at the European level have not appeared to be an issue of particular importance. Democracy has, on the contrary, remained a question of national governments in the first place. This means that the democratic qualities of EC politics have been approached more or less in terms of the national conduct of foreign and European policies and in terms of their openness and parliamentary control. And the more that foreign and security matters have been emphasized as the substance of integration, the less democracy has

---

[24] This concept was not entirely new in Europe, though. The idea of a union between European states already constituted the core of Aristide Briand's plan in the late 1920s (Heater, *European Unity*, p. 133). Different types of unions between European sovereigns constituted the core of integration plans in the early eighteenth century, in particular (see, e.g., Voyenne, *Europatankens historia* (1953), p. 69).

[25] My argument on the novelty of the intergovernmental dimension is based upon the fact that the original federalist and liberal plans of integration included a strategy purporting to *overcome* this dimension, which has recently taken a new grip on the whole process.

appeared as a matter of importance in this connection.

This new direction of European unification has strengthened the intergovernmental qualities of the European Communities. This development culminated in the establishment of a new leading body, the European Council, in the 1970s. Again, the transfer of powers to the communitarian agencies, which was stipulated in the constitutive treaties, was decisively retarded.[26] The dispersion of Union decision-making into several institutional structures has been another typical effect of intergovernmentalism.[27] It has constituted the necessary condition for the enlargement of Union powers over the areas of foreign and security policy, but at the same time it has implied a most radical departure from the original plan for unification. This intergovernmental emphasis has been apt to make worse the state of democratic decision-making in the European Union, which was already suffering from a spill-over of bureaucracy. This has led to a situation where the development of the democratic features of the Union has appeared more and more difficult to realize on the basis of the original plan and where political compromises have therefore grown amorphous.[28]

6   THE PROBLEM OF DEMOCRACY REVISED

Through a historical approach I have intended to show that the democratic deficit is a structural question of the European Union rather than a bare institutional one. It has its origins in the focal conflict of views that has prevailed about the main political characteristics of the Union. First, it seems that the federal type of government bodies were an over-estimation from the beginning, or, that their supranational powers were not sufficient to create loyalties towards a common European government.[29] Secondly, bringing in new sensitive policy

---

[26] One of the most concrete acts of retardation is the Luxembourg compromise of 1966. The planned extension of the powers of the European Parliament was also hampered in many ways in the 1960s (Pinder, *European Community: The Building of a Union* (1991), p. 12).

[27] This development has been heavily opposed by federalists according to whom separate decisional structures threaten the whole existence of the European Union (this opposition can be documented from various sources, e.g., Vandamme, 'The Tindemans Report', in Pryce (ed.), *Dynamic of European Union*; Cardozo and Corbett, 'The Crocodile Initiative'; and concerning the debate around the Maastricht Treaty, see, e.g., the Debates of the EP No. 3–417/70).

[28] The Treaty on European Union includes various compromises whose normative clarity can be questioned (e.g., the legislative processes based upon Art. 189).

[29] The choice between these two statements depends on whether we are more inclined to accept the liberal plan for integration or the federalist one.

areas and new anti-federalist Member States has made the federalist organization a still less apparent basis for democracy in the European Union.

This background being given, I will now proceed to discuss the recent means set out for solving this problem in the European Union. The essence of the European Union being so seriously contested, it seems to me that its democratic deficit can only be solved through a means that is sufficiently acceptable from the point of view of all these very constitutive interests. The recent efforts made to improve the level of democracy in the European Union can be divided into two categories according to the way they relate themselves to the two integration plans constituting the basis for this discussion. Some of these instruments of democracy can be considered as pure prolongations of the original integration plans and the democracy programmes they included. Examples of these old methods are, for instance, the reinforcements of the powers of the European Parliament in the Treaty of European Union (TEU) and the measures taken to increase the degree of openness in Union decision-making. The concept of Union citizenship will be analysed in this category due to the fact that in its very essence it comprises an integral part of the old federalist plan. Brought for the first time into the legal and political system of the Union, the concept of Union citizenship, however, includes such a new, unproved potential for democracy that it must be considered separately from the other elements in this category.

There are two elements in the Maastricht Treaty which have raised great expectations of democracy and which can be treated as new instruments in the sense that their potentials have not yet been proved in Community politics. The concepts of regionality and subsidiarity and their democratic potentials will, however, be discussed last of all in this chapter.

7   ENHANCING DEMOCRACY IN ACCORDANCE WITH THE OLD PLANS

The original integration plans included two contradictory conceptions of the forms that a democratic government should have at the European level. Federalists strove for the establishment of a powerful European government above nation-states. The democratic nature of this planned federal government has been based upon a parliamentary body, the powers of which have been devised much in accordance with parliamentary powers at the national level. From time to time more constitutive political powers, such as powers to stipulate the whole political and legal basis of the European Community, have been demanded for the

European Parliament.[30]

The federalist programme of a European parliamentary democracy has not proceeded very successfully. The European Parliament has not been able to achieve the role of legislative supremacy. Nor does it carry out any decisive control of the political executive. The development of Parliament in this direction has, on the contrary, required political compromises which have rendered the Union's political and legislative system ambiguous and complicated. The Maastricht Treaty takes this original democracy programme some steps further through various channels. It establishes once more a new legislative process at the basis of which Parliament, for the first time, has the right of veto over legislative proposals of certain types. The right of Parliament to make legislative proposals is also slightly strengthened as well as its possibilities of exerting a democratic control of the executive. In addition to the political reasons which have hindered the effective realization of this democracy programme, there have, however, appeared various administrative factors working in the same direction. One of them is the size of the European Parliament, which is apt to put limits on effective functioning as long as it consists of one chamber only. Another hindrance, and connected with the first one, is the ineffective organization of party formation at the European level, which reflects itself in a lack of planning and political coherence in the parliamentary work.

European party formation stands conceptually very close to the more novel federalist element which recent integration politics has raised as one potential solution to the democratic deficit. The concept of Union citizenship is likely to increase the level of Union democracy in various ways. Some of these ways are derived directly from the powers of the European Parliament, while others can be seen to contribute to the democratization of the European Union at a more basic level in the citizenry. The idea of civil and human rights being laid down at the European level has constituted a vital part of the Christian Democrat plan for European unification. The decisive break-through of the idea took place in the draft Treaty of the European Parliament in 1984, after which two major modifications of the constitu-

---

[30] At least twice a European assembly has drafted a 'constitution' for a united Europe. In the years 1952–1953 this task was given to the general assembly of the Coal and Steel Union, which drafted a further form of unification at the basis of the ECSC Treaty and the defence union that was being planned (Cardozo, 'Project for a Political Community', p. 54). At the beginning of the 1980s, the present European Parliament adopted a similar role and drew the outlines for the first large-scale Union treaty of the past few decades (draft Treaty on Political Union).

tive treaties have already been made in this respect.[31] The Maastricht Treaty establishes and recognizes the concept of Union citizenship, but only subsequent legal and political practice will show its concrete significance as well as give the outlines for its further development.

The concept of Union citizenship contributes to the unification of political rights at the Union level. Even if this new federalist element will presumably have a great impact upon Union democracy in the long term, its role will first be essentially bound to the position of the European Parliament. As long as political rights laid down at the Union level are limited to parliamentary participation, the new citizenship will bring no major amendment to the situation of democracy. There is, however, a latent possibility for a more long-term change in two respects. First, I see in the concept of Union citizenship a firm instrument for the reinforcement of the European Parliament. It appears evident that as far as the concept of Union citizenship will strengthen the idea of a Union electorate it will give further legitimacy to the European Parliament and bring it closer to the European people. Another detail of equal importance in this respect is the unitary electoral system.

The other effect of 'citizenship', including and exceeding the first one, relates to the capacity of this concept to constitute not only an electorate, but a citizenry in a broader sense. This is furthermore bound up with the way the formation of parties and other social and political groups proceeds at the European level. A broader justification of the concept of Union citizenship is presumable to lead to an extension of citizens' rights determined at the Union level. All in all this could imply a pressure towards a modification of Union government in a direction which would take better account of the citizens' perspective. As I have tried to show in this chapter, the continuing legitimacy of national sovereignty and the opposition raised against a federal Europe have constituted the main obstacles to this development thus far. This growing 'citizen identity' would imply the emergence of a heavier critique of the bureaucratic and complicated character of Union decision-making.

The concept of Union citizenship has been introduced here as an intermediate form between old and new means of democracy in the European Union. It remains still to be pointed out that in addition to the federalist democracy programme to which this concept gives

---

[31] The Single European Act included a general reference to human and civil rights and the TEU brought in finally the whole concept of 'Union citizenship'. Art. 3 of the draft Treaty established 'Union citizenship' (e.g., Lodge, *European Union*, p. 190) much in the same terms as the TEU (Art. 8).

expression, democracy has recently been pursued by means of the original liberal integration plan. Here democracy has been linked with the openness and transparency of Union decision-making. According to the political declaration attached to the Maastricht Treaty, the European Commission should submit to the Council a report on measures designed to improve public access to information available to the institutions.[32] At the political level the Union agencies have already reached an agreement on certain measures which should be taken in order to increase Union democracy and transparency.[33] Another instrument of democracy which has been of greater importance in the liberal programme is the effective involvement of national parliaments in Union decision-making. Federalists, again, have tended to concentrate more upon the powers of the European Parliament. There is also a declaration attached to the Maastricht Treaty concerning the reinforcement of the role of national parliaments in matters of European integration.[34]

8 SUBSIDIARITY AND REGIONALITY AS MEANS OF DEMOCRACY IN THE EUROPEAN UNION

The concept of Union citizenship constitutes, in theory, a significant instrument for the democratic development of the European Union. Its effective use is, however, likely to be complicated because of its apparently federalist character.[35] It is questionable whether the journey to a democratic European Union is shorter through the principles of regionality and subsidiarity, but the character of these principles is at least more receptive of compromises. The problem of their acceptability is that the traditions of regionalism and subsidiarity belong closer to Catholic Europe, where a stronger attraction towards a united Europe already exists. The link in common between these principles is that they can both be made to work against the principle of state sovereignty and for a fragmentation of political authority without any necessary connection with federalism. Both principles have, however, grown up

---

[32] Declaration on the Right to Access to Information.

[33] Interinstitutional Declaration on Democracy, Transparency and Subsidiarity (Doc. EN\RR\239\239257).

[34] Declaration on the Role of National Parliaments in the European Union.

[35] Denmark has already been allowed to make some important reservations against the concept, while the realization of the rights connected with it has run into great difficulties in other Member States, too (see, e.g., Chapter 6).

in a close interaction with EC government, which appears necessary in order to enable them to cope with the strength of national sovereignty. It seems to me that, at least for the time being, the fragmentation of sovereignties is decisively dependent on the centralized powers of the EU.

The expectations of democracy that have been raised by the principles of subsidiarity and regionality have in both cases been based upon their assumed capacities to work against the centralizing features of the European Union. The principle of subsidiarity originates in the Catholic political tradition. Its democratic essence results from its core idea of making decisions as close as possible to the citizens. Its significance for Union democracy will therefore be connected not only with the division of powers between the Union and the Member States, but also with the division of powers between the Member States and regions, or other political unities in the Member States.

The problems in the application of the principle have already made themselves apparent at both of these levels. In general, the provisions on subsidiarity remain ambiguous in the Maastricht Treaty and have already been provided with various guidelines of interpretation.[36] As a result of the explicit formation of these provisions, subsidiarity has been approached in the first place as a division of power between the Union and the Member States. The ECJ will now play the key role as far as the definition and interpretation of the principle is concerned. It will thus also decide upon the role that the principle of democracy should play as a criterion for its application.

The other new dimension of Union democracy derives from the principle of regionality. This dimension reflects an aspiration to strengthen politically different kinds of historical, cultural and economic regions at the expense of the nation-state. In the context of European integration this kind of political development has been seen as a protection of the elements of plurality and heterogeneity which might otherwise risk being weakened. The importance of regions has been emphasized in various declarations and protocols since the 1980s. In 1988 a consultative board consisting of local and regional authorities was established in the Commission. In the Maastricht Treaty it was given an official status as the Committee of Regions, the powers of which are, however, quite marginal thus far.

Problems arising from the principle of regionality as a means of democracy are closely interrelated with the problems concealed behind

---

[36] E.g., Interinstitutional Agreement on Procedures for Implementing the Principle of Subsidiarity, Doc. PE 176.643, 7–58; 1992 Commission Communication to the Council and the European Parliament on Subsidiarity, Bull. EC–1992/10.

the full use of the rule of subsidiarity. The strength and forms of regionality vary enormously between different Member States of the Union. Wessels and Engel have analysed forms of regionality in European states by dividing these into regionalized, decentralized and unitary states.[37] In addition to a federal Germany, Belgium, Italy and Spain are classified as regionalized states. In all these countries the rights of regions have been stipulated in law. In France and The Netherlands the central government is dominant in spite of the decentralization of regions. Regions are governed by assemblies elected by the people. In unitary states like Denmark, Greece and Ireland the regions are weak, but the role of local government tends to be significant. The European Union intends to support a development of regionality which is in harmony with natural region formation in Europe. It appears evident that as a means of democracy the principle of regionality will be the most successful in those countries in which regionality and regional self-government are based upon a long tradition.

For instance in northern Europe, where regional communities are less natural and the main emphasis is put upon local government, the democratic influence of the principle of regionality is not so self-evident. The same can be said about subsidiarity, which has certainly better chances of decentralizing political power in those Member States which have more serious historical alternatives to state sovereignty.

9   CONCLUSION

The democratic deficit appears to be a much more far-reaching problem of the present unification process than is usually imagined. The problem of democracy is a conflict of forms where federal representative democracy, international institutional democracy and national democracy stand against each other. And there are no signs of the dissolution of this constellation, the origins of which are deep in European cultural and political history. I have tried to show that the democratic deficit cannot be abolished simply by increasing the powers of the European Parliament. The discussion on democracy should therefore be extended and the particular character of the European Union be taken more into account.

The new instruments that the Maastricht Treaty sets up to work against the democratic deficit appear to be too weak to reach the core

---

[37] Kokkonen and Vartiainen, *Alueiden Eurooppa: haasteet alueelliselle kehittämiselle* [The Europe of Regions: Challenges of Regional Development] (1993), p. 15.

of the difficult problem. Their weakness does not lie in the concepts of Union citizenship, subsidiarity and regionality themselves, but rather in their uneven acceptability in various areas of Europe. If this problem can somehow be overcome it will presumably take so long that the Union will be risking its legitimacy in the eyes of the citizens before democratization bears fruit. Democracy, once one of the constitutive forces of European integration, has suddenly turned into its fateful problem. This problem has to be solved before it breaks down the legitimacy of the whole of this historical idea.

3 A EUROPE CLOSE TO THE CITIZEN? THE 'TRINITY CONCEPTS' OF SUBSIDIARITY, TRANSPARENCY AND DEMOCRACY

Nanette A. Neuwahl

1   INTRODUCTION

There are few concepts in European Community law which are as elusive as the concept of subsidiarity, or the principle laid down in Article 3b EC Treaty that the Community should act only where an objective can be better achieved by the Community than by the individual Member States. Article 3b EC Treaty determines the best level of decision-making. But what does it mean? What is subsidiarity exactly: is it about effectiveness, is it about competence, is it about necessity? Can it be enforced by a competent court? Contemporary documents on subsidiarity exist in the form of the 1992 Commission Communication,[1] the 'Edinburgh Annex'[2] and an Interinstitutional Agreement.[3] But they are not conclusive, and a decision by the Court of Justice of the European Communities (ECJ), which could provide an authoritative interpretation of the EC Treaty, is not yet available. Consequently, the literature on the meaning and possible application of the principle flourishes.

An issue where there is yet new ground to be covered is the possible meaning of subsidiarity in the light of a citizens' Europe. In

---

Some of the ideas expressed in this chapter have been presented at the University of Swansea and the European Community Institute of the University of Marmara, Istanbul. The author wishes to thank all participants at the Turku Symposium on a Citizens' Europe on 14–17 July 1994 for their helpful comments. She alone, of course, is responsible for any shortcomings.

[1] 1992 Commission Communication to the Council and the European Parliament on subsidiarity, Bull. EC 10–1992, pt. 2.2.1.

[2] Annex to the Conclusions of the Presidency of the European Council at Edinburgh 11–12 Dec. 1992. See Part One: Overall Approach to the Application by the Council of the Subsidiarity Principle and Article 3b TEU. Bull. EC 12–1992, pt. I.15–I.22.

[3] Interinstitutional Agreement on Procedures for Implementing the Principle of Subsidiarity. Adopted 17 Nov. 1993. Doc. PE 176.643, pp. 7–58.

that context, subsidiarity, transparency and democracy can be seen as a trinity.

The terms 'democracy' and 'transparency' do not appear in the EC Treaty. Nor have they been defined by the ECJ. In a common sense understanding, the term 'democracy' can be used to describe a requirement assuring the adequate involvement, by direct or indirect participation, of citizens or groups of citizens in an area of policy-making within the Community (elective and participatory democracy). Democracy is also about ensuring the protection of the rights of the individual.[4] The concept of transparency in turn is closely related to the latter aspect. 'Transparency' would denote a requirement that acts of government be understandable to the persons concerned and, where appropriate, accessible to the public, reasoned and clearly drafted.

The Community institutions seem to establish some connection between these concepts as the three principles have been the subject of what would appear to be a package of interinstitutional agreements delivered on the same day. Why would this be so? Of course, the Community is bound to Article A of the Treaty on European Union (TEU), which provides that decisions in the Union shall be taken 'as closely as possible to the citizen'.[5] This article is binding on the Community institutions, even if it is not enforceable by the ECJ (see Article L TEU). Because, in a sense, the principles of democracy, transparency and arguably also subsidiarity serve to bring Europe closer to the citizen, it is natural to mention all three notions together and to treat them as norms to be observed by the Community. But apart from this, there is also a 'selfish' motive behind the zeal of the institutions: after the referendums on Maastricht it became clear that the citizens of the Member States would not be queuing up to support further transfers of power to the Community if it is basically an undemocratic organism of which little is known or understood. In these circumstances the long-standing insistence by the European Parliament that these principles be put into practice did not fall on deaf ears with the other institutions. Some guarantee of democracy and transparency it was hoped would instil confidence in the Community, lessen resistance to its actions and foster greater participation in its construction. The principle of subsidiarity serves a similar purpose as it makes clear that the Community is not wholly swallowing the identities of the

---

[4] Mancini and Keeling, 'Democracy and the European Court of Justice', 57 MLR (1994), 175–190, at 181.

[5] In addition, the preamble of the TEU confirms the attachment of the Member States to the principles of liberty, democracy and human rights and fundamental freedoms and of the rule of law as well as to the principle of subsidiarity.

Member States or lower levels of decision-making, but is subject to a rational division of power. So it is not surprising that a series of interinstitutional negotiations dealt with these matters in close connection.

But what exactly is the legal relationship, if any, between these principles? Ought not considerations of transparency and democracy play a role in determining the best level of decision-making (or is it merely the case that these principles have to be strengthened because in some instances there may be no alternative to Community action)? If principles of democracy or transparency are taken into consideration when determining the decision-making level, would this be contrary to Article 3b? In my opinion an interpretation of subsidiarity which leaves factors so important to a citizens' Europe out of account would be too narrow. The debate on the meaning of subsidiarity therefore has to be reopened.

In the next two sections of this chapter I will investigate how subsidiarity is dealt with in the Maastricht Treaty (Section 2) and by the institutions (Section 3). Section 4 deals with the possible role of the ECJ in interpreting subsidiarity. In Section 5 a liberal interpretation of Article 3b is attempted, taking into account the significance of general principles of law. In Section 6 the question of the role played by the principles of democracy and transparency in the assessment of compliance with Article 3b will receive a tentative answer. The conclusion will be that it is not possible to see subsidiarity as a concept wholly detached from the principles of transparency and democracy. Situations may arise where these principles ought to be part of the subsidiarity test itself. Taken as a principle of effectiveness or competence only, subsidiarity cannot bring Europe closer to the citizen. Interpreted in a more flexible way it may.

2   SUBSIDIARITY IN THE TREATY ON EUROPEAN UNION

The determination of the meaning of subsidiarity as a legal concept has to start from a textual analysis of the Maastricht Treaty. The word 'subsidiarity' can be found basically only in the Common Provisions, Article B TEU and Article 3b EC Treaty. According to Article B TEU, the objectives of the Union shall be achieved 'while respecting the principle of subsidiarity as defined in Article 3b of the Treaty establishing the European Community'. This latter provision is definitely more elaborate, as it provides:

The Community shall act within the limits of the powers conferred upon it by this Treaty and of the objectives assigned to it therein. In areas which do not fall within its exclusive competence, the Community shall take action, in accordance with the principle of subsidiarity, only if and in so far as the objectives of the proposed action cannot be sufficiently achieved by the Member States and can therefore, by reason of the scale or the effects of the proposed action, be better achieved by the Community.

Any action by the Community shall not go beyond what is necessary to achieve the objectives of this Treaty.

Several things can be noted on the basis of a textual analysis of this article.

First of all, Article 3b EC Treaty does not really contain a clear definition of subsidiarity. Apart from the fact that the second paragraph is a monster which would not satisfy any test of transparency, it is not plain to see where exactly in the article subsidiarity is defined, if at all. In particular, it is not clear whether one would have to take the meaning of this concept from the second paragraph of Article 3b only, or whether the first and third paragraphs of the article are part of the 'definition', as Article B TEU would seem to imply.

However this may be, the main element of subsidiarity seems to be the rule laid down in the second paragraph that the Community shall act only where an objective can be better attained at the Community level than at the level of the Member States. As such, the principle appears to be a procedural device determining the division of policy-making responsibilities between the Member States and the Community. Arguably, apart from subjecting Community action to certain conditions, the article also imposes a negative obligation on the Member States to refrain from action if the conditions referred to are fulfilled. The principle cannot be used for transferring new powers to the Community, for that would conflict with the preceding paragraph.

In addition, it strikes immediately that Article 3b applies to the relations between national capitals and the Community level only. It does not deal with smaller units like regions, *Länder*, provinces, municipalities or cities. For this reason, it would appear, the principle of subsidiarity in Article 3b cannot be used as an all-round legal device for determining the appropriate level of decision-making in the Community.

Undoubtedly, in the context of Article 3b the powers of decentralized institutions will be taken into account, because if it is considered that the Community level is the most appropriate level of decision-making, this implies that the national, regional or local level is not,[6] and vice versa, but the fact remains that the principle laid down in Article 3b does not explicitly provide for the possibility of devolving powers to subnational authorities. The question whether the Community, in its sphere of competence, can delegate legislative or executive powers to subnational levels of government is not addressed, and the intention seems to be to respect the freedom of the Member States to organize themselves internally.[7]

In addition, Article 3b does not deal with non-state organizations, citizens' movements, employers and trade unions, other social groupings or individuals. It is plain to see, therefore, that the article is far from representing a blueprint for the social organization of the Union.

Within the limited field of application just described, Article 3b lays down two criteria for determining whether a certain objective can be better achieved by the Member States or by the Community: the scale and the effects of the proposed action. These criteria are vague and in need of elaboration (see below).

Another aspect which catches the eye is that the rule that the Community shall act only where an objective can be better attained at the Community level should not apply to 'exclusive' Community competences. This can be criticized. Even in fields of exclusivity Member States at present have not lost their power to act. They merely have lost the power to act autonomously.[8] It could be argued that in fields of exclusivity a subsidiarity test should apply to indicate the expediency of authorizing Member States to act. This is now formally excluded. Nevertheless, whether a 'hands off exclusivity' clause can work in practice of course remains to be seen. In view of constant discussions about the Community's exclusive competences, there is a possibility that subsidiarity arguments will be introduced in the discussion about virtually any measure proposed by the Commission.

In addition, the words 'exclusive' and 'competence' are not entirely clear. Exclusivity, it would seem, is the principle whereby the power to enact legally binding rules on a certain subject matter is reserved to the Community (to the exclusion of the Member States and lower levels of

---

[6] Hessel and Mortelmans, 'Decentralized Government and Community Law: Conflicting Institutional Developments?', 30 CML Rev. (1993), 905–937, at 911.

[7] Cf. Case 96/81, *Commission v The Netherlands*, [1982] ECR 1791. See also the opinion by Advocate General Jacobs in Case C-156/91, *Mundt*, [1992] ECR I 5587, para. 29.

[8] I.a., Case 131/73, *Giulio and Adriano Grosoli*, [1973] ECR 1555, cons. 6; and Case 41/76, *Criel, née Donckerwolcke et al.* v *Procureur de la République et al.*, [1976] ECR 1921, cons. 32.

government).[9] In this sense it is dealt with in the case law of the ECJ. However, it may also be used so as to include other than legislative powers. As a rule, even where the Community has an exclusive legislative power, powers of enforcement or administration and executive power (i.e., power of implementation) in the Community can be delegated to Member States or international organizations.[10] To assume that a test of subsidiarity would apply also in regard to such aspects of the division of powers would certainly not be straining the text of Article 3b. Whether Article 3b can be applied to the (exclusive) power of the Community institutions to enforce competition policy is uncertain.

The third paragraph of Article 3b, which requires that any action of the Community shall not go beyond what is necessary to achieve the objectives of the Treaty, and which is applicable also in areas of exclusive Community competences, may well have to be distinguished from the principle of subsidiarity. Arguably, this paragraph is nothing but the principle of proportionality, which is the subject of a well-established (though not necessarily exhaustive) case law of the ECJ. Somewhat confusingly for lawyers, however, the Commission Communication, the Edinburgh Annex and implicitly also the Interinstitutional Agreement deal with the third paragraph of Article 3b under the heading of subsidiarity. The Edinburgh Annex refers to the principle in the second paragraph as 'subsidiarity in the strict legal sense'. Arguably, the test of proportionality precedes the test set out in the second paragraph of Article 3b, in the sense that only a 'minimal' action by the Community, or in any case only a measure which is 'necessary' to achieve the objectives of the Treaty will be considered and compared with action by the Member States.

In addition, in assessing whether Article 3b is complied with, reference may be taken, if appropriate, to the more specific Treaty articles imposing obligations on the Community and/or setting limits to Community action.[11]

The relationship between Article 3b and Article 235 is not immediately clear, but the best view seems to be that these articles can apply simultaneously, the latter providing for implied powers of the Community, the former specifying the conditions and the way in which they

---

[9] I.e., as long as it does not authorize Member States to act (see above).

[10] On this matter see Lenaerts, 'Regulating the Regulatory Process: "Delegation of Power" in the European Community', 18 EL Rev. (1993), 23–49.

[11] Examples of articles imposing limits to Community action are: Arts 118a, 126, 127, 128, 129, 129a, 129b, 130 and 130g EC Treaty and Art. 2 of the Agreement on Social Policy.

may be exercised.

Finally, it is interesting to note that, since the ECJ is bound by the EC Treaty, its actions may also have to comply with the principle of subsidiarity. If Article 3b is not restricted to legislative measures, arguably it also requires the ECJ to exercise restraint in taking up jurisdiction or in the tenor of its judgments.[12]

3   SUBSIDIARITY AS INTERPRETED BY THE INSTITUTIONS

The Commission, the Council, the European Parliament and the European Council have dealt with the principle of subsidiarity in a number of documents.

Both the Edinburgh Annex and the Commission Communication provide guidelines for assessing compliance with Article 3b EC Treaty. The Commission and the Heads of State or Government focus on (1) the necessity, respectively (2) the intensity of Community action.

(1) In order to enable the assessment of the *necessity* of Community action, the two documents provide some indications for a case-by-case analysis. The Commission Communication is the most informative in this respect, and its suggestions are not out of tune with the rather concise section of the Edinburgh Annex dealing with the same subject. The Commission's sophisticated views certainly do not offer an easy way out of the problem as to what is the best level of decision-making (in the specific instance the various limbs of the rather elaborate cumulative test may point to opposite results), but at least they provide a framework for discussion. The criteria suggested by the Commission would appear to be the following:

(a) The degree of constraint imposed on the institutions, or the question whether there is an obligation of result in the Treaty provisions. Indicatively, the degree of constraint would be highest in fields like the harmonious functioning of the internal market and lowest in fields like education, culture, health.

(b) The comparative effectiveness of the means available to the Community respectively the Member States. This in turn implies: (i) checking that the Member States have at their disposal the means—including the financial means—to the end

---

[12] This matter will not be elaborated in more detail in the context of this chapter. Suffice to say that the interpretation of Article 3b proposed below in Section 5 would appear to be in conformity with such an attitude, should it be required.

(national, regional or local legislation, codes of conduct, agreements between employers, etc.);[13] and (ii) assessing the effectiveness of Community action. This involves questions like: what does Community action add to Member State action, what is its 'critical mass', what is most efficient and cost-efficient, what would be the cost of non-action, and the transnational aspect of the problem that is to be solved?[14]

From the viewpoint of a citizens' Europe, it is the comparative effectiveness criterion which is alarming, since everyone knows that effectiveness *per se* can be the antithesis of both democracy and transparency.

(2) With regard to the question of the *intensity* of Community action, the principle is essentially that where the Community has a choice between several instruments, the instrument which least restricts the Member States should be chosen.

It shall be clear that the interpretation by the Commission and the Heads of State or Government is hardly capable of bringing Europe closer to the citizen. This interpretation, with its emphasis on effectiveness, does not have regard for considerations relating to the direct or indirect participation by citizens, or the adequate representation of their interests. As regards transparency, although the third paragraph of Article 3b in theory should help to reduce the excessive detail of Community legislation, neither the criterion of necessity, nor the criterion of the intensity of Community action in fact guarantees that Community measures are clearly drafted or accessible to the public.

As concerns decision-making levels other than the Community or the national tier of government, only the Commission Communication envisages them, and even there it is not in great detail. Interestingly, the Commission does acknowledge that such interests are to be taken into account in the preparation and examination of proposed Community action, that transfers of powers to the Community shall have 'due regard' for national identity and the powers of the regions, and also that regional agencies can play a role in the management and supervision of the implementation of Community policies and activities.[15] Yet when it comes to assessing the expediency of Community action, the criterion is really that of the effectiveness of such action, not the level

---

[13] The comparative efficiency test.

[14] The value added test.

[15] None of these aspects is dealt with in the Edinburgh Annex or the Interinstitutional Agreement.

of decision-making as such or any substantive or organizational considerations.

The Interinstitutional Agreement basically does not add any criteria for the interpretation of the principle of subsidiarity, as it is focused on procedural aspects. In this agreement it is stipulated by way of preliminary that the procedures shall not call into question the *acquis communautaire* or the institutional balance of power. This can be important for two reasons. First, it may mean that when the Council and the European Parliament have doubts about the compliance of existing Community legislation with the principle of subsidiarity, rather than having recourse to the ECJ, these institutions will have to steer at amendment of those aspects which in their opinion do not conform with the principle by calling for a Commission proposal. Secondly, and more in general, it may prevent the risk that the position of the Commission is weakened through over-frequent, 'unjustified' recourse to an investigation of the principle. This may be relevant notably as regards measures coming in the exclusive competence of the Community.

It is provided that the Commission shall take into account the principle of subsidiarity and show that it is observed. The European Parliament and the Council shall do likewise in exercising the powers conferred on them in Articles 138b and 152 EC Treaty. Since Article 138b refers to the power of the European Parliament to request the Commission to submit proposals on matters on which it considers that a Community act is required for the purpose of implementing the EC Treaty, it shall be clear that this institution is entrusted here with an important task, as well as with a possibility of influencing the further interpretation and application of the principle.

The Interinstitutional Agreement then proceeds to state that compliance with the principle must be shown by the Commission in its explanatory memorandum of a proposal. Compliance with the principle shall be regularly checked, both as regards the choice of legal instruments used and as regards the content of a proposal. Subsidiarity is therefore a dynamic concept.

Examination of the observance of the principle occurs at the same time as the substantive examination of a proposal. Review of compliance shall furthermore take place under the 'normal Community process', which probably means that review by the ECJ is considered possible.

Since none of the documents mentioned is a Community act in the sense of Article 189 EC Treaty, the question of their legal effect arises. Plainly, the Commission Communication is a unilateral interpretation by the Commission of how in its view the principle of subsidiarity should be applied. Formally, it has no binding legal force. The Edinburgh Annex is essentially a political understanding of Article 3b EC Treaty by the Heads of State or Government. This kind of act also has no binding legal force in Community law.

The legal force of Interinstitutional Agreements in Community law is uncertain.[16] Zangl[17] defines such an act as a 'gentlemen's agreement', whose legal force is 'less binding than a formal Council Decision', but better accepted and more likely to be respected. Because these agreements are conceived as gentlemen's agreements, the question of the legal effect of this type of agreement is unlikely to arise directly before the ECJ on the initiative of an institution, but it is not excluded. On the other hand, individuals may not be interested in invoking such agreements, even if they are aware of them, because they usually contain matters of procedural practice.

However this may be, it is conceivable that the three documents on subsidiarity, taken alone or in comparison, have an indirect legal impact, since they can be used informally by the ECJ in order to detect a politically feasible interpretation of the Founding Treaties or an emerging institutional practice. Secondly, it is conceivable that a continued institutional practice creates rights and obligations of its own, either on the basis of legitimate expectations or on the basis of general principles of law (see further below).

4   THE ROLE OF THE COURT OF JUSTICE OF THE EUROPEAN COMMUNITIES

Within the framework of the EC Treaty, the interpretation and application of Article 3b is subject to the jurisdiction of the ECJ in the same way as that of any other provision of Community law. In the view of one writer[18] the principle of subsidiarity will give rise to a floodgate of constant litigation, as both national and Community legislation will be open to challenge, at both national and Community level, on the grounds that it infringes Article 3b.

The question which imposes itself is, how could such questions come before the ECJ? As has been noted above, the recourse to litigation between Community institutions regarding existing Commu-

---

[16] See now Monar, 'Interinstitutional Agreements: The Phenomenon and its New Dimension after Maastricht', 31 CML Rev. (1994), 693–719.

[17] Zangl, 'The Interinstitutional Agreement on Budgetary Discipline and Improvement of the Budgetary Procedure', 26 CML Rev. (1989), 675–685, at 678.

[18] Toth, 'The Principle of Subsidiarity in the Maastricht Treaty', 29 CML Rev. (1992), 1079–1105, at 1101.

nity legislation may well be restricted by the Interinstitutional Agreement, and the institutional balance of power may well prevent attacks by the institutions against newly proposed Community legislation.[19] The most likely litigants are therefore (groups of) individuals, subnational authorities, and the Member States themselves. As regards individuals, since the ECJ is not bound by the Edinburgh Annex (see above), the statement in that document that the principle cannot be invoked by individuals is not determining. Questions in connection with subsidiarity may therefore come before the ECJ via the national judge or, if appropriate, in a direct action provided for by the Treaties. Subnational authorities too may wish to raise a question concerning the validity of a Community measure or a national measure (legislative or other) before a national court, which could then ask for a preliminary ruling. Litigation at the initiative of a Member State challenging Community legislation is less likely because the Member States' governments are represented in the Council, but it is not excluded, especially when the Community act concerned was adopted by majority. In addition, the ECJ may have to decide questions relating to the division of treaty-making power between the Community and the Member States in certain policy areas. In the context of opinions under Article 228(6) EC Treaty, the Council, the Commission or a Member State can request the opinion of the ECJ as to whether an agreement envisaged is compatible with the EC. There is therefore little doubt that the question of subsidiarity will arise at law.

Should any of these matters come up for decision, one may wonder if the ECJ is really in a position to decide whether the objectives of a measure can be better achieved at the Community level or at the national level. The ECJ has never really been willing to decide whether a particular measure is suitable to achieve a given objective or how that objective can best be achieved.[20] In the view of Toth,[21] these are complex economic and political decisions for which the ECJ is not equipped in terms of staff and expertise.

Admittedly, several aspects of subsidiarity will be beyond judicial control. Whereas the ECJ may find less difficulty in applying the principle of proportionality[22] and the principle of *attribution de*

---

[19] In the same way it would appear that an action for failure to act on account of Article 3b would in practice be restricted.

[20] See, e.g., Cases 6/54, 154/78, 136/77, 138/79, 197/80.

[21] Toth, 'The Principle of Subsidiarity', 1102.

[22] On this matter, see further Nolte, 'General Principles of German and European Administrative Law. A Comparison in Historical Perspective', 57 MLR (1994), 191–212.

compétences (laid down in the third and first paragraphs of Article 3b), the control of what the Annex calls 'subsidiarity in the strict legal sense' (the second paragraph of Article 3b) may well be confined to a marginal check on the exercise of powers by political institutions which respects their margin of appreciation.

Yet, even if the ECJ cannot become the ultimate arbiter as to whether the principle of subsidiarity has been observed in a particular case, this would not prevent it from further interpreting Article 3b. This aspect of the role of the ECJ has not been elaborated on very much in the research on subsidiarity, although there clearly is a potential for further development of the Community legal order. Because from the viewpoint of a citizens' Europe a conception of subsidiarity centring mainly on efficiency or comparative effectiveness would appear to be too narrow, the ECJ could interpret Article 3b in a way which goes further than the institutions have done.

The ECJ may want to establish clearly, for instance, that non-state interests are to be taken into account when judging the necessity of Community action in the second and/or third paragraphs. But other factors may be equally important. For instance, in an intervention by Jacques Delors at the Interinstitutional Conference in November 1992, the President of the Commission suggested that the question whether money of the European citizens was involved could be a criterion for Community action.[23] Similarly, the need to establish direct effect could be a criterion for establishing Community action. For instance, traditionally, GATT rules are considered to have no direct effect as long as there is no internal Community legislation giving them such effect. The desirability of establishing the direct effect of GATT provisions may be a criterion justifying the necessity of Community legislation granting such effect.

It shall be clear that, from the viewpoint of a citizens' Europe, any development of this kind could provide a valuable incentive to the development of higher standards both in the Community and/or within the individual Member States. Arguably, therefore, the role of the ECJ in connection with the principle of subsidiarity is more important than might first appear.

One final remark has to be made in this context. It may not be advisable to think of subsidiarity as a concept which needs to be refined solely for the purpose of enforcement. As Brinkhorst remarks: 'The more one attempts to be precise, the greater the difficulties there

---

[23] Delors, 'Intervention à la conférence interinstitutionelle tenue à Bruxelles, le 10 Novembre 1992'. Mimeo.

will be in achieving either Community or national action.'[24] Instead of tightening up the screws on subsidiarity, it is also possible that the ECJ might 'soften up' the principle in respect of the requirements laid down by the other institutions. This is especially expedient if one takes the view that the interpretations given by the institutions in the documents referred to above are not adequate, because, centring as they do on efficiency and comparative effectiveness, they disregard aspects of central importance to the citizen.

Many scholars have focused on the role of the ECJ as an enforcement mechanism for subsidiarity. This then has led to the conclusion that subsidiarity could not be enforced for lack of legal precision, as if that would be a major concern. Yet a legal rule is not binding only if it is enforceable by a court. Because non-enforceable aspects of the EC Treaty can have as much decisive effect on the daily running of the Community as enforceable ones, perhaps it is time to devote more attention to some areas at the 'borderlines' of the ECJ's jurisdiction.

5 A LIBERAL INTERPRETATION OF ARTICLE 3B, TAKING INTO ACCOUNT GENERAL PRINCIPLES OF LAW

It is one thing to say that the criteria laid down by the institutions should not be the only ones to determine the best level of decision-making under Article 3b. To prove that other factors must or can be taken into account is quite another matter.

In the interpretation of subsidiarity, it will be necessary to investigate the area of general principles of law, and this for two reasons. First, if there are any such principles, they give rise to enforceable rules of Community law. It is general knowledge among lawyers that by using general principles of law the ECJ can resolve what is unclear or fill in gaps, or even strike down Community law, and surely, even without pronouncement by the ECJ, the detection of general principles of law can give an indication of the way in which Community law ought to be interpreted at a given moment in time. Secondly, if there are no such principles we are safely in the political arena: if all sources of Community law have been exhausted, any political solution which does not come into conflict with such norms represents an acceptable course of action in the Community framework.

One may observe that on the Community level few principles have

---

[24] Brinkhorst, 'Subsidiarity and European Environmental Policy', in *Subsidiarity: The Challenge of Change—Proceedings of the Jacques Delors Colloquium 1991* (1991), pp. 89–100, at p. 91.

evolved as regards the principle of subsidiarity itself. It may be too early to say, for instance, that the practice by Community institutions of taking subnational interests into account when determining whether Community action is better/necessary has given rise to a general principle of Community law which requires this to be done.

On the other hand, one will readily accept that provisions of the EC Treaty have to be interpreted in the light of human rights principles binding on the Community. Arguably, a requirement of transparency is part of the rule of law which the Community of necessity has to observe. In July 1994 the British newspaper the *Guardian* took the Council before the Court of First Instance for its refusal to give them access to certain preparatory documents and minutes of the Council in conformity with the pertinent Council regulation of 20 December 1993.[25] The *Guardian* claimed, *inter alia*, that this violated the fundamental right of access to documents along the lines set out in one of the Declarations annexed to the TEU. The respect of the right of public access to government information, the paper argued, is becoming a real necessity in the Community because the Union suffers from a 'lack of democratic control'.

In addition, one may want to know if any further rules of relevance to subsidiarity can be derived from the legal systems of the Member States.[26] Of course, the notion of 'democracy' can scarcely be considered a general principle of law. Surely, there is no Member State which would deny being a democratic state, but it is of little avail to say that 'democracy' is a legal norm in all the Member States, as the concept is both hard to define and of little use if not made specific in prescriptive rules.

Prescriptive rules apply, for instance, in the budgetary sphere, and perhaps these can help to provide an answer to some of the practical problems with which the Community is confronted. Former Commission President Jacques Delors gives an account of how it had been suggested to the Commission that a special Community inspectorate be established to check, *inter alia*, the quality of drinking water in Seville or bathing water on British beaches. Reflecting on how this would fit in with the principle of subsidiarity, Delors states that in his view, whenever money is being spent by the Community, that level itself should exercise control to ensure that it is properly spent.[27]

---

[25] *Europe*, 16 July 1994, 14.

[26] General principles of law can also be found in the international legal order, but it is difficult to see what this could add to the analysis presented here.

[27] Delors, 'Intervention à la conférence'.

In order to determine the existence of general principles derived from the systems of the Member States, one would have to undertake a careful comparative analysis of the legal systems concerned. This involves analysing constitutions, legislation as well as case law. It should not be a prerequisite that any specific principle exists in each of the Member States. When there is no rule of law governing a certain situation and a norm must be found in order to prevent a denial of justice, it may be sufficient if such a rule is available only in some of the legal orders of the Member States, whilst the others remain silent.[28]

The situation is different when the national legal orders offer divergent solutions for the same problem. If two or more legal orders present solutions which cannot be reconciled, then there is no general rule common to the laws of the Member States, and therefore, no general principle of Community law. Thus, there does not seem to exist a general principle of subsidiarity that powers *ought to* be devolved to subnational levels, because the legal system of one or more of the Member States may well object to such an interpretation. Also it is uncertain whether any support can be derived from the national legal systems for a Community rule that subnational interests have to be taken into account when determining whether or not action at a higher level is better or necessary.

As stated before, however, even from the absence of general principles conclusions may be drawn: in that case any solution which does not come into conflict with the formal norms of Community law represents an acceptable course of action. For instance, there does not seem to exist a general principle which *per se* forbids any devolution of (executive) power to subnational governments.[29] As a result, the devolution of certain powers to, for instance, regional levels through a Community act can lawfully take place, provided, of course, that this would be necessary to achieve the Community's objectives. The latter may perhaps be difficult to show, but if the legislative should think it is, it would be difficult to maintain on legal grounds that it exceeded its discretion. For that reason, should a Community rule be adopted which provides for a devolution of power, it would probably stand. The authority of local government is therefore not or no longer the province of individual national governments.[30]

---

[28] Schermers, *Judicial Protection in the European Communities* (1987, 4th edn), paras. 42–164.

[29] On delegation of powers, see Lenaerts, 'Regulating the Regulatory Process', 29–31.

[30] Another matter is, which voting procedure would be required to establish such an act. Would unanimity be required? If a Member State votes against a devolution of power to the subnational level, would it be bound by such a measure if it is adopted by majority?

In sum, the angle of general principles may provide valuable insights into the validity of decisions taken in view of subsidiarity. Even a negative conclusion—that no such principle exists—would be an important one, for if no general principle of law exists with which a gap in the Treaties may be filled or a piece of Community legislation quashed, then we are firmly in the political arena. Thus, it seems possible to argue that the criteria developed by the institutions are not determining for the question whether Community or national action is necessary. As long as the adoption of any given solution is not contrary to the very wording of Article 3b or the more specific Articles of the Treaty, a limitation of the criteria to those laid down by the institutions would appear to be arbitrary.

6   DEMOCRACY AND TRANSPARENCY

On the basis of the foregoing it is possible to give a tentative answer to the question whether 'democracy' and transparency can play a role when determining compliance with Article 3b EC Treaty.

The term 'democracy' was used broadly to refer to the principle requiring the adequate involvement and representation of citizens or groups of citizens in an area of policy-making within the Community and the guarantee that these interests can be protected at law. The concept of transparency in turn is closely related to the latter aspect. 'Transparency' would denote a requirement that acts of government be understandable to the persons concerned and, where appropriate, accessible to the public, reasoned and clearly drafted. In my opinion such aspects ought to be taken into consideration. Just because in practice some form of democracy and some form of transparency are being observed both in the Community and in the Member States, this does not mean that, when it comes to choosing the appropriate level of decision-making we are free to concentrate on criteria of efficiency, effectiveness and transnationality only. Situations may still arise where the interest of the citizen is at stake. Three examples may serve to illustrate this point:

(1) In the context of GATT, it would be in the interest of European citizens that provisions of this agreement be invoked in national courts. In the present state of integration, to grant such effect in the Community would require Community legislation to be issued. Supposing that the subject matter concerned is not firmly in the exclusive power of the

---

Since there is no compelling legal principle which pleads against devolution, it seems that such a Member State would indeed be bound.

Community and the effectiveness/efficiency test applies, then it may not be easy to pass the legislation required. Such legislation may not be the most effective way to promote the objectives pursued by the Community in the context of GATT, and in any case it is not really efficient as it would 'double' the work done in the international context. Yet it would be desirable that this legislation is enacted.

(2) In the context of immigration, intergovernmental decision-making is notoriously inaccessible to the public, and it is not subject to direct democratic control.[31] If the same decisions were taken in the Community framework, the European Parliament would have to be heard.[32] As it is not certain that decision-making at the Community level is more effective than the intergovernmental level, Community legislation may not pass the subsidiarity test if this is interpreted narrowly.[33]

(3) At present, there is a tendency for some Member States to press for the inclusion of very detailed rules in Community legislation in order to get around the problems of the transformation of Directives into national law and the inability of the national courts to fill in gaps left by such measures. Whereas this pressure may well assist in making Community law more precise, the result may not comply with the second or the third paragraph of Article 3b, as it goes further than strictly 'necessary'. These are just three examples where the interest of the citizen may have to be taken into account when determining the best level of decision-making.

Taking such factors into account does not conflict with the wording of the second paragraph of Article 3b EC Treaty, as the term 'effects' is broad enough to accommodate them. A recommended approach by the ECJ might therefore involve a statement that the term 'effects' in Article 3b EC Treaty is to be interpreted broadly, allowing regard to be had for direct effect, greater transparency, participatory democracy, or indeed any general principle of law such as, perhaps, compliance with requirements of fiscal supervision.

---

[31] See, e.g., Groenendijk, 'Three Questions about Free Movement of Persons and Democracy in Europe', in Schermers et al. (eds.), *Free Movement of Persons in Europe—Legal Problems and Experiences* (1992), pp. 391–402.

[32] Broadening the test so as to include aspects of democracy raises the question whether decision-making at the Community level is indeed more democratic, and if not, what to do about it.

[33] Another question is whether the subsidiarity test actually applies to immigration policy. Arguably, this matter is exclusively regulated by Arts K.9 TEU and 100c EC Treaty and the latter creates an exclusive power to which subsidiarity does not apply. For a critical view of the 'hands off exclusivity' approach of Art. 3b, see Section 2 above.

Obviously, the broader the term 'effects' is interpreted, the more likely the potential for real or apparent conflict between the different elements taken into account. For instance, in the first example given above, although it may be desirable to establish the direct effect of GATT, enacting Community legislation may not seem the most efficient, as an international agreement already exists.

The ECJ may not always be the appropriate institution for solving such kind of choices, but at least in most cases it will be in a position actively to uphold a choice of policy once it is made.

Interestingly, a precedent for an active stance of the ECJ with regard to democratic principles already exists in a slightly different context. The case in question does not relate to the application of Article 3b as such, but to the application of a similar principle laid down in more specific provisions of Community law. In the *Titanium Dioxide* case[34] the ECJ established that a Council Directive on procedures for harmonizing the programmes for the reduction and eventual elimination of waste from the titanium dioxide industry should be based on Article 100a EC Treaty rather than on the joint basis of Articles 100a and 130r, because the latter option would have had as a result that the European Parliament would merely have to be consulted. This would circumvent the cooperation procedure and the 'fundamental democratic principle that the peoples should take part in the exercise of power through the intermediary of a representative parliament'. The Directive in question was annulled.

In this instance the ECJ did not decide the subsidiarity issue as such, but it probably did influence the extent to which it is applicable. In practice, subsidiarity, it seems, would apply only in the context of environmental policy (Article 130r), not in the context of the internal market (Article 100a), because of the requirement in Article 100a of a 'high level of protection' as a basis for Community action and the absence in practice of scope for diversity of approach between Member States.[35] The ECJ's statement therefore comes down to saying that considerations of comparative effectiveness may in certain cases have to give way to considerations of 'democracy'.

---

[34] Case C-300/89, *Commission of the European Communities* v *Council of the European Communities*, [1991] ECR I-2867.

[35] Brinkhorst, 'Subsidiarity and European Environmental Policy', p. 91.

7   CONCLUSION

The present analysis would confirm the view of many authors that subsidiarity is essentially non-justiciable in the sense that the ECJ only has a limited say in its enforcement. Nevertheless it is important to note that subsidiarity, as much as being a political concept, is a rule of primary Community law. It is important that the ECJ interprets it, as this may affect the way in which it will be applied. If the institutions take a view of subsidiarity which is too narrow, this may be detrimental to the Community edifice, as desirable legislation may be difficult to enact unless it fulfils the narrow criteria elaborated by the institutions.

The ECJ may not be there to solve problems of an essentially political character, but it can establish a framework within which the discussion is to take place, and to broaden it in order to enable sound decisions to be taken.

If subsidiarity were only about comparative effectiveness it would become nugatory. If instead other factors are taken into account, it might be an incentive on both planes.

4 UNION CITIZENSHIP: PIE IN THE SKY?

Hans Ulrich Jessurun d'Oliveira

1 THE CONCEPT OF UNION CITIZENSHIP

The insertion into the Treaty establishing the European Community of Articles 8–8e on Union citizenship is the first official move of a streetcar which already started its clattering journey a long time ago. As early as 1974, at the Paris Summit of the Heads of State or Government, a working party was established to study 'the conditions under which the citizens of the ... Member States could be given social rights as members of the Community'.[1] A year later the Report 'Towards European Citizenship' proposed the introduction of 'special rights', to be granted by the Member States to nationals of other Member States. These 'special rights' consisted of some civil and political rights, a nucleus of elements linked with citizenship which could be extended, as preferential treatment to privileged foreigners. The Tindemans Report repeated the desirability of extending special rights to nationals of other Community Member States.[2]

A Community parlance developed in which reference was made to a 'citizens' Europe'[3] and 'European citizens', without any clarity about the meaning of these admittedly suggestive terms. Still, the frequent use of the terms by the institutions of the Community indicated the consciousness that something was missing in the build-up of the new legal order: full participation by those who are subjected to its impact.

During the run-up to Maastricht many documents were to pave the way. The Dublin Summit had asked how the Union could include and extend the notion of Union citizenship carrying with it specific rights.[4]

A few months later the Council in its Rome session established the link, missing in Dublin, between the definition of European citizenship

---

[1] Bull. EC 12–1974/7, item 11.

[2] Tindemans Report, Supplement 1/76 – Bull. EC.

[3] See, e.g., Pascal Fontaine, *A Citizen's Europe* (1991). This book features the catchy sub-title 'Europe on the Move'.

[4] Sessions of the European Council, Dublin, 25 and 26 June 1990, Annex I on Political Union, in *Conclusions of the Sessions of the European Council* (1975–1990), 388.

and democratic legitimacy of the Union.[5] At the end of 1990, on the occasion of the Rome session of the Council, although European citizenship did not appear in its conclusions concerning democratic legitimacy, it mentioned European citizenship separately as an aspect of the European Union. Indeed, political rights were not mentioned separately any more in this document, although they may be thought to be hidden under the heading of 'civil rights', which continues to indicate 'participation in elections to the European Parliament in the country of residence; possible participation in municipal elections'.[6]

One of the proposed answers was framed by the Spanish government, to be examined at the Rome meeting of the group of personal representatives of the Heads of State or Government in preparation for the Maastricht Summit.[7] This Spanish document, 'Towards European Citizenship', complained that the notion that nationals of other Member States were nothing more than 'privileged foreigners' had not been overcome, and urged a major qualitative step 'towards European citizenship'. It defined this citizenship as a

> personal and inalienable status of citizens of Member States, which, by virtue of their membership of the Union, have special rights and tasks, inherent in the framework of the Union, which are exercised and protected specifically within the borders of the Community, without this prejudicing the possibility of taking advantage of this same quality of European citizens also outside the said borders.

It indicated roughly—as to the content of this European citizenship—five areas of rights:

---

[5] *Conclusions of the Sessions of the European Council*, 404.

[6] Ibid., p. 416. The whole text concerned with European citizenship reads as follows: 'The European Council notes with satisfaction the consensus among Member States that the concept of European citizenship should be examined. It asks the Conference to consider the extent to which the following rights could be enshrined in the Treaty so as to give substance to this concept:
—civil rights: participation in elections to the European Parliament in the country of residence; possible participation in municipal elections;
—social and economic rights: freedom of movement and residence irrespective of engagement in economic activity; equality of opportunity and of treatment for all Community citizens;
—joint protection of Community citizens outside the Community's borders.
Consideration should be given to the possible institution of a mechanism for the defence of citizens' rights as regards Community matters ('ombudsman').
In the implementation of any such provisions, appropriate consideration should be given to particular problems in some Member States.'

[7] See *Europe Documents*, 2 Oct. 1990.

1   The central core would consist of the full freedom of move-
    ment, free choice of place of residence and free participation in
    the political life of the place of residence.
2   Parallel to the transfer to the Community of policies in the
    areas of social relations, health, education, culture, environ-
    mental protection, consumers etc., the European citizen would
    have to acquire specific rights in these domains.
3   European citizens should receive a higher degree of assistance
    and diplomatic and consular protection by other Member
    States.
4   Access to Community institutions should be facilitated and
    reinforced, especially the right of petition to the European
    Parliament, and the setting up of a European Ombudsman
    system could be envisaged, in order to provide the protection
    of the specific rights of the European citizen.
5   Other possible developments could be proposed, such as the
    recognition and validity of obligations of military service or
    alternative service.

These proposals for the introduction of this *dynamic concept* of European
citizenship have found their echo in the Maastricht Treaty, without
however having been accepted lock, stock and barrel.

We shall now try to delineate the contours of European citizenship
as defined in the TEU. But it may be helpful as an analytical tool,
briefly to indicate two dimensions which are generally recognized, be
it in different ways, as belonging to the notion of citizenship. In the first
place, if a category of persons, endowed with certain rights (and duties)
is created or defined, then, by the same token, other persons are
excluded. The *inclusion* of certain groups implies the *exclusion* of others.
Citizenship takes as its corollary non-citizens. One of the points of
establishing citizenship is the exclusion of others from the rights and
entitlements granted to these citizens, and from the duties attached to
such citizenship. It may be useful to investigate in which ways non-
citizens are excluded from those rights attached to citizenship of the
Community or the Union.

The demarcation line between citizens and non-citizens, between
those who 'belong' and those who don't, is formed by the criterion of
nationality. Thus we shall have to say something about this ticket to
Union citizenship, and especially approach the question about the
competence of the Union or the Community to deal with the nationality
laws of the Member States.

In the second place there is the matter of the *extension* of the rights
and duties which form the conditions for participation in the public life

of a community which may be called citizenship. Here we will be primarily interested in the question of whether the Maastricht Treaty makes a difference to the status quo which has already been established by the European legal order and its constituent parts—Single Act, secondary legislation, decisions by the European Courts—and whether a real improvement of the status of those who 'belong' to this society or the Community has been attained.

Furthermore, in so far as the Community or the Union is something different from the Member States, and in so far as citizenship of a Member State is something different from citizenship of the Union, we may distinguish the specific rights and duties *vis-à-vis* the Union from those *vis-à-vis* the Member States. Inevitably, we will encounter in this (vertical) dimension problems of demarcation between Member States and Union, especially where Community law dictates that there be a certain status in the body politic of a Member State for nationals of other Member States. The typical example of this troublesome definitional conundrum concerns voting rights in the political bodies of the Member States granted to non-nationals of that state. Is this a right attached to Community citizenship, or is this an extension of Member State citizenship, or both?

2 NATIONALITY AND THE UNION

Although the logic of EC law suggests the assumption that nationality is a Community law term, to be defined according to Community law canons and principles, this is not the case. The considerations which the Court of Justice of the European Communities (ECJ) has devoted in various decisions to the concept of 'worker', as used in Article 48 of the Treaty, with the objective of establishing a Community definition of the term 'worker' in order to avoid a multitude of variations according to the laws of the Member States, are not valid for the definition of 'national of a Member State'. Although these considerations militate also for 'nationals', and the linkage of the term 'worker' with that of 'national' is exclusive and strong, nevertheless there is an overriding argument which prohibits making the term a Community term: the fact that nationality is central to the existence of the Member States. It is not an ordinary legal term, but defines both the status of the Member States and that of the Community more than any other term would. As long as the Community consists of independent and sovereign Member

States, the competence to define their nationals belongs to each state.[8] This is expressed in an important and revealing Declaration annexed to the Maastricht Treaty, reading as follows:

> The Conference declares that, wherever in the Treaty establishing the European Community reference is made to nationals of the Member States, the question whether an individual possesses the nationality of a Member State shall be settled solely by reference to the national law of the Member State concerned. Member States may declare, for information, who are to be considered their nationals for Community purposes by way of a declaration lodged with the Presidency and may amend any such declaration when necessary.

Such a declaration, by a Member State, as referred to in this Declaration, then, is simply an indication for the other Member States and Community institutions about which persons are considered nationals by the state concerned. It is information about the law of the state involved, and does not bind that state.

The recipients of the message, however, are safe in being guided in their actions by it, as long as the declarations have not been changed. Without these declarations the other Member States and the Community have to delve into the nationality law of the other states at their own risk, and are obliged to accept as such nationals those who can show valid passports or other identity documents.

These declarations, of which in particular those of the United Kingdom and the Federal Republic of Germany must be mentioned here, have been accepted by the other Member States and the Community. In the case of the United Kingdom, these declarations had the effect of restricting the number of UK citizens for Community purposes; in the case of the Federal Republic of Germany on the contrary, the implication has been to include some 20 million persons whose nationality of the German Federal Republic was, to say the least, doubtful. Nevertheless, the Member States have shown themselves to be prepared to abide by these declarations, and have accepted the expansion of the EC with some 20 million newcomers (members of the former GDR and *Aussiedler*) without audible protest. Negotiations on accession of the GDR would have caused more complications than the anodine accession of five *Länder* to the territory of the FRG. In a way, the German unification can be seen as the melting together of two nationalities. The problem whether a bipatride with a Member State nationality and a third-country nationality can be considered as a

---

[8] See also Verhoeven, 'Les citoyens de l'Europe', 2 *Annales de Droit de Louvain* (1993), 165–191, at 169.

Member State national for Community law purposes such as the right of establishment and freedom of movement has recently been decided by the ECJ in the *Micheletti* case.[9] The Court held that:[10]

> La définition des conditions d'acquisition et de perte de la nationalité relève, conformément au droit international, de la compétence de chaque Etat Membre, compétence qui doit être exercée dans le respect du droit communautaire. Il n'appartient pas par contre à la législation d'un Etat Membre, de restreindre les effets de l'attribution de la nationalité d'un autre Etat Membre, en exigeant une condition supplémentaire pour la reconnaissance de cette nationalité en vue de l'exercice des libertés fondamentales prévues par le Traité.

The ECJ refers to international law in holding that it is for each Member State to define the conditions for acquisition and loss of nationality. This may be taken as a reference, *inter alia*, to Article 1 of the Hague Convention of 1930 on Certain Questions relating to Conflict of Nationality Laws, which codifies the law on the subject and states that:

> It is for each State to determine under its own law who are its nationals. This law shall be recognized by other States insofar as it is consistent with international conventions, international customs and the principles of law generally recognized with regard to nationality.

That the ECJ restricts this 'reserved domain' by the phrase that the jurisdiction has to be exercised 'dans le respect du droit communautaire' is in line with Article 1 of the Hague Convention, which mentions that the exercise must be in line with 'international conventions', of which the EC Treaty is an example. Which specific restrictions the EC Treaty would imply is not clear.[11]

In shorthand the Heads of State or Government repeated their position when deciding at the Edinburgh Summit of December 1992 on the problems raised by Denmark on the Treaty on European Union. According to the conclusions of the Presidency concerning citizenship, they stated that: 'The question whether an individual possesses the

---

[9] Case C-369/90, *Mario Vicente Micheletti and Others* v *Delegación del Gobierno en Cantabria*, [1992] ECR I-4239, 30 CML Rev. (1993), 623–637, with my note. See also d'Oliveira, 'Plural Nationality and the European Union', in d'Oliveira (ed.), *Plural Nationality, New Trends* (forthcoming).

[10] Ibid., at para. 10.

[11] See d'Oliveira (ed.), *Plural Nationality*.

nationality of a Member State will be settled solely by reference to the national law of the Member State concerned.'[12]

The Member States did not adopt the ECJ ruling in *Micheletti* that these national laws must be in accordance with Community law. This may indicate that they were not prepared to accept inroads upon their reserved domain, and may have been an attempt to at least humour Danish and other sensibilities.

3   THE CONTENT OF CITIZENSHIP

The magic wand of performative speech acts is waved in Article 8(1), which bravely declares: 'Citizenship of the Union is hereby established.' This feat, reminiscent of the first verses of the Gospel according to St John, defies the incredulity of doubting Thomases who believe that *'ex nihilo nihil'*.

The first thing we must note about this citizenship is that it is not of the Community but of the Union, which is based on the Community but also includes forms of intergovernmental cooperation. This means that not only the legislative instruments of the Community are available for the definition of the content of European citizenship, but agreements within the framework of intergovernmental activities as well, including the Maastricht Treaty itself. The establishment of a European Union is intimately connected with the establishment of this Union citizenship, as is borne out by one of the recitals of the preamble explicitly demonstrating the resolution of the Member States 'to establish a citizenship common to nationals of their countries'.[13] One of the objectives of the Union listed in Article B is: 'to strengthen the protection of the rights and interests of the nationals of its Member States through the introduction of a citizenship of the Union.'

Citizenship is, of course, a very nice word indeed, but, one may ask, is it any more potent than those mirrors and beads with which natives of other continents were gratified in the colonial past? The Maastricht Treaty affirms in Article 8(2) that it is more: 'Citizens of the Union shall enjoy the rights conferred by this Treaty and shall be

---

[12] European Council in Edinburgh 11–12 Dec. 1992, Conclusions of the Presidency, Part B, Annex 1, 53.

[13] Is it significant that this consideration does not speak of 'the nationals' but of 'nationals'? Or is this one of the many slips of the pen? Is there the possibility of a category of nationals of Member States who are excluded from Union citizenship? I would answer negatively, unless hereby is tacitly implied that there are nationals who are not nationals 'for Community purposes'.

subject to the duties imposed thereby.' This provision seems to give at least a clear indication as to where to look for the bundle of rights and duties attached to the concept of Union citizenship: it is 'this Treaty' which yields the answer. But *which* treaty is 'this Treaty'? Is it the TEU as signed in Maastricht on 7 February 1992, or is it the Treaty establishing the European Economic Community as amended by Article G of the Maastricht Treaty? In other words, do we have to take into account only Title II of the Maastricht Treaty, consisting of Article G, which inserts the Articles 8–8e into the Rome Treaty, or does the provision refer to the Maastricht Treaty as a whole? This should make a difference in the interpretation of the concept of Union citizenship.

In my opinion, 'this Treaty' refers back to the Maastricht Treaty. This is suggested, in the first place, by its name: *Union* citizenship. It would be somewhat strained to see this Union citizenship defined solely by the Rome Treaty on the European (Economic) Community. I would, in the second place, draw attention to the fact that Article 8(2) refers to 'the duties imposed thereby'. It is very difficult to detect any duties for citizens laid down in the Rome Treaty, however carefully one reads Articles 8–8e. Even if one accepts that in some Member States for instance the right to vote is construed as a duty, one still has to accept that this construction is not reflected in the wording of Article 8b, where the word 'right' is systematically used to indicate the content of Union citizenship. It would be remarkable, finally, to contend that Union citizenship would not be influenced by the common provisions of Title I of the Maastricht Treaty or by the provisions of Titles V and VI on a common foreign and security policy and on cooperation in the fields of justice and home affairs. If Union citizenship were excluded from these important political areas, it would be devoid of sense to use the term and it would be clearer to use the term 'Community citizenship'. In my view, then, the third pillar is influenced by Union citizenship and plays a role in its definition.

3.1 The core of Union citizenship

From a comparative point of view it is highly interesting to note that the core and origin of Union citizenship is the right to free movement. Mobility is the central element, around which other rights crystallize. Article 8a confers 'the right to move and reside freely within the territory of the Member States'. This is not normally considered to be a political right linked up with democratic systems of government, but forms part of the fundamental economic freedoms of the European market: the mobility of economically active persons has now been elevated to the core of European citizenship and expanded into mobility for persons generally. In other words, the economically irrelevant people have been promoted to the status of persons.

It is only as a secondary issue that 'the right to vote and to stand as a candidate at municipal elections in the Member State in which he resides' is mentioned,[14] whereas the right to vote and stand for election to the European Parliament is conferred on every citizen, even those who reside in Member States other than their 'own'.

In Article 8d the right is given to citizens to petition the European Parliament and to apply to an Ombudsman whose office is to be established, with complaints about instances of maladministration in the activities of the Community institutions or bodies (European Courts excepted).

Finally in Article 8c an 'entitlement' is bestowed on the citizen to protection in third countries where his or her own country is not represented. There he or she is entitled to 'protection by the diplomatic or consular authorities of any Member State, on the same conditions as the nationals of other Member States'.[15]

3.2 Scattered rights

The TEU itself permits us, as has been mentioned earlier in this chapter, to seek out hidden treasures concerning Union citizenship. I have referred already to Article B which states as one of the objectives of the Union the strengthening of 'the protection of the rights and interests of the nationals of its Member States through the introduction of a citizenship of the Union' of which Part Two of the EC Treaty forms an element of its implementation.

Furthermore, and at least as important, is Article F(2) TEU which explicitly states, for the first time that:[16]

> The Union shall respect fundamental rights, as guaranteed by the European Convention for the Protection of Human Rights and Fundamental Freedoms ... and as they result from the constitutional traditions common to the Member States, as general principles of Community law.

It will be interesting to follow the development of this very general reference to the 1950 Rome Convention and its common constitutional provisions; splendid surprises are not to be discounted.

---

[14] Art. 8b.

[15] See also Art. 138e.

[16] Art. F(3) is an article in itself and would have merited a separate lettering or numbering.

Given the history of the development of the concept of Union citizenship, in which fundamental rights have been mentioned regularly,[17] it is plausible that these are seen as an element of this citizenship, an intensional part of the definition. The fact that fundamental rights and freedoms are not reserved for nationals of Member States, but that others under the jurisdiction of the Member States and the Community are entitled to their exercise is not decisive. We will see[18] that this is the case for most aspects of Union citizenship.[19]

These historical and structural indications are important reasons for the statement that the boundaries of Union citizenship are not drawn by Title Two of the EC Treaty, but that rights and entitlements, appertaining to citizenship, may be found elsewhere in and around the Treaty. It ultimately depends upon the notion, the concept of citizenship, a partly ideological, political, contextual concept, where the line will be drawn between rights belonging to citizenship and other rights, and where these rights (and duties) may be found.

The citizens of the Union are mentioned elsewhere in the Treaty as well, especially in Article 138 et seq. Thus Article 138a contains an exclusive, ideological statement to the effect that political parties at European level are important as a factor for 'integration within the Union. They contribute to forming a European awareness and to expressing the political will of the citizens of the Union.' This newly inserted provision, of which the legally binding contents are neither here nor there, has indeed been displaced from Part Two[20] to the title concerning the European Parliament. In this Part Five on Community institutions we again find articles laying down detailed provisions concerning the right to petition the European Parliament[21] and the creation of an Ombudsman system;[22] furthermore, the articles concern-

---

[17] See, e.g., the text adopted at the Dublin meeting of the European Council (see note 4 above).

[18] See below Section 5.

[19] Verhoeven, 'Les citoyens de l'Europe', 187, seems to include fundamental rights in the notion of Union citizenship as well: 'Il avait certes été fréquemment question, avant la signature du Traité de Maastricht, d'inclure les droits fondamentaux parmis les attributs de la citoyenneté européenne. Il n'en est cependant pas fait mention dans l'article G du Traité de Maastricht qui introduit celle-ci dans le Traité de Rome. Il ne s'ensuit pas toutefois que ces droits aient été écartés. Tout au contraire, leur respect par l'Union est expressément visé à l'article F, comme l'une des exigences fondamentales de celle-ci.'

[20] Art. 8 et seq.

[21] Art. 138d.

[22] Art. 138e.

ing direct universal suffrage for the European Parliament have been maintained as slightly amended.[23]

Finally, mention must be made of the provisions concerning such topics as social policy, education, vocational training (Title VIII), culture (Title IX), public health (Title X), consumer protection (Title XI), environment (Title XVI) which all have implications for the intensional aspects of the term citizenship. They have been mentioned in the important Spanish document mentioned earlier. This is not an exhaustive list of elements of citizenship, rather an indication that rights connected with citizenship are scattered throughout the Treaty, and that lack of formal coherence is hiding behind the declaration that it concerns a 'dynamic concept'. How dynamic is this Union citizenship, as compared with the status quo?

The question has its weight, as one of the factors accounting for Danish reluctance to ratify the TEU stems from the unwillingness to accept any creeping dynamics adding to or reducing rights which exist under Community or Danish law. This aloofness is apparent from the unilateral Declaration which Denmark intended to associate to the Danish Act of Ratification of the TEU. Here Denmark emphatically states that:[24]

> 1. Citizenship of the Union is a political and legal concept which is entirely different from the concept of citizenship within the meaning of the Constitution of the Kingdom of Denmark and of the Danish legal system ...
> 2. Citizenship of the Union *in no way in itself* gives a national of another Member State the right to obtain Danish citizenship or any of the rights, duties, privileges or advantages that are inherent in Danish citizenship.
> ... Denmark will fully respect all specific rights *expressly provided for* in the Treaty and applying to the nationals of the Member States.

While Denmark is apparently afraid of blurred edges between national citizenship (and nationality) and Union citizenship, the Edinburgh Summit tries to explain that there are clear demarcation lines between the two. Whether this separation is watertight remains to be seen: where a number of rights are granted to take part in the public and political life of the Member States, the citizenship involved may not be full, but is still amounting to partial citizenship in the Member States. As long as there is no agreement among the Member States on the

---

[23] Art. 138(3).

[24] See Conclusions of the Presidency, Edinburgh, 12 Dec. 1992, Part B, Annex 3, 57–59 (emphasis added).

concept of citizenship, as distinguished from nationality, Union citizenship may have the potential of becoming the sum total of the citizenships in the Member States combined, which, of course, will mean the end of the Member States.

4 NOVELTIES INTRODUCED BY UNION CITIZENSHIP

The *word* 'citizenship' is primarily new. It gives some coherence to certain rights which are conferred upon certain categories of persons, especially those who possess a nationality of a Member State. If one looks closely, however, the TEU has frozen the existing status of nationals of Member States, and has only marginally added new and relevant elements to it.

Let us take the example of the freedom of movement. This freedom, considered as the nucleus of citizenship, dealt with in Article 8a, and conferred on 'every citizen' (read: all nationals of Member States) is certainly not dramatically larger than the one existing under the Single European Act (SEA) and secondary legislation: the citizens are told explicitly that their freedom of movement and residence is 'subject to the limitations and conditions laid down in this Treaty and by the measures adopted to give it effect'. This amounts to declaring that not every citizen has the right to move and reside freely within the territory of the Member States, given the existing limitations and conditions.[25] What is given with the one hand is taken back with the other.

It is only in the future that the freedom of movement may be developed to a fuller extent, and it is in the procedure leading to new legislation in this area that something new can be detected. Although Article 8a(2) takes as its starting-point that the 'Council shall act unanimously on a proposal from the Commission and after obtaining the assent of the European Parliament' to facilitate the exercise of the rights referred to in paragraph 1, which makes the road rather narrow, it allows for exceptions as well, and these seem to be the rule. In various modes Articles 49, 54, 56 and 57 have been revised with the introduction of the famous Article 189b procedure for the issue of new directives or regulations to bring about freedom of movement of workers, freedom of establishment, freedom to take up and pursue activities as self-employed persons, and so on. In this area acting by qualified majority will then prevail, and unanimity will be the

---

[25] On the present state of affairs, but not without desiderata, see O'Keeffe, 'The Free Movement of Persons and the Single Market', 17 EL Rev. (1992), 3–19, at 3. See also Chapter 5.

exception. It remains to be seen whether Article 189b will yield the hoped-for results of acceleration and deepening of the decision-making process.

Although it may be regarded as a step forward that the TEU has now made available, at least in principle, the freedom of movement for *all* citizens, that is, for *all* nationals of Member States, whether economically active as workers and self-employed or not, the road towards the fulfilment of this arcadian objective nevertheless still seems long.

On 8 May 1992, the European Commission submitted a Communication on the Abolition of Border Controls to the European Parliament and to the Council of Ministers. In this communication the Commission reaffirmed that controls of persons at the internal borders must be abolished by 1 January 1993.[26] At the General Affairs Council on 11 May, however, the British Foreign Secretary, Douglas Hurd, confirmed the refusal of Great Britain to accept the abolition of controls at British borders and thus refused to accept the Commission's interpretation of Article 8a SEA.[27] The Commission takes the position that this Declaration, saying that the deadline of 31 December 1992 for establishing the internal market did not create any legal consequences, cannot change the binding force of a Treaty provision, and has considered taking measures against countries which have not implemented Article 8a by 1 January 1993, or interpret the provision in such a way as to exclude third-country nationals from the freedom of movement within the internal market. This will presumably take the form of placing a complaint at the ECJ against Member States that refuse to accept the consequences of Article 8a SEA.[28] The European Commissioner for the Internal Market, Vanni d'Archirafi, took a more cautious stand in a meeting of European Parliament's Committee on Civil Liberties and Internal Affairs. This was not appreciated and led to a Resolution by the European Parliament inviting the Commission to take action against Member States failing to fulfil their obligations under Articles 8a, 100 and 235 of the Treaty. In case the Commission and Council come up with answers falling short of the demands of the European Parliament, 'it will not hesitate to use all the measures at its disposal, and in particular its right under Article 175 EC Treaty to obtain that the obligations clearly deriving from Article 8a are fully complied with and

---

[26] *Agence Europe*, 7 May 1992. See also *Agence Europe*, 9 May 1992.

[27] *List of Events ESMV*, May 1992. See also *Agence Europe*, 13 May 1992; and *Migration News Sheet* (hereafter referred to as MNS), June 1992.

[28] *Agence Europe*, 2 Jan. 1992.

applied without delay.'[29] Thus the new cautiousness of the Commission is met with a collision course by the European Parliament. Recently, the new French government issued statements to the effect that it would not abolish its internal borders as long as effective measures at the external borders of other Member States such as Italy were not put into place, and it furthermore withdrew its intention to deposit the instrument of ratification of the Schengen Implementing Agreement with the Government of Luxembourg according to Article 139 of the Agreement.

The Dublin Convention on crossing external borders, one of the 'necessary' flanking measures, still has to deal with its 'stone' of contention, Gibraltar.[30]

If the effort with which the abolition of internal borders is being engaged in is symbolic for the value which the Community attaches to the freedom of movement of persons as the core of citizenship, then the ranking of this objective leaves no doubt. The abolition of internal borders for persons is a complete failure.

Similar remarks can be made concerning the right to vote and stand for elections to the European Parliament. The *via dolorosa* of the implementation of Article 138(3) EC Treaty is a well known example of the legal, technical and political barriers to a uniform procedure for elections by direct universal suffrage in all Member States. The Act concerning the elections of the representatives of the European Parliament,[31] with its Article 7(2) stating that 'the electoral procedure shall be governed in each Member State by its national provisions', bears witness to this defeat. There is no uniformity whatsoever. Since the 1976 Act, the goal of a common procedure is still out of reach. Differences of perspective and view concerning nearly all elements of such a procedure reign supreme.[32]

The Maastricht Treaty now deals with one aspect of the right to vote and stand for election in the European Parliament: the position of citizens of the Union residing in another Member State than that of which he or she possesses the nationality. Already before Maastricht the laws of some Member States granted these rights to nationals of other

---

[29] MNS, March 1993. On 21 Oct. 1993, the Legal Affairs Committee of the European Parliament recommended that its President introduce a complaint before the ECJ against the Commission for not insuring the full implementation of Art. 8a. See MNS, Nov. 1993.

[30] See d'Oliveira, 'Expanding External and Shrinking Internal Borders: Europe's Defense Mechanisms in the Areas of Free Movement, Immigration and Asylum', in O'Keeffe and Twomey (eds), *Unresolved Legal Issues of the Maastricht Treaty* (1993).

[31] Annexed to Council Decision of 20 Sept. 1976, O.J. 1976, L 278.

[32] See Doc. A3–0152/91 of 29 May 1991 (interim report De Gucht).

Member States, others did not. In some Member States, as Italy, Spain and The Netherlands, even nationals resident in third countries are entitled to vote in European Parliamentary elections.

The TEU does not really *add* to the existing voting rights for the European Parliament, but specifies that the situation of Member State nationals resident in other Member States has to be dealt with. It complicates matters considerably by adding that this specific problem shall be tackled 'by the Council, acting unanimously, on a proposal from the Commission and after consulting with the European Parliament', however, 'without prejudice to Article 138(3) and to the provisions adopted for its implementation'. Thus Article 8b(2) introduces *two* procedures to arrive at a solution for one and the same problem: that of structuring a uniform procedure for European Parliament elections. How a 'prejudice' can be avoided is extremely problematic given the European Parliament's right to propose a regime for its elections. It is clear that the European Parliament will oppose all initiatives of the Commission in this area as infringing upon its own right of initiative.[33]

Thus, Article 8b(2) does not merely add nothing to the existing entitlements or rights of citizens, but is furthermore framed with a complete lack of awareness of the fact that it forms part of such a supposedly important part of the Treaty, in which the central rights of the citizens of the Union are enumerated. One might have expected that the general principles for active and passive voting rights for the European Parliament would have been mentioned, instead of appearing as a detail,[34] that *one* procedure would have been indicated. Presumably an urge to create a parallel provision to Article 8b(1) concerning 'the right to vote and stand as a candidate at municipal elections in the Member State in which he resides' has led the framers of this Part Two astray: the two voting rights are very different in nature.

Certainly a new element in the TEU is the introduction of 'the right to vote and stand as a candidate at municipal elections in the Member State in which he resides, under the same conditions as nationals of that State'. There is of course a logical ambiguity in the provision. If a Member State does not allow its own nationals to take part in municipal elections if they are residing abroad, the formal equality principle

---

[33] The Council Directive 93/109 of 6 Dec. 1993 on the right to vote and eligibility for election to the European Parliament only adds a minimum of uniformity in the electoral system, O.J. 1993, L 329/34.

[34] Compare, e.g., a constitution stating merely that: 'Nationals residing abroad may vote in the elections for our Parliament', instead of: 'Nationals who have been residing abroad may vote in the election of etc.'

of Article 8b(1) leads to the conclusion that nationals of other Member States resident in this Member State are excluded in the same way, because they are residing 'abroad'. Although I do not presume that this was indeed the intention of the framers, this interpretation nevertheless would fit into the rationale to extend voting rights to citizens resident in another Member State: the idea that the lives of these citizens are directly affected by decisions on the local level concerning housing, education, public services, etc. Those resident abroad are less directly involved in the life of the municipality.

But there is on the theoretical level a more important issue: can the right to participate in local elections be considered as an aspect of citizenship of the Union? Taking part in the political life in a municipality of a Member State is a far cry from European citizenship: exercise of voting rights for national elections would be a much more relevant aspect of European citizenship, given the involvement of (some) national bodies of representation in the framing and implementation of the European legal and political order.

Again, it is on the national level that the really important basic and general policies will be developed that concern aliens. As the European Parliament has not seen its powers increased by much in the TEU, there is a tendency in national parliaments to take back the powers they had in practice yielded earlier in controlling governmental activities on the European level.[35]

I submit that granting rights at local elections have more to do with unexpressed endeavours to dissolve the identities of the Member States, and indeed their statehood, than with democracy on a European level. One may question how far Article F, in solemnly evoking that 'the Union shall respect the national identities of its Member States', is compatible with Article 8b(1) which imposes the breaking up of those direct links, which until recently existed between the definition of the legitimation of the state in terms of the sovereignty of the people belonging to that state on the basis of nationality, and the exercise of political powers in the state concerned.[36] To my mind, the two

---

[35] See, e.g., a circular letter by the French Prime Minister Balladur on increased involvement of the French Parliament in the European legislative process, reported in *Libération*, 24 July 1994. Similar developments can be shown in The Netherlands. The Danish position on this topic is well known. See also the statement on behalf of the presidents of the Twelve, Rita Süsmuth, concerning an envisaged consultation process on involving national parliaments in the revision of the Maastricht Treaty in 1996. *Agence Europe*, 14 Sept. 1994.

[36] See, e.g., Art. 20(2) of the German Basic Law and judgment of the German Constitutional Court, BVerfGE 83, 60.

provisions are mutually exclusive. In so far as Article 8b(1) entails revisions of constitutions of certain Member States, as is the case in Germany, France and possibly in Luxembourg[37] as well as other states, one may conclude that the Union does not respect the national identity of the Member States, assuming that a constitution could qualify as a repository of the national identity. This remark is not to imply that I am not in favour of extending voting rights to non-nationals, but simply that Article F is untrue; and that the TEU speaks with at least two tongues.[38]

The dynamics of the concept of Union citizenship show various speeds: the right to participate in local elections shall, according to the Treaty, be put into place by arrangements to be adopted before the end of 1994, a year later than those for the European Parliament. Optimism or lack of realism? We shall see.[39] *Per ultimo* October 1994, the European Parliament in its consultative capacity agreed upon a text which now lies on the desk of the Council which has two months to take a unanimous decision.

As for the right to petition the European Parliament as laid down in Article 8d(1) and Article 138d, it must be remarked that this right existed already under the Rules of the European Parliament. Thus the Article, as the reference to Article 138d shows, has only a systematic, token value; it does not add to the connotation of citizenship any right which did not already exist and may have an impact on the speediness and adequacy of the response by the European Parliament.

The Ombudsman, however, is a new institution designed to reinforce the position of those who are 'subject to instances of maladministration in the activities of the Community institutions or bodies'.[40] However, it is to be noticed that this remit reduces the rights of Union citizens to those of Community citizens, as the Ombudsman is not empowered to conduct enquiries and to report to the European

---

[37] This country will avail itself of the derogations offered by Art. 8b.

[38] Cf. Chapter 7.

[39] Whether these voting rights, granted under Art. 8b, are indeed rights or are to be conceived as obligations or duties, as they are under the laws of some Member States, will be for the Council to decide. If they opt to construe this political participation as a duty (which I consider rather improbable) it would be one of the very few examples of duties imposed on the Union citizens, mentioned in Art. 8. If fundamental freedoms are included in the concept of Union citizenship, and one accepts some forms of horizontal effect of these rights and freedoms, there is room for construing corresponding fundamental duties or obligations (*Grundpflichte*).

[40] Art. 138e, of which s. 4 instructs the European Parliament to 'lay down the regulations and general conditions governing the performance of the Ombudsman's duties'. This has been accomplished by decision of 9 March 1994, O.J. 1994, L 113/15–18.

Parliament concerning complaints about the functioning of institutions or bodies, executive committees, or other pillars of the Union than that of the Community. The same goes for the right of petition to the European Parliament, which is restricted to 'a matter which comes within the Community's field of activity'. Here too only Community citizenship, which does not exist as such, is involved. There is no outlet for complaints about matters concerning the way Union bodies operate, which are not at the same time Community bodies or institutions, or are not functioning in their Community capacity. This is an especially deplorable vacuum concerning the activities of bodies such as the one set up by Article K.4, a Coordinating Committee with far-reaching powers without corresponding parliamentary or judicial control.

A few words on the diplomatic protection of Union citizens.[41] This entitlement is granted on the level of the Member States, not of the European Union or Community. In theory it would have been possible to create the competence for the Union or Community as a subject of international law, and international person, comparable to the United Nations,[42] to exercise diplomatic protection, not only as regards staff members of the EC, but also for Union citizens at large.[43] The Maastricht Treaty opted, however, for a more 'horizontal' form: diplomatic protection by Member State A for nationals of Member State B. Whether third countries will accept that a Member State will act on behalf of nationals of other Member States remains to be seen. There are many instances in which a country represents the rights and interest of other states, especially if diplomatic relations with the host state are strained or broken, but this protection by proxy has to be accepted by the host country. The real question therefore is whether the Member State which will take upon itself to exercise diplomatic protection *vis-à-vis* a national of another Member State, can act unilaterally in this respect. Does the Union afford a 'genuine link' or does it constitute a 'supranationality' of the claim in such a way that the third state has to accept the diplomatic protection whether it agrees or not? The Maastricht Treaty

---

[41] See also Verhoeven, 'Les citoyens de l'Europe', 185, 187.

[42] See the Advisory Opinion of the International Court of Justice in the *Bernadotte* case, *Reparation for injuries suffered in the service of the United Nations, Advisory Opinion: I.C.J. Reports 1949*, p. 174.

[43] It is understandable that the Maastricht Treaty opted for a 'safe' solution: even for staff members the capacity of the EC to exercise diplomatic protection was at that time denied. See, e.g., Pescatore, 'Les relations extérieures des Communautés européennes', RdC (1961-II), 219. Cf. Brownlie, *Principles of Public International Law* (1979), p. 684. See also Blumann, 'L'Europe des citoyens', (1991) RMC, 283–292, at 283, who urges the exercise of diplomatic protection by Community institutions, such as the Presidency or the troika.

seems to start from the assumption that this type of diplomatic protection is to be negotiated for and cannot be unilaterally relied on. It is furthermore to be taken from the text of Article 8c that the details of this diplomatic protection by proxy have to be agreed upon in intergovernmental negotiations between the Member States and that the Union as such is not to lay down rules in this respect.

Whether the Member States will be able to develop a uniform regime for the diplomatic protection of nationals of other Member States is doubtful, given the large discrepancies between Member States. On the other hand, it is not very practical to charge the diplomatic missions of the EC with this task.[44]

Finally, an interesting but not very transparent solution has been found for the fundamental rights and freedoms, which will be respected by the Union.[45] These will not be seen as fundamental principles of the Union, but as 'general principles of Community law'. Does this imply that the Union, in so far as it is something else or something more than the Community—and this follows from Article A—is subjected to general principles of Community law? How are these Community principles upheld in the Union in areas where the European Courts have no competence? One of these fundamental rights being access to the courts, it is doubtful whether the respect for fundamental rights is indeed not much more than sanctimonious lip service as long as it is not accompanied by access to Union courts for citizens of this Union.

To sum up: if it is asked just how dynamic a concept this notion of Union citizenship is, the answer must be that it is for the time being nothing more than a new name for a bunch of existing rights, a nice blue ribbon around scattered elements of a general notion of citizenship. The dynamism is—apart from a few additions to existing rights—pie in the sky, the promise of future developments. Instead of bringing order to the notion of citizenship, one must look for important aspects elsewhere than in Part Two of the Treaty establishing the European Community, which is supposedly devoted to the topic. It is thus more adequate in this area to talk about the Community legal disorder, the European disunited legal non-system.

---

[44] There are EC missions in places such as Ankara, Athens, Caracas, Geneva, Montevideo, New York, Ottawa, Santiago, Tokyo and Washington. Cf. Schermers, *Inleiding tot het Internationale Institutionele Recht* (1985), p. 285.

[45] Art. F(2).

5   UNION CITIZENSHIP AND EXCLUSION

The previous section detailed the rights, which may collectively form ingredients for the notion of Union citizenship. This Union citizenship functions inside the Union as indicating those who are entitled to participate in the life of the Union or the collectivity which constitutes this Union. As stated earlier, it also has the function of distinguishing those who 'belong' from outsiders: the function to *exclude* others. The question must now be asked, whether the bundle of rights connected with the notion of Union citizenship indeed fulfils this function of exclusion. It is implied from the outset, that if there is only little differentiation in terms of the rights connected with citizenship as compared with the rights which are granted to various groups of non-citizens, then citizenship does not fulfil this function properly.

The question then to be asked is whether persons who do not possess the nationality of one of the Member States are excluded from the rights which are presently being bestowed upon Union citizens. Let us begin by considering local elections. This Community right must be realized on the level of the Member States, although it is introduced as an aspect of Community law. Member States, when designing the introduction of this right, will certainly be confronted with the question whether there is reason to grant similar rights to resident non-nationals of Member States. There are already several Member States who have answered this question positively and have granted this category of 'non-communitarians' the right to vote and to be elected in local elections.[46] The debate is premised by a whole range of factors, including the demographic set-up of each country in terms of national-ities of the resident population: if, as in Luxembourg, more than 25 per cent of the population is non-national the readiness to accept the political influence of such a large body is less likely than in a country like Ireland or Portugal, where the foreign population does not exceed 1 per cent. The breakdown of the foreign population under several perspectives in the various countries also plays a role in these public debates.

---

[46] See generally Sieveking, Barwig, Lörchen and Schumacher (eds), *Das Kommunalwahlrecht für Ausländer* (1989), with a large bibliography on the topic; see in particular Sieveking, 'Kommunalwahlrecht für Ausländer in den Mitgliedstaaten der EG—ein europäischer Vergleich', pp. 69–90. Ireland, Denmark and The Netherlands have introduced voting rights in local elections for all non-nationals who comply with certain criteria (age, residence, etc.); the UK and Portugal allow certain categories of foreigners to vote, whereas in other Member States sometimes very lively debates—e.g., in Germany and France—are ignited by the prospects of Community action. See also Chapter 7.

It is not clear whether international law permits differentiation between nationals of Member States and others when granting voting rights, and whether this does not amount to discrimination direct or indirect, either on the basis of nationality or on other characteristics of the excluded groups. The reasons put forward to allow Member State nationals to participate in local elections are not exclusively linked up with the emergence of a Community or Union collectivity, or with central elements of Community law, but refer also to principles of democracy. Article F furthermore, in a phrase which may be as normative as it looks descriptive, mentions 'the principles of democracy' on which the systems of government of the Member States are founded. One may ask whether it is reconcilable with this principle of democracy to include nationals of Member States and to exclude all other residents from (local) elections, and thus to distinguish between a group of nationalities and all other nationalities. To create first-class and second-class citizens in this respect will *prima facie* only then not amount to discrimination and lack of democracy, if there are very good reasons for this distinction. I do not think that the social and political ties between the Member States amount to such a good reason as to exclude persons who otherwise fulfil the conditions but do not possess the nationality of a Member State. It is interesting to notice in this context, that it is this type of reasoning that led Denmark to extend the election rights granted to nationals of the other Scandinavian countries, on the basis of the social links between these countries, to all foreigners. In other countries, like The Netherlands, the distinction between nationals and resident foreigners has from the outset been seen as a democratic problem, especially in view of the integration of minorities. Thus, whether or not the exclusion of non-nationals of Member States from local elections violates non-discrimination rules of international law, my forecast is that wherever these voting rights are introduced, they will sooner or later be granted to *all* foreigners, regardless of nationality, who otherwise comply with residence conditions.

Mention should here be made of the Council of Europe's Convention on the Participation of Foreigners in Public Life at Local Level.[47] Article 6 of this interesting convention is explicitly devoted to the right to vote in local authority elections; each party to the Convention undertakes 'to grant to *every foreign resident* the right to vote and to stand for election in local authority elections'.[48] It is clear that any

---

[47] Strasbourg, 5 Feb. 1992, ETS No. 144.

[48] Emphasis added. Art. 6 reduces this to the right to vote only, and Art. 7 explicitly allows Member States to reduce the required period of residence.

foreign resident, not only nationals of Member States of the European Community, is granted this right.

As for the right to address a petition to the European Parliament, Article 138d explicitly grants this not only to citizens, but to 'any natural or legal person residing or having its registered office in a Member State' generally, and they are furthermore entitled to petition the European Parliament 'individually or in association with other citizens or persons'. In other words, the right to petition does not differentiate between 'citizens' and other persons, though it must be noted that it seems to differentiate between these two categories as regards residence: Union citizens wherever residing, even in third countries, and others residing in a Member State, are entitled to this right. Thus, for citizens the link of nationality of a Member State seems to suffice, whereas for others residence must furnish this link.[49]

The same situation is to be found concerning the availability of the Ombudsman. Both categories of persons—any citizen of the Union or any natural ... person residing in a Member State—have access to the Ombudsman. Here again there is no significant differentiation.

As far as human rights and fundamental freedoms are concerned, Article F(2) solemnly declares that the Union shall respect them as general principles of Community law, and it refers to the Convention for the Protection of Human Rights and Fundamental Freedoms (European Convention on Human Rights; ECHR) and the constitutional traditions common to the Member States. Article 1 ECHR grants the rights embedded in the Convention to all those who are under the jurisdiction of the Parties.

This jurisdiction includes, at the least, all persons on the territories of the Parties to the Convention, whether nationals or foreigners. As foreigners are humans, human rights are theirs as well, and this truism finds its enshrinement in the common constitutional traditions. In other words, the enjoyment of human rights and fundamental freedoms only marginally distinguishes between Union citizens and others; they are to be enjoyed by 'everyone'.

Similar observations can be made concerning collective rights and entitlements such as the protection of *human* health,[50] consumer

---

[49] There are cases, concerning matters which come under the Community's (Union's?) field of activity, affecting non-Community nationals or legal persons residing outside the Community Member States. Would the European Parliament indeed deny a right of petition here?

[50] Art. 129.

protection,[51] protection of the environment, of which one of the objectives is again the protection of human health.[52]

Again, as regards the very restricted position which individual persons have under Article 173 concerning access to the ECJ, no distinction is made between nationals of Member States and others.[53]

The right to participate in the elections for the European Parliament, however, is reserved for an as yet undecided category of citizens of the Union, and non-citizens are disfranchised. Here then, one finds a clear differentiation, and thus only citizens of the Union are characterized as having active and passive voting rights for the European Parliament.

It is, however, questionable whether this should be the case. If the Union, or the Community, demands of the Member States that they grant the right to take part in local elections to foreigners, or at least a category of foreigners (which will entail, if not logically then at least empirically, the extension to other groups as well), then the logical step would be to grant voting rights to the European Parliament to 'foreigners' as well. Foreigners in terms of the European Union or Community are those who do not possess the quality of national of any Member State, but who otherwise fulfil the conditions to take part in the elections, primarily residence in one of the Member States. It is inconsistent to use residence as the criterion for voting in municipal elections and for the European Parliament, and to exclude from the latter elections those who are as 'foreign' to the Community or the Union, as nationals of other Member States are (in local elections) to the Member States.

Apart from such logical considerations one may reflect on the desirability, in terms of democracy, of the disfranchisement of increasingly large groups of the permanent population of the territory of the Member States of the Union, who are subject to myriads of rules and regulations stemming from the Community, without representation on the level of the decision-making process. The more important the European Parliament becomes and the more involved in the communitarian legislative process, the less acceptable it seems to exclude millions of persons who are directly touched by this legislation. Fear for *Überfremdung* is undemocratic.

---

[51] Art. 129a.

[52] Art. 130r.

[53] It is clear from this provision that the exclusion of non-resident non-citizens from the work of the Ombudsman or enquiries by the European Parliament goes too far, and indeed is more restrictive than the provision on access to the ECJ.

Finally, there is the right to move and reside freely within the territory of the Member States, the nucleus around which all other rights crystallize to form the concept of European Community or Union citizenship. Here for sure, is the dividing line to be found between citizens and non-citizens. But there are some very important groups of non-citizens who are nevertheless beneficiaries of this central right to move and reside freely, which, one should remind oneself, has only imperfectly been realized at the present stage of the development of the Community.

In the first place, the residence directives contain the right for various groups of relatives of the primary beneficiaries, irrespective of their nationality. Their right of residence and right to freedom of movement is predicated upon the right of the Union citizen, but tends to emancipate itself somewhat from it. Thus spouses of 'workers' will retain their freedom of movement and residence after dissolution of the marriage by death or divorce, according to a (revised) commission proposal for amending Regulation 1612/68 and Directive 68/360.[54] Directive 91/439/EEC[55] on driving licences, to give another example, is a contribution 'to facilitate the movement of persons, settling in a Member State other than that in which they have passed a driving test'.

This Directive is seen as a step forward as compared with Directive 80/1263/EEC which obliges drivers to exchange driving licences and which 'constitutes an obstacle to the free movement of persons', which is 'inadmissible in the light of the progress made towards European integration'.[56] Article 1 allows for mutual recognition of driving licences issued by Member States. The nationality of the holder of such a driving licence, issued by a Member State, is irrelevant. In other words, *everyone* in possession of such a driving licence is entitled to its recognition in the other Member States; this contribution to the freedom of movement is bestowed upon 'holders' of driving licences, irrespective of their nationality.

In the second place, a very important inroad into the exclusivity of the freedom of movement or residence for Union citizens must be mentioned, one which involves all economically active European Free Trade Association (EFTA) Member State nationals. In the Third Part of

---

[54] See COM 88/815 final – SYN 185 (29 March 1989); see also the amendments proposed by the European Parliament that extend the categories of persons to, e.g., persons with whom the worker lives in a *de facto* union recognized as such for administrative and legal purposes, O.J. 1990, C 68.

[55] Council Directive of 29 July 1991 on Driving Licences (91/439/EEC), O.J. 1991, L 237.

[56] See Preamble Directive 80/1263/EEC, O.J. 1991, L 237.

the Agreement on the European Economic Area (EEA),[57] entitled 'The Free Movement of Persons, Services and Capitals', the freedom of movement of workers is granted in Article 28. This freedom implies the abolition of all discrimination based on nationalities between workers of the Member States of the EC and those of the EFTA Member States (Article 28(2)), in accordance with the general anti-discrimination provision Article 4. Thus the approximately 25 million citizens of Sweden, Finland, Norway, Iceland and Austria enjoy the central feature of Union citizenship as well, to the extent that they are workers, self-employed or providers or receivers of services. With the EEA, their potential mobility equals that of Union citizens.

There is, in view of this development, even less reason to refuse this freedom to other categories of non-Member State nationals legally resident in the EC territory. The more non-Member State nationals enjoy freedom of movement within the European Community the stronger the case that it amounts to unacceptable discrimination to refuse this right to others who have migrated to one of the Member States and settled there.[58]

One should bear in mind that German unification furnished 18 million Member State nationals overnight, which is a much larger figure than that of the category of resident 'foreigners'. There is a real danger that the population of the European Community will be divided into 'citizens' and an underclass mostly originating from the Middle East and the African continent, primarily the Maghreb countries.[59]

6   CONCLUSION

Up till now, as far as citizenship is concerned, the European market is a 'futures' market. Citizenship is, in other words, nearly exclusively a symbolic plaything without substantive content,[60] and in the Maast-

---

[57] As signed in Porto on 2 May 1992. The agreement entered into force on 1 Jan. 1994, one year late. As from 1 Jan. 1995, Austria, Finland and Sweden will become full Union members, whereas Iceland and Norway will continue to belong to the EEA.

[58] In Art. K(1) under 3 of the TEU, mention is made of 'policy regarding nationals of third countries' as one of the matters of common interest which lend themselves to intergovernmental cooperation. See Groenendijk, 'Europese Migratiepolitiek na Maastricht: uitbreiding en beperking van vrijheden', *Migrantenrecht* (1992), pp. 76–86. See also Chapter 9.

[59] I leave the Association agreements with several of these countries aside, although they contain some important provisions on entry into the EC.

[60] In the same vein, Groenendijk, 'Europese Migratiepolitiek', p. 79.

richt Treaty very little is added to the existing status of nationals of Member States. It is worth noting that, whereas in the Member States the notion of citizenship historically accrued around the *political* rights of the individual, it is around the freedom of movement that the notion of Union citizenship is crystallizing.

It is unclear which rights and duties together are connected with Union citizenship because there is no cohesive notion of this new citizenship, and because the political dimension of citizenship here is underdeveloped. The instruments for participation in the public life of the Union are lacking as this public life itself, as distinguished from public life in the Member States, is virtually non-existent: a weak Parliament, next to no direct access to the European Courts, and so on.

Furthermore, the rights and obligations of the European citizen as granted by the Maastricht Treaty do differentiate only very partially between citizens and non-citizens. Several rights, such as the freedom of movement, are granted to large categories of non-nationals, such as nationals of the EFTA countries, or even to 'everyone', or normally to those legally resident in the territory of one of the Member States. Thus, European citizenship is not only severely underdeveloped, but also insufficiently distinctive between those who 'belong' and those who do not. In this situation, and also for policy reasons, it is better to forge a Union citizenship not only for nationals of Member States, but for resident aliens as part of the population of the Member States of the Union as well. This would increase rationality and cohesiveness of such a larger concept, and would reinforce democratic access to participation in the cultural, political and economic life of the Union and Community of the resident population of the Member States.

One must not forget, after all, that the creation, albeit in an as yet very rudimentary form, of a concept of citizenship which is related to a community of states, marks a significant departure from the traditional link between nationality and citizenship in the nation-state. It represents a loosening of the metaphysical ties between persons and a state, and forms a symptom of cosmopolitization of citizenship. The rising concept of European citizenship is not the concept of national citizenship writ large: its quality has changed in that it does not presuppose any more a large set of common or shared values. It is a clear indication of a phenomenon which is also to be observed in the component parts of the European Community: that the Member States have to a large extent become multicultural and multi-ethnic societies which may be bound together not in the first place by a set of common values, but by a developing competence of persons to deal with differences in their dealing with others who do not necessarily share the same values and with redefined institutions. It is this competence to deal with differences which may be the nucleus of modern active citizenship,[61] and European citizenship may be useful as a laboratory for this procedural concept of proto-cosmopolitan citizenship.

As it stands, Union citizenship is misleading in that it suggests that the Union is a state-like entity. This connotation is less adequate than ever as the Union moves more and more away from federal and supranational aspirations. It is furthermore misleading as the elements added to the European Community, and especially the third pillar of the Union, are inaccessible to the political influence of the so-called citizens. Nobody in his or her right mind would use the word citizen to describe the relationship between people and international organizations like GATT or the Hague Conference for private international law. To indicate the position of people under the Maastricht Treaty as citizenship is nearly as gross a misnomer. The populations of the Member States have not asked for citizenship; it has graciously been bestowed upon them as a cover-up for the still existing democratic deficit. As an alibi it may please Brussels; whether it changes anything in the sceptical attitude and weak position of the populations of the Member States is, in my view, rather improbable.

---

[61] Cf. van Gunsteren et al., *Eigentijds Burgerschap* [Contemporary Citizenship], publication by the Wetenschappelijke Raad voor het Regeringsbeleid (1992).

5 UNION CITIZENSHIP AND THE EQUALITY PRINCIPLE

Andrew Evans

1 INTRODUCTION

The evolution of Union citizenship does not depend simply on the technical quality of legislative proposals for the introduction of the rights perceived to be entailed. Given that the first such proposal was produced three decades ago,[1] technical problems might be expected to have been overcome by now. Nor does it depend simply on the 'political will' of Member States and their representatives in the Council of the Union to approve such proposals. They adopted the idea of introducing 'special rights' two decades ago.[2] Its evolution also depends on its relationship with the Union legal system and the more general social context.

This chapter seeks to situate Union citizenship within the Union legal system and, hence, within integration processes. The prominence acquired by the 'four freedoms' within these processes and the reluctance of the Union legislature to act under other EC Treaty provisions mean that the original tendency, manifested in Article 48(4) of the Treaty, to treat citizenship issues within the framework of free movement provisions has been perpetuated. For similar reasons, it is within this framework that related issues of nationality law and fundamental rights have tended to be considered. Such consideration has concentrated on the relationship between nationality and citizenship, and the former has been treated as providing the link between citizenship and integration. A result has been to narrow the debate and to focus discussions on politically sensitive issues as to the implications of Union citizenship for the existing nationalities of the Member States. A further result has been to limit exploration of the potential for

---

[1] Art. 12 of the *projet de convention sur l'élection de l'Assemblée parlementaire européenne au suffrage universel direct* of 17 May 1960 (J.O. p. 834/1960).

[2] Para. 11 of the *Communiqué* of the Heads of State or Government, Paris, 10 Dec. 1974 (Bull. EC 12–1974, point 1104).

dynamism in the relationship between citizenship and fundamental rights.

Such results may reflect the fact that Union citizenship, even though it might be portrayed simply as an extension of the principles of free movement and equality, fits uneasily within the Union legal system. On the one hand, the core of integration processes concerns market integration, and efforts are made in provisions such as Article 48(4) of the Treaty and in legislative treatment of nationality as a condition for free movement to insulate the essence of the nation-state from the effects of such integration. On the other hand, important developments, such as insertion of Article 8 into the EC Treaty by the Treaty on European Union (TEU),[3] have resulted from intergovernmental bargaining rather than from the supranationalism which is supposed to characterize EU integration.

Investigation of the underlying problems may be assisted by recognition that citizenship is essentially an equality problem. If it is to be at all meaningful, holders of Union citizenship must be equal in relation to some matters of importance. Yet, the fundamental character of European integration, which attaches significance to the 'bond of nationality',[4] implies that major differences must remain. Existing arrangements for representation in the Union institutions are only intelligible if some differentiation is maintained between persons 'belonging' to one Member State and those belonging to another. For example, Article 137 EC Treaty refers to the European Parliament as representing 'the peoples of the States',[5] and according to the Parliament itself, 'the development of a federal type of European Union has not yet reached a sufficiently advanced stage for proportional representation in the European Parliament to be introduced.'[6] In other words, processes of inclusion and exclusion are inherent in the concept of

---

[3] According to the *Bundesverfassungsgericht* in *Manfred Brunner and Others* v *The European Union Treaty*, [1994] 1 CMLR 57, at para. 40, 'with the establishment of union citizenship by the Maastricht Treaty, a legal bond is formed between the nationals of the individual member-States which ... provides a legally binding expression of the degree of *de facto* community already in existence.'

[4] Case 149/79, *Commission of the European Communities* v *Kingdom of Belgium*, [1980] ECR 3883, 3900; [1982] ECR 1845, 1851.

[5] The French *Conseil Constitutionnel* preferred 'de chacun des peuples de ces Etats', Judgment of 30 Dec. 1976, Dall. (1977) J. 201.

[6] Resolution of 10 June 1992 (O.J. 1992, C 176/72) on a uniform electoral procedure: a scheme for allocating the seats of Members of the European Parliament (para. 2).

citizenship,[7] the essential question being the criteria on the basis of which these processes operate.

The consequence is that application of the equality principle can no more offer a simple solution to the difficulties of developing Union citizenship than established models of citizenship and nationality can. However, analysis based on this principle—a principle which by its nature is incapable of reduction to individual legal rules alone—may assist exploration of the relationship between individual legal provisions and more general features of the Union legal system which both structure the operation of, and are structured by, these provisions.

The importance of this relationship is implicitly recognized by the Commission. According to the Commission, the TEU implies that the nature of the rights entailed by Union citizenship, which are 'essentially dynamic in nature', has been 'fundamentally altered',[8] and such rights have been granted 'constitutional status' by the TEU. The capacity of the Union legal system to accommodate this 'alteration'[9] may be expected to be critical for the development of Union citizenship. In the following sections its capacity to do so will be explored, having regard to practice concerning free movement, nationality law and fundamental rights.

2   FREE MOVEMENT: THE LIMITATIONS OF MARKET IDEOLOGY

Practice concerning Articles 48–66 EC Treaty, which originates principally[10] in concern to liberalize the movement of persons as factors of production, suggests that free movement has three aspects. The 'domestic' aspect concerns activity 'wholly internal' to a Member State, the 'Union' aspect concerns activity between Member States, and the 'international' aspect, which is dealt with elsewhere in this volume,[11] concerns movement between the Union and third states.

---

[7] See Chapter 4.

[8] *Report on the Citizenship of the Union*, COM (93) 702, 2.

[9] On expiry of the deadlines laid down therein, much of Art. 8 may become directly effective. See Verhoeven, 'Les citoyens de l'Europe', 2 *Annales de Droit de Louvain* (1993), 165–191, at 183. To the extent that this provision does so, its operation will no longer be 'controllable' by representatives of Member States in the Council of the Union.

[10] Though the evolution of these provisions as an element of Union citizenship may have been anticipated by some. See Ophuls, 'La relance européenne', (1958) *European Yearbook*, 3–15, at 13; and Presidenza del Consiglio dei Ministri, *Comunita Economica Europea* (1958), p. 106.

[11] See Chapter 9.

2.1 Domestic aspect

EC Treaty provisions governing the free movement of persons have been interpreted by the Court of Justice of the European Communities (ECJ) as not affecting national regulation of domestic activity. Such an interpretation has precluded the ECJ from following the views of certain Advocates General, such as Advocate General Warner in *Saunders*,[12] and subjecting Member States to prohibitions based on the concept of 'reverse discrimination'. In judgments such as *Morson*[13] the ECJ has ruled that nationals of a Member State may only invoke rights of entry and residence in relation to their own Member State under provisions such as Article 48 of the Treaty where they have already exercised their freedom of movement in order to carry on an economic activity in another Member State.[14] In other circumstances the issues are treated as 'wholly internal'[15] to the Member State concerned or as being without 'any element going beyond a purely national setting'.[16] As a result, a Member State may be permitted by the Treaty to impose restrictions on the entry and residence of its own nationals which would be prohibited by the Treaty in the case of nationals of other Member States.

2.1.1 Textual considerations　　The terms of particular Treaty provisions by no means preclude prohibition of 'reverse discrimination'. Article 48(1) simply provides for freedom of movement for workers to be secured, Article 48(2) for the abolition of discrimination based on nationality between workers of the Member States and Article 48(3) for such persons to enjoy rights of entry and residence for the purposes of employment. The only reference to national treatment is found in Article 48(3)(c), which requires that beneficiaries of freedom of movement should be subject to the law of the host Member State

---

[12] Case 175/78, *Regina v Vera Ann Saunders*, [1979] ECR 1129, 1142–1143.

[13] Joined Cases 35 and 36/82, *Elestina Esselina Christina Morson v State of the Netherlands and Head of the Plaatselijke Politie within the meaning of the Vreemdelingenwet; Sewradjie Jhanjan v State of the Netherlands*, [1982] ECR 3723.

[14] Ibid., at 3736. The rationale may be that nationals of Member States might otherwise be deterred from exercising their rights in relation to a Member State other than their own. See Case C-370/90, *The Queen v Immigration Appeal Tribunal and Surinder Singh, ex parte Secretary of State for the Home Department*, [1992] ECR I-4265, I-4294–4295. The same rationale may have important implications for nationality law. See Section 3.1 below.

[15] Case 175/78, *Regina v Vera Ann Saunders*, [1979] ECR 1129, 1135. Cf. regarding indirect effects, Case C-1/93, *Halliburton Services BV v Staatssecretaris van Financiën*, [1994] ECR I-1137.

[16] Case 20/87, *Ministère Public v André Gauchard*, [1987] ECR 4879, 4896.

governing the employment of its own nationals. As regards rights of entry and residence, there is nothing in Article 48 which might seem to justify rulings permitting discrimination by a Member State against its own nationals.

2.1.2 Political considerations   An analogy with *Peureux*[17] suggests that political concerns may override textual considerations. Here the ECJ ruled that Article 95 of the Treaty did not prohibit the imposition on domestic products of internal taxation in excess of that on imported products. Such disparities resulted, in the view of the ECJ, from special features of national laws which had not been harmonized in spheres for which Member States were responsible. Apparently, in relation to domestic activity, development of the liberalization requirements of individual Treaty provisions is limited by general conclusions drawn from the framework provided by the Treaty, which are influenced by state-centred conceptions as to the limitations on judicial decision-making within the Union legal system. If domestic activity is to be liberalized and, hence, the equality of treatment traditionally associated with 'negative' integration[18] is to be fully secured, participation by representatives of the Member States in 'positive' integration through harmonization is required. In the absence of the necessary participation, the free movement provisions of the Treaty do not affect state regulation of the domestic activity of Union citizens.

However, such participation may not be forthcoming or, indeed, may not even be sought. For example, Directive 93/109[19] limits itself to conferring rights to vote and stand as a candidate in direct elections to the European Parliament on 'Community voters' resident in a Member State other than that whose nationality they possess. This limitation reflects the fact that, according to the Commission, 'the aim is not ... to achieve overall approximation of Member States' electoral laws'.[20] Since the original proposal for this measure was drawn up

---

[17] Case 86/78, *S.A. des Grandes Distilleries Peureux* v *Directeur des Services Fiscaux de la Haute-Saône et du Territoire de Belfort*, [1979] ECR 897, 913.

[18] See, e.g., Pinder, 'Positive Integration and Negative Integration: Some Problems of Economic Union in the EEC', 24 *The World Today* (1968), 88–110.

[19] Of 6 Dec. 1993 (O.J. 1993, L 329/34) laying down detailed arrangements for the exercise of the right to vote and stand as a candidate in elections to the European Parliament for citizens of the Union residing in a Member State of which they are not nationals.

[20] Commission Proposal of 27 Oct. 1993, COM (93) 534, 9. The Preamble to Directive 93/109 also states that to take account of the principle of proportionality set out in Art. 3b of the Treaty, the content of Union legislation in this sphere must not go beyond what is

before the coming into force of the TEU,[21] it seems that Article 3b of this Treaty enshrines rather than creates the obstacles to the development of Union citizenship associated with the subsidiarity principle.

2.1.3 Legal instability   The legal position may be somewhat unstable. If a national of a Member State enjoys under the Treaty a right of residence in his own Member State after having exercised his freedom of movement to carry on an economic activity in another Member State, he may apparently acquire this right after merely having received a service in another Member State[22] or having gone there to shop.[23] Hence, the right may only effectively be restricted to the extent that the concern of Advocate General Slynn in *Morson*[24] to prevent the Treaty being employed simply as a device to evade secondary immigration control is shared by the ECJ itself.[25] In other words, the real limitations imposed on free movement may be less serious than is suggested by the language of the relevant judgments.

More fundamentally, Article 8a of the Treaty refers to the right of every Union citizen to move freely within the territory of the Member

---

necessary to achieve the objective of Art. 8b(2). More particularly, 'electoral territory' is left to depend on the 1976 Act on Direct Elections (O.J. 1976, L 278/5). See Art. 2(1) of Directive 93/109. The European Parliament, however, considers further harmonization to be necessary. See the Resolution of 17 Nov. 1993 (O.J. 1993, C 329/130).

[21] SEC (93) 1021.

[22] Tourists who go to another Member State as recipients of services benefit from freedom of movement. See Case 186/87, *Ian William Cowan* v *Trésor public*, [1989] ECR 195.

[23] The right to go to another Member State to shop is guaranteed by the Treaty (see Case C-362/88, *GB-Inno-BM* v *Confédération du Commerce Luxembourgeois Asbl*, [1990] ECR I-667), even if the shopper is carrying no means of payment (see Advocate General Tesauro in Case 68/89, *Commission of the European Communities* v *Kingdom of the Netherlands*, [1991] ECR I-2637, I-2647). According to the ECJ itself in the latter ruling, questions may be put in order to establish whether a national of a Member State is entitled to enter, but only 'upon the issue of a residence card or permit' (para. 12). Expiry of the deadline in Art. 7a of the Treaty may have further consequences. According to the Commission, this provision 'refers to all persons, whether they are economically active and irrespective of nationality'. See the Communication on the abolition of border controls, SEC (92) 877, 10.

[24] Joined Cases 35 and 36/82, [1982] ECR, 3742 (see note 13 above).

[25] Cf. regarding evasion of national legislation regulating vocational training, Case C-61/89, *Marc Gaston Bouchoucha*, [1990] ECR I-3551, I-3568. Cf. also, regarding the need for persons to be genuinely travelling between Member States for purposes of tax exemption for goods contained in their personal luggage, Case 278/82, *Rewe-Handelsgessellschaft Nord mbH and Rewe-Markt Herbert Kureit* v *Hauptzollamt Flensburg, Itzehoe and Lübeck-West*, [1984] ECR 721, 763.

States,[26] subject to the limitations and conditions laid down in this Treaty and by the measures adopted to give it effect. It would seem incompatible with this provision for a national of a Member State wishing to acquire a right under the Treaty to reside in his own Member State to have first to move to another Member State. It might also be argued that it would be inconsistent with the definition of the internal market in Article 7a of the Treaty for rights to depend on the prior crossing of frontiers which are supposed to have been abolished at the end of 1992.

If free movement were to be developed on the basis of the concept of Union citizenship, which is apparently bound up with plans for political union,[27] or on the demands of the internal market, it might be argued that the development was specific to the framework provided by the EC Treaty. On the other hand, it might be observed that the ECJ has so far only ruled on the position of those wishing to work in their own Member State. Where the persons concerned had not themselves previously moved to another Member State, the ECJ felt able to rule that no situation governed by the Treaty had been presented. However, in the case of those in their own Member State wishing, for example, to receive a service from a person who had exercised his right to establish an undertaking in that Member State or from a person established in another Member State, such a situation would apparently be present, and so the would-be recipients might be able to invoke rights of entry and residence in their own Member State under the Treaty. In other words, it may not be easy to contain activity as 'wholly internal' to a Member State.[28] Indeed, recognition of such rights by

---

[26] The Charter of Fundamental Social Rights, adopted by the European Council on 9 Dec. 1989 (Bull. EC 12–1989, point 1.1.10), referred in Art. 1 to free movement over the 'whole territory' of the Union. Art. 8 of the Declaration of Fundamental Rights and Freedoms of the European Parliament of 12 March 1989 (O.J. 1989, C 120/51) referred to movement 'within the Community territory'.

[27] See, e.g., the Commission Opinion of 21 Oct. 1990 on the Proposal for Amendment of the Treaty Establishing the European Economic Community with a View to Political Union (COM (90) 600), 9–10.

[28] Cf. Advocate General Darmon in Case C-61/89, *Marc Gaston Bouchoucha*, [1990] ECR I-3551, I-3559. Cf. also Advocate General Mancini in Case 352/85, *Bond van Adverteerders and Others* v *The Netherlands State*, [1988] ECR 2085, 2115, regarding the 'provision of services which is without frontiers'; and Case 311/85, *VZW Vereniging van Vlaamse Reisbureaus* v *VZW Sociale Dienst van de Plaatselijke en Gewestelijke Overheidsdiensten*, [1987] ECR 3801, 3828, regarding travel agencies.

analogy with *Phil Collins*[29] might be possible. In that ruling the ECJ recognized that industrial property rights were such as to affect trade in goods and services and competitive conditions *'à l'intérieur de la Communauté'.*[30] Hence, the prohibition of discrimination in Article 6 of the Treaty was found to be applicable in relation to such rights, without it being necessary to establish the applicability of specific rules in Articles 30, 36, 59 and 66.[31]

Adoption of an analogous approach to the movement of persons without reference to the concept of the internal market or that of Union citizenship might be relevant for interpretation of agreements with third states, particularly the European Economic Area (EEA) Agreement.[32] On the other hand, application of free movement provisions to domestic activity or even mere prohibition of 'reverse discrimination' would be extremely intrusive into national policy-making. The ECJ seems wary of such intrusion on the basis of the EC Treaty, and such wariness might be all the greater in the case of an agreement with a third state.

2.2 Union aspect

Application of EC Treaty provisions governing free movement to activity which takes place within the Union but goes beyond the domestic setting of a single Member State, that is, to the movement of persons between Member States, is comparatively well developed. However, such application is not without problems.

2.2.1 Country of origin principle
In *Debauve*[33] Advocate General Warner argued that Articles 59–66 of the Treaty were designed to create a Common Market in the provision of services, and not merely to abolish discrimination between providers of services. Certainly, Article 59 provides for restrictions on the freedom to provide services to be progressively abolished during the transitional period in respect of

---

[29] Joined Cases C-92/92 and C-326/92, *Phil Collins v Imtrat Handelsgesellschaft mhH; Patricia Im- and Export Verwaltungsgesellschaft GmbH v EMI Electrola GmbH,* [1993] ECR I-5145, I-5179–5180.

[30] More particularly, in Case C-118/92, *Commission of the European Communities v Grand Duchy of Luxembourg,* [1994] ECR I-1891, the ECJ accepted the argument of the Commission that 'all workers, be they nationals of the host state or of other Member States' were entitled to participate in elections within trade unions and related bodies.

[31] Cf. regarding student fees and Art. 6, Case C-47/93, *Commission of the European Communities v Kingdom of Belgium,* [1994] ECR I-1593.

[32] The free movement of persons is provided for in Part III of the Agreement.

[33] Case 52/79, *Procureur du Roi v Marc J.V.C. Debauve and Others,* [1980] ECR 833, 872.

nationals of Member States who are established in a Member State other than that of the person for whom the services are intended. No reference is made to the prohibition of discrimination as between nationals of the Member State where the service is provided and providers of services from other Member States. The implication is that restrictions may have to be abolished, even if they do not entail such discrimination. In other words, freedom of movement requires more than equality of treatment in the country of destination.

The same implication might be drawn from Article 65, which provides that as long as restrictions on freedom to provide services have not been abolished, each Member State shall apply such restrictions without distinction on grounds of nationality or residence to all persons providing services. This language seems to confirm that a measure may constitute a restriction on the freedom to provide services, even though it does not discriminate against providers of services from other Member States, and this was the conclusion drawn by the Advocate General in *Debauve*.[34]

According to the ECJ itself, the restrictions to be abolished under these provisions include all requirements imposed on the person providing the service by reason in particular of his nationality or of the fact that he does not habitually reside in the Member State where the service is provided, which do not apply to persons established within the national territory or which may prevent or otherwise obstruct the activities of the person providing the service.[35] The principal aim of Article 60(3) is to enable the provider of the service to pursue his activities in the Member State where the service is provided without suffering discrimination in favour of nationals of that Member State. However, it does not follow from that paragraph that all national legislation applicable to nationals of that Member State and usually applied to undertakings established therein may be applied in its entirety to the temporary activities of undertakings which are established in other Member States.[36]

---

[34] It is true that the third paragraph of Art. 60 provides that the person providing a service may, in order to do so, temporarily pursue his activity in the Member State where the service is provided, under the same conditions as are imposed by that Member State on its own nationals. This provision does not, however, clearly purport exhaustively to define the requirements of the freedom to provide services.

[35] Case 33/74, *Johannes Henricus Maria van Binsbergen* v *Bestuur van de Bedriffsvereniging voor de Metaalnijverheid*, [1974] ECR 1299, 1309; Case 39/75, *Robert Gerardus Coenen* v *the Sociaal-Economische Raad*, [1975] ECR 1547, 1555.

[36] Case 205/84, *Commission of the European Communities* v *Federal Republic of Germany*, [1986] ECR 3755, 3802.

Similarly, social security legislation, adopted under Article 51 of the Treaty, aims to remove obstacles in the way of full achievement of the free movement of workers, especially those arising from inequalities which place migrants at a disadvantage in comparison with nationals of the host Member State.[37] The implication is that such an obstacle may arise and be prohibited, even in the absence of any such inequality. Certainly, Article 51 envisages aggregation of social security benefits in the case of migrant workers, even though it is not clear that non-aggregation would entail discrimination between migrants and nationals of the host Member State.

The purpose of Articles 48–51 is not simply to prohibit such discrimination. Rather, these provisions seek to ensure that, as a consequence of the exercise of their right to free movement, workers do not lose the advantages in the field of social security which are guaranteed to them by the laws of a single Member State.[38] Accordingly, in cases such as *Van der Veen*[39] and *de Moor*[40] the ECJ compared the situation of a worker before migration with his position after migration rather than the respective situations of migrants and nationals of the host Member State who had never migrated.

As the ECJ ruled in *Iorio*,[41] Articles 48–51 are intended to give workers established in one Member State free access to employment in other Member States without regard to their nationality. Thus these provisions are to be interpreted as precluding national legislation which might be unfavourable to persons wishing to extend their activities beyond the territory of a single Member State.[42]

In short, free movement under Articles 48–66 of the Treaty entails that beneficiaries should be as free to engage in economic activity elsewhere in the Union as they are in their state of origin. Any restrictive measure is, in principle, prohibited by virtue of application of the 'state of origin' principle to free movement requirements.

---

[37] Advocate General Trabucchi in Case 66/74, *Alfonso Farrauto* v *Bau-Berufsgenossenschaft*, [1975] ECR 157, 168.

[38] Case 254/84, *G.J.J. De Jong* v *Bestuur van de Sociale Verzekeringsbank*, [1986] ECR 671, 682.

[39] Case 100/63, *Mrs J. Kalsbeek (née J.G. van der Veen)* v *Bestuur der Sociale Verzekeringsbank*, [1964] ECR 565, 574.

[40] Case 2/67, *Auguste de Moor* v *Caisse de Pensions des Employés Privés*, [1967] ECR 197, 206–207.

[41] Case 298/84, *Paolo Iorio* v *Azienda autonoma delle ferrovie dello Stato*, [1986] ECR 247, 255.

[42] Case 143/87, *Christopher Stanton and SA belge d'assurances L'Étoile 1905* v *Inasti (Institute national d'assurances sociales pour travailleurs indépendants)*, [1988] ECR 3877, 3894.

2.2.2 Competition requirements   Discrimination in the Member State of destination may be a sufficient condition for the restrictive measure concerned to be prohibited, because an impediment to movement beyond the state of origin would be implied, and the Treaty seeks to eliminate such impediments. Prohibited impediments are not only those directly regulating economic activity. Thus, for example, it is prohibited to deny tourists from other Member States access to a state compensation scheme.[43] If such a denial is prohibited by the Treaty, it is difficult to see why discrimination against nationals of other Member States regarding voting rights should be permissible, the link with economic activity, viewed solely in terms of the impact on free movement, being no more tenuous in relation to the latter than in relation to the former. Moreover, even in the absence of such discrimination, movement beyond the state of origin may be treated as being impeded by a state measure, and so the latter may be prohibited.[44] The apparently logical conclusion would be that non-discriminatory restrictions on the political activity of nationals of other Member States would be prohibited.

The classic concept of equality may, subject to certain modifications, be capable of capturing the requirements of free movement which are entailed. This concept may prohibit differential treatment of what are alike and like treatment of what are different. Without more, such a concept would be inoperable, not least within the Treaty context. Persons from the various Member States will usually be alike in some respects and different in other respects. Hence, criteria are necessary to determine which similarities demand like treatment and which differences demand differential treatment.

These criteria may be provided by market unification demands, or more particularly the requirement that individuals should be free to engage in economic activity beyond the confines of a single Member State. Thus differential treatment is prohibited where persons are sufficiently similar that such treatment impedes exercise of such freedom, and like treatment is prohibited where they are sufficiently different that such treatment has this effect. In other words, differential treatment depending on origin and like treatment failing to take account of different origins may be prohibited. In essence, market unification demands apparently underlie an interaction between the equality principle and the prohibition of action which interferes with

---

[43] Case 186/87, *Ian William Cowan* v *Trésor public*, [1989] ECR 195, 221.

[44] Cf. regarding the free movement of goods, Joined Cases 60 and 61/84, *Cinéthèque SA and Others* v *Fédération rationale des cinémas français*, [1985] ECR 2605.

extension of economic activity beyond the confines of the domestic market into the Union market.

Market unification demands do not entail that application of any measure restricting the activity of migrants is prohibited, even in principle. It is inherent in the idea of market unification that freedom to compete is protected. Restrictions which do not affect the competitive position of migrants are not, therefore, prohibited. Were they prohibited, distortions of competition incompatible with the requirement in Article 3(f) of the Treaty of undistorted competition in the Common Market would be created. Such creation would differ from the failure of the Treaty to liberalize domestic activity, because a distortion would not simply be replaced by another but would be created where none existed before.

In other words, the dynamic of the relationship between the equality principle and the state of origin principle is provided by competition requirements. Such requirements, based as they are on market ideology,[45] cannot play the same role in relation to the movement of persons as an element of Union citizenship.[46] Some other dynamic has to be found to justify and control intrusion into national policy-making, if free movement is to evolve in accordance with the needs of such citizenship. In essence, a substitute has to be found to structure 'spill-over' from market unification issues to 'higher' or, perhaps, 'core' politics. In the absence of such a substitute, application of the equality principle to political participation could have extreme consequences. It could mean that almost any national regulation of political participation would, subject to public policy considerations and 'mandatory requirements', be inapplicable to nationals of other Member States because it entailed restrictions on their political participation which did not apply to them in their own Member State and, in this sense, restricted their free movement. Little scope for political diversity within the Union would remain.

---

[45] See, regarding the importance of 'market access' issues for the operation of Article 30 of the Treaty in Joined Cases C-267 and C-268/91, *B. Keck and D. Mithouard* (not yet reported). However, even within its 'proper' field, market ideology provides a basis for judicial decision-making that is by no means unproblematic. Note the formal rejection of precedent (ibid.) and compare, regarding the question whether there is a distinct market for bananas, Case 184/85, *EC Commission of the European Communities* v *Italian Republic*, [1987] ECR 2013 and Case 27/76, *United Brands Company and United Brands Continentaal BV* v *Commission of the European Communities*, [1978] ECR 207.

[46] Attribution of freedom of movement to 'Union citizens' may have implications for the formal link between this freedom and economic activity. Note the original 1979 proposal of the Commission (O.J. 1979, C 207/14).

To avoid such an eventuality, the equality principle is diluted by the Union institutions. For example, according to the Preamble to Directive 93/109, the right to vote and stand as a candidate in elections to the European Parliament in the Member State of residence, laid down in Article 8b(2) of the Treaty, is an instance of the application of the principle of non-discrimination between nationals and non-nationals and a corollary of the right to move and reside freely enshrined in Article 8a. The Commission considers that, in view of the equality principle, nationals of other Member States should be subject to the same conditions as nationals of the host Member State for participation in elections to the European Parliament.[47] To preclude effective discrimination, Article 5 provides that where a national of a Member State must have completed a minimum period of residence in his own Member State to be eligible to vote there, an equivalent period of residence for 'Community voters' in another Member State will suffice. On the other hand, requirements of a minimum period of residence in order to vote in a particular locality are unaffected. Nationals of the Member States concerned are more likely to be able to meet such requirements than nationals of other Member States. As a result, the latter may not be as free to participate in such elections if they move to another Member State as if they stay in their own. Thus the Union legislature is unwilling to go as far in securing equality in the field of political participation as the ECJ has gone in the field of market participation.

3 NATIONALITY: THE LIMITATIONS OF STATIST IDEOLOGY

Problems with the development of Union citizenship may be complicated by the operation of nationality as the condition for access to the rights entailed, these complications apparently being a reflection of underlying conflict between market and statist ideologies. Article 8(1) of the Treaty states that all persons having the nationality of a Member State are citizens of the Union.[48] This condition may be seen as

---

[47] Explanatory memorandum to the Proposal of 27 Oct. 1993, COM (93) 534, 8.

[48] It is questionable whether Art. 8 refers to 'Community nationals' or 'Union nationals'. Art. 3 of the draft Treaty of European Union of the European Parliament (O.J. 1984, C 77/33) went further and expressly stated that citizenship of the Union could not be acquired or lost independently of the citizenship of a Member State. Art. 25(3) of the Declaration of Fundamental Rights and Freedoms of the European Parliament (O.J. 1989, C 120/51) also limited citizenship to nationals of Member States. Note, however, the possibility in Art. 25(2) thereof that the rights concerned might be extended to other

offering the nation-state a defence against the effects of integration. It implies dependence of Union citizenship and that the link between an individual and his or her state of nationality constitutes the basis for his participation in integration processes. Such thinking implies, in turn, a conviction that the demands of these processes can be satisfactorily met by limited extension of rights by Member States to each other's nationals on a reciprocal basis.

The result has been a series of intergovernmental reports, such as the Addonino Report,[49] which envisage bargains between Member States. These bargains may take the form of Summit Declarations, such as that of December 1974,[50] but they may also be reflected in amendments to the EC Treaty, such as those introduced by the Single European Act and the TEU.[51] Such practice has an inherent tendency to be unsystematic and to emphasize the nationality condition. Thus, for example, the 1974 Summit Declaration[52] described the rights involved as 'special rights'[53] to be secured for nationals of Member States on a reciprocal basis.[54]

The consequences may include the apparent legitimation of, first, the nonoperability of Union citizenship in relation to domestic activity and, secondly, separate treatment of intra-Union movement by nationals of Member States and that of third-country nationals, despite the potential for disruption of the internal market associated therewith.[55] Indeed, to the extent that Member States are left free to determine the holders of their nationality for Union law purposes, even the Union aspect of Union citizenship may be undermined.

---

persons.

[49] Supplement 7/85 – Bull. EC.

[50] Bull. EC 12–1974, point 1104.

[51] Note also the Resolutions of the Representatives of the Member States of 23 June 1981 (O.J. 1981, C 241/1) and 30 June 1982 (O.J. 1982, C 179/1) regarding a 'European passport' Cf. the 'European driving licence,' established by Directives 80/1263 (O.J. 1980, L 375/1) and 91/439 (O.J. 1991, L 237/1).

[52] Point 11.

[53] Cf. the idea of Union citizenship as 'en quelque sorte une citoyenneté "d'attribution", par rapport à la citoyenneté "de droit commun" qu'est la citoyenneté étatique', in Kovar and Simon, 'La citoyenneté européenne', (1993) CDE, 285–315.

[54] Recognition of local electoral rights for nationals of other Member States in Art. 88(3) of the French Constitution is subject to a reciprocity condition.

[55] Evans, 'Third Country Nationals and the Treaty on European Union', 5 EJIL (1994), 119–219.

3.1 Definition of nationality

The Declaration concerning nationality of a Member State,[56] annexed to the TEU,[57] declares that whenever the EC Treaty refers to nationals of Member States, the question whether an individual possesses the nationality of a Member State shall be settled solely by reference to the national law of the Member State concerned.[58] Member States may declare, for information, who are to be considered their 'nationals for Community purposes' by way of a declaration lodged with the Presidency and may amend any such declaration when necessary. According to the Commission, this Declaration 'spells out' that in Article 8(1) EC Treaty and implies that rules on the acquisition and possession of the nationality of a Member State fall within the scope not of the EC Treaty, but of the national law of the Member State concerned.[59]

To the extent that a Member State may unilaterally alter its definition of nationality for Union law purposes, free movement may be precarious.[60] Indeed, discrimination might be entailed. Those whose residence rights are affected by changes in the nationality law of the state to which they 'belong' may enjoy some protection under international law against that state.[61] However, the same protection would not apparently be available in relation to any other Member State to which such persons, in the exercise of their free movement, had chosen to move.

Even if a Member State were precluded by Union law from unilaterally altering its definition of nationality, the exercise of free

---

[56] The legal status of the Declaration is unclear. See Verhoeven, 'Les citoyens de l'Europe', 170.

[57] See also Part A of the Decision of the Heads of State or Government, meeting within the European Council, concerning certain problems raised by Denmark in relation to the Treaty on European Union (Bull. EC 12–1992, I.35).

[58] See also Kovar and Simon, 'La citoyenneté européenne', 285–315. Cf. the acceptance of this position in the case of ships in Case C-280/89, *EC Commission v Ireland*, [1992] ECR I-6185, I-6200 and Case C-286/90, *Anklagemyndigheder v Peter Michael Poulsen and Diva Navigation Corp.*, [1992] ECR I-6019, I-6054.

[59] Explanatory memorandum to the Commission Proposal of 27 Oct. 1993 regarding rights to participate in elections to the European Parliament, COM (93) 534, 11. This means, *inter alia*, that determination whether persons originating in overseas countries or territories covered by Art. 227(3) are entitled to participate in direct elections is a matter exclusively for the legislation of the Member State with which there is a special relationship.

[60] Cf. regarding definition of 'workers', Case 75/63, *Mrs M.K.H. Hoekstra (née Unger)* v *Bestuur der Bedrijfsvereniging voor Detailhandel en Ambachten*, [1964] ECR 177, 184–185.

[61] 13 *Yearbook of the European Convention on Human Rights* (1970), 928.

movement might still be jeopardized. For example, under United Kingdom law descendants of persons born to British citizens who have exercised their freedom of movement may be denied British citizenship.[62] In the sense that persons who exercise their free movement may only be able to pass on a 'second-class' citizenship, their exercise of this freedom may be said to expose them to discrimination in comparison with those who do not exercise it. While nationality law provisions may reflect national traditions, their application may be problematic where they are employed as instruments of immigration control incompatible with integration requirements.[63]

Hence, in *Micheletti*[64] the ECJ ruled that the competence of each Member State to define the conditions for acquisition and loss of its nationality 'doit être exercée dans le respect du droit communautaire'.[65] This obligation was presumably regarded as the necessary corollary of the obligation of Member States to recognize the Treaty rights of nationals of other Member States[66] and thus as a necessary condition to ensure that the application of free movement did not vary from Member State to Member State. However, Union law rules in this area are at best rudimentary,[67] and it is difficult to see how they can be significantly developed by case law alone. The European Parliament has responded to the problems raised by urging Member States to effect the harmonization of their nationality laws necessary to reduce statelessness.[68] More particularly, the Parliament considers that free movement and 'extension of European citizenship call for the replacement of the principle of *ius sanguinis* by the principle

---

[62] S. 2 of the British Nationality Act 1981. Cf. Bonner, 'British Citizenship: Implications for UK Nationals in the European Communities', 6 EL Rev. (1981), 69–75.

[63] An analogy might be drawn with criminal law, which remains in principle within the competence of Member States but which cannot operate in such a way as to impede free movement. See, for example, Case 203/80, *Criminal Proceedings against Guerrino Casati*, [1981] ECR 2595.

[64] Case C-369/90, *Mario Vicente Micheletti* v *Delegación del Gobierno en Cantabria*, [1992] ECR I-4239.

[65] Ibid., at I-4262.

[66] Even where the persons concerned are also their own nationals. See Case 292/82, *Claude Gullung* v *Conseils de l'ordre des avocats du barreau de Colmar et de Saverne*, [1988] ECR 111, 136.

[67] See, regarding the absence of such rules, Advocate General Tesauro, [1992] ECR I-4239, I-4254.

[68] O.J. 1981, C 260/100.

of *ius soli* as a basis for citizenship'.[69] Such harmonization may have a role to play, particularly given that the 'new approach' to harmonization would obviate the need for comprehensive Union regulation of nationality issues, though technical complications of harmonization in this field may limit the extent to which it can be achieved.

In other words, there may be severe limitations to the capacity of the Union, whether through legislative harmonization or case law, to develop its own definition of nationality and, hence, to the viability of statist conceptions of nationality as a basis for the development of Union citizenship. While a focus on definition of nationality of Member States for Union law purposes, as opposed to that for other legal purposes, might defuse certain political sensitivities, underlying problems would apparently remain.

Such considerations may be amongst those which underlie occasional challenges to the secondary effects of nationality law (rather than control of the rules of nationality law themselves) and thus challenges to nationality as the exclusive basis for recognition of entitlement to Union citizenship or at least enjoyment of rights entailed by such citizenship.[70] For example, the nationality requirement applies for the purposes of rules governing the social security rights of migrants at the time of acquiring such rights.[71] The Commission has also proposed that derived rights for the spouse and dependants of a national of a Member State exercising his freedom of movement should subsist his death or the dissolution of the marriage.[72] In both cases a right which is originally based, directly or indirectly, on a nationality

---

[69] Para. 93 of the Resolution of the European Parliament of 11 March 1993 (O.J. 1993, C 115/178) on respect for human rights in the European Community (annual report of the European Parliament).

[70] Art. 8 of the Treaty does not expressly provide that Union citizenship, let alone the rights entailed thereby, is limited to nationals of Member States. According to the *Communication on Immigration and Asylum Policies*, COM (94) 23, 34, 'the logic of the internal market implies the elimination of the condition of nationality for the exercise of certain rights.'

[71] Case 10/78, *Tayeb Belbouab* v *Bundesknappschaft*, [1978] ECR 1915.

[72] O.J. 1989, C 100/6. The explanatory memorandum described the right as conditional on 'a tie to the employment market of a Member State' (COM (88) 815, 22). The European Parliament considers that such rights should be unaffected by the death of the primary beneficiary or divorce or *de facto* separation. See O.J. 1990, C 175/90, in the case of pensioners; see O.J. 1990, C 175/96, in the case of students, though here protection against the effects of dissolution of the marriage rather than separation was envisaged. In the case of those exercising their right of residence under the draft of what became Directive 90/364 (O.J. 1990, L 180/26), protection against the effects of 'final separation' was envisaged (O.J. 1990, C 175/849).

condition may develop into one which is exercisable independently of this condition.

Protocol 3 to the British Accession Act, on the Channel Islands and the Isle of Man, goes further. Article 2 provides that Channel Islanders and Manxmen shall not benefit from the free movement of persons and services. However, according to Article 6, those who have 'at any time been ordinarily resident in the United Kingdom for five years' are not considered to be Channel Islanders or Manxmen for these purposes. Thus entitlement to free movement may be founded on ordinary residence in a Member State for a given period.

An analogy with the Council of Europe Convention on the Legal Status of Migrant Workers[73] suggests that such tendencies could be developed much further. This instrument applies to nationals of a Contracting Party who have been authorized by another Contracting Party to reside in its territory in order to take up employment there.[74] Given that the operation of Union law is supposed to be independent of strict reciprocity requirements,[75] an analogy would entail that lawful residence within the Union could provide a basis for enjoyment of rights of Union citizenship.

3.2 Naturalization

Naturalization law may exaggerate or, potentially, mitigate problems that would arise from a failure to develop residence as a condition for enjoyment of rights of Union citizenship. For example, a Member State may deter its nationals from integrating into a Member State to which they have moved[76] by depriving them of their nationality if they are

---

[73] ETS No. 93.

[74] It is argued by the Committee on Civil Liberties and Internal Affairs that the principle of territoriality should, whenever possible, be a decisive criterion for conferring rights and duties and for receiving effective protection from the state. See the Annual Report on respect for human rights in the European Community, EP Doc. A3–0025/93, p. 58. Similarly, lawful residence in a Member State might appropriately condition enjoyment of free movement for third-country nationals generally within the Union. Cf. Council Recommendation 92/441 of 24 June 1992 (O.J. 1992, L 245/46) on common criteria concerning sufficient resources and social assistance in social protection systems, which seeks to further the social protection of all such persons.

[75] Thus operation of the equality principle cannot be dependent on the existence of a specific reciprocal agreement between Member States. See Case C-20/92, *Anthony Hubbard* v *Peter Hamburger*, [1993] ECR I-3777, I-3795.

[76] According to the Commission, naturalization is 'potentially an important legal instrument to facilitate the integration of resident immigrants and subsequent generations born in the country.' See the Communication on Immigration and Asylum Policies, COM (94) 23, 35.

naturalized there.[77] Likewise, the host Member State could impede their integration by refusing to naturalize them or by requiring them to relinquish their previous nationality or nationalities.[78] For such reasons, reform of naturalization law, involving increased acceptance of plural nationality,[79] is advocated. For example, the European Parliament has called upon Member States 'to ensure unimpeded access to citizenship for third-country nationals after a reasonable period of legal residence' on their territory.[80] Such a reform might not only render equal treatment more accessible in the case of third-country nationals but might also facilitate efforts by nationals of a Member State to integrate into the society of another Member State. The extent to which reform would be a consequence of interpreting existing Union law provisions as prohibiting application of naturalization law in such a way as to impede free movement and the extent to which legislative harmonization would be necessary are uncertain questions. What seems more clear is that such reforms, like attempts at more general harmonization of nationality law, may only play a limited role in the development of Union citizenship.

4 FUNDAMENTAL RIGHTS

Fundamental rights considerations may imply the need for reforms which, being constrained neither by market nor statist ideology, are both more radical and more practicable. While Union practice tends generally to follow state practice in linking citizenship issues with nationality and separating them from fundamental rights issues, in

---

[77] According to the European Parliament, the exercise of the fundamental right to leave any country and return to one's country cannot be penalized by the withdrawal of citizenship rights. See para. 95 of the Resolution of 11 March 1993 (O.J. 1993, C 115/178) on respect for human rights in the European Community (annual report of the European Parliament).

[78] In general terms, obstacles to the acquisition of nationality are a source of discrimination which is unjustified in present-day Europe (ibid., para. 94).

[79] Plural nationality may be regarded as positively desirable, at least in certain circumstances, rather than as a source of practical problems. See Recommendation 1081 (1988) of the Council of Europe Parliamentary Assembly on problems of nationality in mixed marriages. The Second Protocol amending the Convention on the Reduction of Cases of Multiple Nationality and Military Obligations in Cases of Multiple Nationality, ETS No. 149 lifts opposition to multiple nationality, so as to encourage the integration of immigrants.

[80] The Committee on Civil Liberties and Internal Affairs of the European Parliament has suggested that there should be a right 'to apply for nationality' five years after a third-country national has acquired a right of residence. See EP Doc. A3–0284/92.

essence, European integration processes are incompatible with reservation of citizenship rights in relation to a particular Member State to nationals of that state. In other words, these processes pose a challenge to the established distinction between fundamental rights of general availability and fundamental rights available to individuals in relation to their state of nationality. If the implications of these processes go unrecognized, not only may the potential of fundamental rights for tackling problems in the development of Union citizenship be disregarded, but also its development may entail discrimination contrary to the Convention for the Protection of Human Rights and Fundamental Freedoms (European Convention on Human Rights; ECHR).

4.1 Containment

Under Article K.2 TEU matters of common interest in the field of justice and home affairs are to be dealt with in accordance with the European Convention on Human Rights. The underlying concern seems to be to contain Union encroachment on such rights rather than to treat Union law as an instrument for promoting them.

The case law of the ECJ seems to imply that the function of such rights within the Union legal system is even more narrow. The ECJ requires that, in exercising their powers under provisions such as Article 48(3) EC Treaty and Directive 64/221[81] to restrict the movement of nationals of other Member States on public policy grounds, Member States respect principles enshrined in the European Convention on Human Rights.[82] A contrast may be drawn with *Demirel*,[83] where provisions of the Turkish Association Agreement[84] were at issue. The ECJ noted that the free movement of workers was, by virtue of Article 48 of the Treaty, one of the fields covered by the Treaty and did not accept that the Member States entered into commitments to Turkey concerning this freedom in the exercise of their own powers. These commitments fell within the powers conferred on the European Community by Article 238 of the Treaty.[85] However, they merely set out programmes and were 'not sufficiently precise and unconditional

---

[81] J.O. p. 850/1964.

[82] Case 36/75, *Roland Rutili v Minister of the Interior*, [1975] ECR, 1219, 1232.

[83] Case 12/86, *Meryem Demirel v Stadt Schwäbisch Gmünd*, [1987] ECR 3719.

[84] J.O. p. 3687/1964.

[85] [1987] ECR 3719, 3751.

to be capable of governing directly the movement of workers'.[86] The ECJ did not address the question of whether in implementing these commitments the Member States had to respect the Treaty and, more particularly, fundamental rights[87] embodied in Union law.

Such practice renders availability of fundamental rights dependent on (impracticably conceived) integration requirements rather than vice versa. Family reunification, for example, is treated as 'a necessary element in giving effect to the freedom of movement of workers [and] does not become a right until the freedom which it presupposes has taken effect'.[88]

Adverse consequences of such practice may not necessarily be limited to third-country nationals. It is recognized in the European Parliament that although nationals of Member States are not subject to immigration control within the Union, they may suffer bureaucratic oppression and discrimination. Moreover, the restrictions which form part of national immigration policies help to foster fear and distrust or even hatred of foreigners generally,[89] which may ultimately lead to threats to democracy in Europe.[90] In other words, lack of a real fundamental rights dimension[91] to integration processes may be detrimental to the processes themselves and, more particularly, to effective enjoyment of the rights which are supposed to be entailed by Union citizenship.

---

[86] Ibid., at 3753.

[87] Weiler, 'Thou Shalt not Oppress a Stranger: on the Judicial Protection of the Human Rights of Non-EC Nationals—A Critique', 3 EJIL (1992), 65–91. Cf. the argument regarding national implementation of the obligation to hold direct elections in Evans, 'Nationality Law and European Integration', 16 EL Rev. (1991), 190–215, at 208.

[88] Advocate General Darmon in Case 12/86, *Meryem Demirel* v *Stadt Schwäbisch Gmünd*, [1987] ECR 3719, 3745. According to the ECJ itself, such a right would depend on a provision defining the conditions in which family reunification must be permitted (ibid., 3754).

[89] Freedom of movement is seen as contributing to the fight against social exclusion and thus to 'real citizenship'. See *Towards a Europe of Solidarity: Intensifying the Fight against Social Exclusion, Fostering Integration*, COM (92) 542, 27.

[90] Report of the Committee on Social Affairs and Employment of the European Parliament on the communication from the Commission of the European Communities to the Council on guidelines for a Community policy on migration together with a draft Council resolution, EP Doc. A2–4/85, 16–17.

[91] See, e.g., the Resolution of the European Parliament of 15 July 1993 (O.J. 1993, C 255/184) on European immigration policy.

4.2 ECHR breaches

Ultimately failure to utilize the potential of Union law for promoting fundamental rights in the case of third-country nationals may lead to clashes with the requirements of the European Convention on Human Rights.[92] If the general tendency of Union law is to permit, or even to encourage, discrimination between third-country nationals and nationals of Member States, a containment policy may be inadequate to prevent breaches of this Convention.

For example, although the Convention does not guarantee rights of entry and residence as such and the Fourth Protocol thereto only guarantees such rights in the case of nationals of the Member State concerned, expulsion of aliens may involve action contrary to other rights which are guaranteed by the Convention. Thus expulsion of a third-country national related to someone resident in a Member State may constitute a violation of the right to respect for family life in Article 8 of the Convention.[93] The possibility of a violation of the Convention occurring in such circumstances is apparently heightened where discrimination of the kind prohibited by Article 14 is involved.[94] Hence, expulsion of such a person on grounds which would not lead to the expulsion of a national of a Member State might be contrary to the Convention. Differential treatment of different categories of aliens, i.e. nationals of other Member States and nationals of third states, may not necessarily be easy to justify,[95] where the right to family life is involved. Parties to the Convention and its Protocols cannot lawfully derogate from the rights embodied therein simply by concluding agreements, even one as important as the EC Treaty, amongst themselves.[96] There is no equivalent in the Convention of Article XXIV of

---

[92] Cf. regarding the combined operation of the principle of the right to respect for family life in Art. 8 of the European Convention on Human Rights and the provisions of Regulation 1612/68, Case 249/86, *Commission of the European Communities* v *Federal Republic of Germany*, [1989] ECR 1263, 1290.

[93] See, e.g., Application No. 8244/78, *Uppal Singh*, Decisions and Reports 17, 149.

[94] First Report of the Home Affairs Sub-Committee on Race Relations and Immigration: *Proposed New Immigration Rules and the European Convention on Human Rights* (1979–1980) HC 434, memorandum by F. Jacobs, para. 4.

[95] Art. 1(3) of the International Convention on the Elimination of All Forms of Racial Discrimination (G.A. Res. 2106A(XX)) prohibits discrimination against a particular nationality.

[96] According to the ECJ, it was not contrary to the prohibition of discrimination as between nationals of different Asian, Caribbean and Pacific States (ACP) in the Lomé Convention for a Member State to reserve more favourable treatment to nationals of one ACP State, provided that such treatment resulted from the provisions of an international

GATT, and it is unclear whether Union citizenship, which lacks the historical foundation of, for example, Commonwealth citizenship or the special treatment accorded Irish nationals in the United Kingdom, could always provide an objective justification for such differentiation.[97] It is equally unclear whether it could be justified by reference to the demands of European Union or, indeed, that it would be desirable.[98]

The need for a more liberal approach may be rendered all the more pressing by the EEA Agreement. This Agreement provides for extension of freedom of movement and the prohibition of discrimination to benefit nationals of EFTA states which are parties to the Agreement.[99] Thus persons lacking the nationality of a Member State will enjoy the protection of the very principles which lie at the heart of Union citizenship. Indeed, their rights are described as 'identical' to those of nationals of Member States.[100] It, therefore, becomes increasingly implausible to treat as dependent on possession of the nationality of a Member State or, perhaps, 'EEA nationality' rights which might constitute fundamental rights and be protected as such by Union law.

Such considerations may underlie calls for legislative reform, as for example in relation to the Commission draft of what became Directive 90/364[101] on the right of residence for nationals of Member States not covered by other measures. The European Parliament proposed that the Directive should provide for a 'European Resident's Card' to be issued to legal residents from third countries under the same conditions as to nationals of Member States. More particularly, the right of residence should be available to third-country nationals who, before having reached the age of six years, were resident in a Member State and had since regularly resided there as well as to recognized political refugees and displaced persons residing in a Member State.[102]

---

agreement comprising reciprocal rights and obligations. See Case 65/77, *Jean Razanatsimba*, [1977] ECR 2229, 2239. However, fundamental rights issues were not explicitly put to the ECJ.

[97] Though there may be attractions for national authorities. The status of British dependent territories citizens from Gibraltar as UK nationals for Union law purposes was used in s. 5 of the British Nationality Act 1981 to delimit the beneficiaries of the right of registration as British citizens under this provision.

[98] See, generally, Evans, 'Nationality Law and European Integration', 190–215.

[99] See, generally, Art. 4 of the EEA Agreement; and Evans, *European Community Law, including the EEA Agreement* (1994), Chapter 9.

[100] Art. l(l)(a)(iii) of the draft Convention of 10 Dec. 1993 on controls on persons crossing external frontiers, COM (93) 684.

[101] Of 28 June 1990 (O.J. 1990, L 180/26) on the right of residence.

[102] O.J. 1990, C 175/84.

In the case of pensioners,[103] the Parliament proposed insertion of a clause in the Preamble to the draft of what became Directive 90/365[104] on a right of residence for pensioners, envisaging future measures to recognize rights for third-country nationals identical to those of nationals of Member States. The Directive itself should apply to third-country nationals who had lived on a regular basis in a Member State since the age of six, as well as to political refugees and to stateless persons[105] recognized as such in a Member State and residing there.[106] The European Parliament also proposed inclusion of a clause in the Preamble to the Commission draft of what became Directive 90/366[107] on the right of residence for students, to the effect that the EC Treaty envisaged a 'right of people to choose to reside in any one of the Member States without any distinction whatsoever'. The Directive should, according to the Parliament, be a point of reference for the extension of the right of residence to students from third countries.[108]

Related procedural rights, including appeal rights, access to supporting evidence and legal aid, may also be envisaged.[109] According to the Commission proposal concerning illegal migration, Member States were to take the necessary measures to ensure that persons sentenced for taking up illegal employment might appeal against their sentences. Where the sentence was one of deportation, appeal should

---

[103] O.J. 1990, C 175/89.

[104] Of 28 June 1990 (O.J. 1990, L 180/28) on the right of residence for employees and self-employed persons who have ceased their occupational activity.

[105] Arts. 1 and 2 of Regulation 1408/71 (J.O. 1971, L 149/2) expressly assimilate stateless persons and admitted refugees and their relatives to nationals of Member States for social security purposes. See earlier the declaration of the Representatives of the Governments of the Member States (J.O. p. 1225/1964) that refugees within the meaning of the Geneva Convention on the Status of Refugees who were resident in one Member State should be treated as favourably as possible if they wished to enter another Member State for the purposes of taking employment there. See later O.J. 1985, C 210/2, regarding self-employed refugees.

[106] See earlier the Resolution of 17 April 1980 (O.J. 1980, C 117/48).

[107] Of 28 June 1990 (O.J. 1990, L 180/30) on the right of residence for students.

[108] O.J. 1990, C 175/96.

[109] It is considered necessary to speed up the procedures for recognizing the status of political refugees. This would make it easier for these refugees to enter the labour market. See the Opinion of the Economic and Social Committee of 25 Oct. 1984 (O.J. 1984, C 343/28) on migrant workers. Such persons were 'a very special category of migrants'.

involve a stay of execution.[110] Member States were also required by the amended version to ensure that an illegal migrant, whether or not subject to deportation, should be given every opportunity to assert his rights and those of his family before the proper authorities, have access to all possible supporting evidence and, where applicable, free legal aid.[111] According to the European Parliament, there must be at least the right to information and legal aid, and rules governing the legal consequences of unlawful or improper action by the authorities were required. Such protection must be afforded not only to nationals of Member States but to all those legally resident in the Union.[112]

More particularly, recognition of the right to family life is advocated. In its Resolution of 15 November 1977[113] the European Parliament requested the Member States to adopt, in their legislation, as liberal an attitude as possible when it came to regularizing the position of illegal migrants and their families.[114] Even electoral rights may be

---

[110] Art. 4 of the Proposal of 4 Nov. 1976 (O.J. 1976, C 277/2) for a Council Directive on the harmonization of laws in the Member States to combat illegal migration and illegal employment.

[111] Art. 7(3) of the Proposal of 5 April 1978 (O.J. 1978, C 97/9) for a Council Directive concerning the approximation of the legislation of the Member States in order to combat illegal migration and illegal employment. The European Parliament proposed insertion of a new Art. 4(b), which would require Member States to grant in a general way to illegal workers every practical means of upholding their rights in criminal, administrative and civil proceedings, enabling them to rely on all possible proofs and to obtain, where necessary, free legal assistance. See the Resolution of 15 Nov. 1977 (O.J. 1977, C 299/16). The Economic and Social Committee favoured amendments not merely to secure a greater measure of protection for illegal migrant workers but also to ensure that the laws, regulations and administrative provisions governing the residence and employment of workers from outside the Union were not interpreted in a narrow manner by national authorities. Protection should involve the possibility of giving illegal migrant workers permission to stay once they had become *de facto* employees. See the Opinion of 24 Feb. 1977 (O.J. 1977, C 77/9) on the proposal for a Council Directive on the harmonization of laws in the Member States to combat illegal migration and illegal employment.

[112] Resolution of 22 Jan. 1993 (O.J. 1993, C 42/250) on the setting up of Europol.

[113] O.J. 1977, C 299/16 embodying the Opinion of the European Parliament on the proposal from the Commission of the European Communities to the Council for the harmonization of laws in the Member States to combat illegal migration and illegal employment.

[114] See also the Report of the Committee on Social Affairs, Employment and Education on the amended proposal from the Commission of the European Communities for a Directive concerning the approximation of the legislation of the Member States in order to combat illegal migration and illegal employment, EP Doc. 238/78, 12; and the Opinion of the Economic and Social Committee of 30 May 1974 (O.J. 1974, C 109/52) on employment and the changed situation in the Community.

advocated.[115] According to the European Parliament,[116] resident third-country nationals should be entitled to vote and stand for election at the local level.[117]

To the extent that denial of such rights to third-country nationals is contrary to the European Convention on Human Rights and its Protocols, according to the ECJ, the principles embodied therein are part of Union law, their denial may also be contrary to existing Union law. Even in the absence of legislative reform, then, there may be scope for judicial recognition of the rights entailed by Union citizenship as fundamental rights available throughout the Union.

Whether legislative reform or case law evolution takes place along these lines, a general extension of the equality principle, the content and beneficiaries of this principle depending on interpretation of integration requirements in the light of such rights, would be entailed. In essence, the consequence would be to reduce the exclusivity of nationality as a condition for access to equality and to allow for the operation of alternative conditions, notably that of residence. Residence for a given period could operate as an appropriate connecting factor for individuals to be regarded as belonging to a particular Member State for the purposes of full participation in the political life of that state. Union citizenship would function not so much as the basis for enjoyment of the rights concerned but, rather, as a concept denoting their recognition by Union law.

5   CONCLUSION

This chapter has discussed three possible approaches to the development of Union citizenship within the context of European integration processes. These approaches, which may not only be of analytical utility but also, to the extent that they have been and are pursued by Union

---

[115] Art. 6 of the Council of Europe Convention on the Participation of Foreigners in Public Life at the Local Level (ETS No. 144) accords the right to vote and stand as candidates in local elections to aliens who have been resident in the Member State concerned for five years or more.

[116] O.J. 1990, C 175/80. See, most recently, the Resolution of 21 April 1993 (O.J. 1993, C 150/127) on the resurgence of racism and xenophobia in Europe and the danger of right-wing extremist violence, where the Parliament also advocated action regarding access to citizenship for third-country nationals, grant of citizenship to all children born in the Union and adoption of a Resident's Statute for 'non-nationals'.

[117] See also the Opinion of the Economic and Social Committee of 25 Jan. 1989 (O.J. 1989, C 71/2) on the proposal for a Council Directive on voting rights for Community nationals in local elections in their Member State of residence.

institutions, may have normative impacts, need not necessarily be mutually exclusive. However, market ideology alone may be too limited a basis for development of such citizenship within the context of the wide-ranging integration sought by the TEU. Statist ideology might be compatible with the development of Union citizenship along with the creation of a 'European State'. However, the established character of European integration processes, not to mention economic and political developments, often expressed in terms of networks and globalization, may also render such a solution inadequate.

Treatment of citizenship rights as fundamental rights may offer a solution which does not seem to go beyond the capacity of the Union legal system, is adapted to the needs of integration processes seeking more than mere market unification and is not constrained by statist models of nationality and citizenship. It may offer a basis for justifying and controlling development of free movement, whether domestic or Union activity is involved, in accordance with the ideas underlying the concept of Union citizenship. Within the scope of such rights 'reverse discrimination' could be eliminated, and equality could be more fully secured as between nationals of different Member States. Such equality could fully encompass electoral rights as between nationals of the host Member State and nationals of other Member States who had resided in the former for a sufficient period to be regarded as 'belonging' to that state for the purposes of the rights concerned. Moreover, if the basic implication in Union law—that exercise of citizenship rights should not be conditional on possession of the nationality of the Member State in which such rights are claimed—were taken to its logical conclusion, third-country nationals might also qualify for such rights on the basis of residence in a Member State. Such treatment of citizenship rights would mean that nationality law would no longer provide the basis for excluding substantial numbers of individuals from participation in the political life of their state of residence. Indeed, introduction of a right to naturalization, such that nationality law would acquire as its primary function that of promoting the integration of migrants into the host society, might be rendered less controversial.

The extent to which such reforms may be achieved through judicial interpretation of existing Union law and the extent to which legislative harmonization or even Treaty amendment may be necessary depend on the impact of the 'constitutionalization' of Union citizenship by the TEU and, ultimately, on the relationship between Union law and its social context. However, a form of Union citizenship uninspired by such a pervading fundamental rights dimension, even if it were not sought to link this citizenship with possession of the nationality of a Member State, might be an inadequate response to the demands of European integration processes. It might, indeed, be an inadequate response to the demands of Union citizenship itself.

6 POLITICAL FREEDOMS IN THE EUROPEAN UNION

Erik Lundberg

1 INTRODUCTION

According to Article 8b of the Treaty on European Union (TEU), every citizen of the Union residing in a Member State of which he or she is not a national[1] shall have the right to vote and stand as a candidate at municipal elections and in elections to the European Parliament in the Member State in which he or she resides, *under the same conditions as nationals of that state*. These rights are to be exercised subject to 'detailed arrangements' which 'may provide for derogations where warranted by problems specific to a Member State'.[2] This Article is clearly one of the most controversial provisions of the TEU, since political rights have traditionally been seen as rights belonging exclusively to the citizens of a given state.[3]

The purpose of this chapter is to analyse some of the consequences of this extension of the Community principle of equal treatment into the field of electoral rights. It is submitted that the proper implementation of the rights set out in Article 8b TEU will necessarily have certain

---

[1] Today some five million citizens of the Union are living in Union Member States of which they are not nationals (see Commission draft proposal laying down the detailed arrangements for the exercise of the right of Union citizens to vote and to stand as a candidate in municipal elections in their Member State of residence, COM (94) 38 final 23.02.1994, 3).

[2] In the case of elections to the European Parliament these arrangements have already been adopted (see Council Directive 93/109 of 6 Dec. 1993, laying down detailed arrangements for the exercise of the right to vote and stand as a candidate in elections to the European Parliament for citizens of the Union residing in a Member State of which they are not nationals, O.J. 1993, L 329/34). As regards municipal elections, the detailed arrangements have not yet been adopted (but cf. Commission proposal for a Council Directive laying down the detailed arrangements for the exercise of the right to vote and stand as a candidate in municipal elections for citizens of the Union residing in a Member State of which they are not nationals, COM (94) 38 final 23.02.1994). The deadline set by the TEU is 31 Dec. 1994.

[3] Evans, 'The Political Status of Aliens in International, Municipal and European Community Law', 30 ICLQ (1981), 20–41, at 20.

113

implicit effects on the overall regulation of the political participation of non-nationals in the Union Member States. It is furthermore argued that the rights of Union citizens to vote and stand as a candidate under the same conditions as nationals cannot become genuine and effective rights without full guarantees for political freedoms. By political freedoms we understand, above all, freedom of expression, assembly and association. These are fundamental human rights which lie in the overlapping zone between civil and political rights and are each, in a special way, part of the democratic process.[4] Whereas the provisions of the TEU provide for no explicit guarantees for such political freedoms of Union citizens, the protection of these rights by the Union will, nevertheless, become necessary in order to guarantee that the new political rights are exercised *'effectively'* and *'under the same conditions as nationals of that state'*.

Our starting-point and frame of reference is a brief analysis of the most important restrictions on the political freedoms of non-nationals in international human rights law and in national legislation. This examination is related to the demands and the possibilities provided for by Community law in the area of political participation.

2 THE POLITICAL FREEDOMS OF NON-NATIONALS IN INTERNATIONAL HUMAN RIGHTS LAW

Making distinctions between citizens and aliens as regards their participation in the political life of the state is widely accepted. Generally speaking, both international human rights law[5] and national law[6] permit states to restrict the right to vote, and the right to stand as

---

[4] See Nowak, *UN Covenant on Civil and Political Rights—CCPR Commentary* (1993), p. 385; and Humphrey, 'Political and Related Rights', in Meron (ed.), *Human Rights in International Law: Legal and Policy Issues* (1984), pp. 171–203, at p. 172.

[5] See Art. 25 of the 1966 International Covenant on Civil and Political Rights (CCPR) and Art. 23 of the American Convention on Human Rights. See, however, also Art. 21 of the 1948 United Nations Universal Declaration of Human Rights (UDHR) and Art. 3 of Protocol No. 1 to the 1950 Convention for the Protection of Human Rights and Fundamental Freedoms. As far as the two last-mentioned norms are concerned, it is not entirely clear whether they apply only to citizens (see Chapter 7).

[6] All Union Member States restrict participation in national parliamentary elections to their own citizens (Irish citizens may, however, take part in parliamentary elections in the United Kingdom and vice versa). Pending the adoption of the 'detailed arrangements' provided for by Article 8b TEU, the situation with respect to municipal elections is that half of the Union Member States restrict participation to their own nationals, whereas the other half allow certain specific categories or all foreigners to participate, subject to certain

a candidate in elections to their own citizens. Several Member States have, moreover, circumscribed the electoral rights of citizens living abroad.[7]

As regards the political freedoms, however, the possibilities of making distinctions between citizens and foreigners are more limited. International human rights instruments tend to give states a certain 'margin of appreciation' with respect to the concrete application of these rights.[8] The general rule, nevertheless, is that freedom of expression, assembly and association are to be seen as universal human rights, which are to be granted to all persons without any distinction, such as nationality.[9]

The only important express exception to this rule is Article 16 of the Convention for the Protection of Human Rights and Fundamental Freedoms (European Convention on Human Rights; ECHR). This provision provides that: *'Nothing in Articles 10, 11 and 14 shall be regarded as preventing the High Contracting Parties from imposing restrictions on the political activities of aliens.'*

The imposition of special restrictions on the freedom of expression, assembly and association of aliens guaranteed in Articles 10 and 11 ECHR is thus acceptable in so far as the exercise of these rights take the form of 'political activity'.[10]

As Article 16 does not mention any specific purpose, it would

---

conditions regarding, e.g., residence and/or reciprocity (see COM (94) 38 final 23.02.1994, 3).

[7] This is the case, e.g., in Denmark, Ireland, Luxembourg and The Netherlands.

[8] See, e.g., Arts 19, 21 and 22 CCPR and Art. 10 and 11 ECHR. Any derogation from the rights set out in these articles should, however, be 'prescribed by law', 'necessary in a democratic society' and pursue a 'legitimate aim'. Moreover, all derogations from the rights set out in the two above-mentioned Conventions should be of a non-discriminatory character and in accordance with the rule of proportionality (see, e.g., Kiss, 'Permissible Limitations on Rights', in Henkin (ed.), *The International Bill of Rights* (1981), pp. 291–310; and Nowak, 'Limitations imposées aux droits de l'homme dans une société démocratique', (1992) RUDH, 391–409).

[9] See Lillich, *The Human Rights of Aliens in Contemporary International Law* (1984), p. 43; Elles, *International Provisions Protecting the Human Rights of Non-Citizens* (1980), p. 42; and The UN Human Rights Committee, General Comment No. 15 on the position of aliens under the Covenant, 15 Oct. 1986, 1 IHRR (1994), No. 2, 16.

[10] See, e.g., Cohen-Jonathan, *La convention européenne des droits de l'homme*, (1989), p. 547; Velu and Ergec, *La convention européenne des droits de l'homme* (1990), p. 157; and Wölker, *Zu Freiheit und Grenzen der politischen Betätigung von Ausländern* (1987), pp. 106–107. Some writers contend that the possibility of discriminating to the detriment of aliens applies to all the rights guaranteed by the ECHR, in so far as 'political activities' are involved (see van Dijk and van Hoof, *Theory and Practice of the European Convention on Human Rights* (1991, 2nd edn), p. 560).

appear to provide national authorities with a fairly wide margin of appreciation. There are, however, certain limits to the use of Article 16. To begin with, it is placed under the rule of proportionality, which permeates the entire Convention system (see Article 18 ECHR). Most commentators, moreover, seem to agree, based, for instance, on the 'spirit of the Convention', that there is a limit as to how widely national authorities may interpret the concept 'political activities'.[11] The question of whether in a particular case a 'political activity' is involved will ultimately have to be judged by the Convention organs.[12]

Whereas the European Court on Human Rights has not yet interpreted Article 16 ECHR in its jurisprudence, the European Commission on Human Rights has commented upon this article in a recent decision.[13] The Commission notes 'que les rédacteurs de la convention, en introduisant cet article dans la convention, reflétaient une conception prédominante à l'époque en droit international, autorisant de facon général et illimitée des restrictions aux activités politiques des étrangers'.[14] The Commission, however, goes on to say that the Convention is *'un instrument vivant, qui doit être lu à la lumière des conditions de vie d'aujourd'hui et de l'évolution de la société moderne'.*[15]

Whereas the Commission refrains from giving any clear general guidelines on how the concept 'political activity' should be interpreted in the world of today, it does consider the specific matter of who is to be considered an alien for the purposes of Article 16 ECHR. The issue

---

[11] See, e.g., Mascagni, 'Le restrizioni alle attivita' politiche degli stranieri consentite dalla Convenzione europea dei dritti dell'uomo', 60 RDI (1977), 526–537, at 537; Frowein and Peukert, *Europäischen Menschenrechtskonvention: EMKR-Kommentar* (1985), pp. 336–337; Wölker, *Zu Freiheit und Grenzen,* pp. 106–123; van Dijk and van Hoof, *Theory and Practice,* pp. 560–562; Velu and Ergec, *La convention européenne,* pp. 155–157. Article 16 would not seem to offer justification for limitations on trade union activities of aliens (Tomuschat, 'Freedom of Association', in Macdonald, Matscher and Petzold (eds), *The European System for the Protection of Human Rights* (1993), pp. 493–513, at p. 512). It is also highly questionable whether the mere expression of a political idea by an alien could be considered as 'political activity' within the meaning of Art. 16 ECHR (see, e.g., Bullinger, 'Freedom of Expression and Information: An Essential for Democracy', 28 *German Yearbook of International Law* (1985), 88–143, at 99).

[12] Until recently it has been uncertain whether an individual application by an alien concerning the rights set out by Arts 10 and 11 ECHR would be considered admissible (see, e.g., Swart, 'The Legal Status of Aliens: Clauses in Council of Europe Instruments Relating to the Rights of Aliens', 11 NYIL (1980), 3–64, at 44; and Application No. 7729/76, *Agee v The United Kingdom,* Decisions and Reports 7, 164–188).

[13] Requêtes No. 15773/89 and 15574/89, *Dorothée Piermont contre France,* Rapport de la Commission, (Adopté le 20 janvier 1994).

[14] Ibid., para. 58.

[15] Ibid., para. 59.

at stake was a decision by the French authorities to expel a German national, a certain Mrs Piermont, from French Polynesia. Mrs Piermont, who at that time was a member of the European Parliament, took part, on the invitation of some local political parties, in an authorized, peaceful demonstration in support of the independence of French Polynesia and in opposition to French nuclear tests in the area. During this demonstration Mrs Piermont also addressed the crowd. In its observations the Commission concluded that to the extent that the plaintiff *'agissait en sa qualité de membre du parlement européen, la requérente ne peut être considérée comme une "étranger" au sens de l'article 16 de la convention'*. This observation, taken in conjunction with the opinion that the measure taken by the French authorities *'n'était pas proportionnée au but légitime poursuivi'* led the Commission to conclude that Mrs Piermont's freedom of expression under Article 10(1) ECHR had been violated.[16]

This Commission decision raises two important issues of principle. First, it indicates that the question of who is to be considered an alien for the purposes of Article 16 ECHR is open to interpretation. In the application discussed above the plaintiff was a member of the European Parliament. The Commission decision does not *per se* preclude other categories of non-nationals from being excluded from the scope of application of Article 16 either, provided that proper justification for this is deemed to exist. Secondly, it implicitly raises the question of whether Article 16 in its present unqualified form can be seen to be compatible with 'the living conditions of the world of today' or 'developments in modern society'?[17] It is submitted that the pervasive force of this provision has been weakened, *inter alia*, by the subsequent adoption of other international human rights instruments, which do not foresee similar limitations on the political use of the freedoms of expression, assembly and association on grounds of nationality.[18]

---

[16] Ibid., paras 69 and 77. The application is now pending before the Court of Human Rights.

[17] The Parliamentary Assembly of the Council of Europe called for the amendment of Article 16 ECHR as early as 1977 (see Recommendation 799 (1977) on the political rights and position of aliens, 25 Jan. 1977). On the other hand, recent discussions indicate that there still exists reluctance to delete or amend this provision (see Project Group 'Human Rights and Genuine Democracy' (CAHDD) Research and priority action plan, Second draft interim progress report to the Committee of Ministers, 20 Oct. 1994, CAHDD (94) 7 prov., 25).

[18] See, e.g., the 1966 CCPR and the 1969 American Convention on Human Rights. Germany, France, Austria and Belgium, however, when ratifying the 1966 UN Covenant made reservations as regards the possibility of resisting the political activities of aliens in accordance with Art. 16 ECHR (see CCPR/C/2/Rev.3, 12 May 1992, 8, 10, 14 and 15).

Another instrument manifesting a change in outlook within the European framework is the Council of Europe Convention on the Participation of Foreigners in Public Life at Local Level.[19] This convention provides for a combination of guarantees for fundamental human rights and political rights for aliens in one single package. Each Party to the Convention undertakes to grant all foreign residents, subject to a minimum period of residence of five years, freedom of expression, peaceful assembly and association and the right to vote and to stand as a candidate in local authority elections.

3   POLITICAL FREEDOMS OF NON-NATIONALS AND NATIONAL LEGISLATION

Efforts to determine the exact scope and relevance of the different national rules restricting the political activities of non-nationals are complicated, *inter alia,* by the fact that administrative practices often tolerate activities going beyond the scope of legal guarantees. Moreover, the range of permitted political activities cannot, in some cases, be ascertained without a detailed analysis of rules relating to expulsion. Given the limited scope of this chapter, an exhaustive analysis of all relevant national rules is out of the question.[20] In view of the specific purpose of this chapter, the following review will be confined to determining whether there are any 'common constitutional traditions' to be discerned in this area and to giving a few examples of national rules and practices which might affect the effective exercise of the rights set out in Article 8b TEU.

To begin with, a distinction in principle is made between freedom of expression, on the one hand, and the freedoms of assembly and association on the other. The latter two freedoms involve organized political participation and clearly tend to be subjected to more severe restrictions than the former freedom. Most Member States grant

---

[19] Adopted on 5 Feb. 1992, see ETS No. 144. This convention has been signed by Denmark, Italy and the United Kingdom and ratified by Sweden and Norway (19 May 1994).

[20] To my knowledge, the most recent and comprehensive analyses of the law and praxis of the Union Member States in this field are Frowein and Stein (eds), *The Legal Position of Aliens in National and International Law* (Beiträge zum ausländischen öffentlichen Recht und Völkerrecht, No. 94/1, 1987); Grabitz (ed.), *Grundrechte in Europa und USA* (1986); Özsunay, 'The Participation of the Alien in Public Affairs (Political and Associative Life)', in *Human Rights of Aliens in Europe* (1985), pp. 197–254; and Wölker, *Zu Freiheit und Grenzen.* A general overview is given, e.g., by Rengeling, *Grundrechtsschutz in der Europäischen Gemeinschaft* (1992).

'everyone' freedom of expression at the constitutional level.[21] Thus, it would seem that the view according to which persons of any nationality whatsoever have the right to express themselves freely on any matter, subject only to specific limitations laid down by law and applying in the same way to everyone, is fairly well rooted in the 'common constitutional traditions' of the Member States. It is, nevertheless, noteworthy that the German Aliens Act states that *all political activities of aliens* may be limited or prohibited, for example, in order to protect public security and public order or to prevent the impairment of the formation of the political will in Germany and to protect other matters of substantial concern (sonstige erhebliche Belange) to Germany.[22] Article 15 of the Portuguese Constitution, moreover, excludes aliens from engaging in any political activities whatsoever, subject to the express or tacit permission of the government.[23]

As regards the freedoms of assembly and association, the situation of non-nationals is less clear cut.[24] Comparative studies seem to indicate that, in practice, they tend to enjoy the same level of protection as nationals in almost all areas.[25] Notwithstanding a predominately liberal practice in most Member States it is, however, remarkable that only one out of twelve guarantee freedom of association and assembly for non-nationals at the constitutional level.[26] Member States thus tend to see freedom of assembly and association as rights belonging exclusively to citizens, which *may* be given to non-nationals to the extent that they choose to do so through special legislation and/or

---

[21] The UK has no written constitution and in Spain and Ireland the constitutional guarantees for free expression only concern citizens. In practice, however, non-nationals appear to enjoy freedom of expression on equal terms with nationals in all these countries.

[22] See Art. 37 Ausländergesetz, 9 July 1990 (Bundesgesetzblatt I, 1354, 1356). See also Kanein and Renner, *Ausländerrecht* (1992), pp. 186–191.

[23] See Art. 15 of the Portuguese Constitution. Citizens of Portuguese-speaking countries are, however, in a more favourable position than other aliens, since they may by way of an international convention, with some exceptions and subject to reciprocity, be granted political, and other, rights not conferred on foreigners in general (Art. 15.3). Thus, Brazilian citizens have the same political rights as Portuguese citizens due to a bilateral Convention signed in 1971 (see Özsunay, *Participation of the Alien*, p. 206; and Silveira, 'Le régime juridique des étrangers en droit portugais', in Frowein and Stein (eds), *Legal Position of Aliens*, pp. 1257–1301, at p. 1285.).

[24] See in general *Freedom of Association* (1994), proceedings of a seminar organized by the Secretariat General of the Council of Europe in collaboration with the Ministry of Justice of Iceland, Reykjavik, 26–28 August 1993.

[25] See Frowein, 'Concluding Report', in Frowein and Stein (eds), *Legal Position of Aliens*, pp. 2069–2090, at p. 2087.

[26] See Arts 7 and 9 of the Constitution of the Kingdom of The Netherlands.

administrative practice.

Some Member States, such as the United Kingdom, tend to entertain a liberal practice as far as the exercise of political freedoms by foreigners is concerned. There may, nevertheless, exist grey zones; for instance, the British system contains almost no limits as far as expulsion is concerned. In certain cases it might be difficult to determine whether expulsion could be used as a means of preventing political activities of foreigners which are deemed inappropriate.[27]

Despite the lack of any statutory basis for this view, aliens in France have traditionally been expected to maintain a certain *'obligation de réserve'*, as far as political activities are concerned.[28]

A lack of explicit statutory guarantees, however, results in a weaker and more unstable basis for the exercise of freedom of assembly and association by non-nationals, especially as far as sensitive areas such as organized political activities are concerned. The right to join and to form political parties provides a good example of this problem. The regulation of this issue in law and praxis varies considerably in the different Member States. The role and status of political parties is dealt with at the constitutional level in six of the Member States, which tend to consider political parties, *inter alia*, as an important factor for the concretization of the principle of popular sovereignty at the national level.[29] In one of these Member States, Portugal, aliens may neither form nor join political parties.[30] Others, such as Germany, restrict the possibilities of non-nationals to form and join political parties.[31] Alien membership in political parties and, in particular, alien political parties have, moreover, been controversial issues also in Italy and Spain.

Only six of the present Member States refrain from imposing any

---

[27] See Plender, 'The Legal Position of Aliens in National and International Law in the United Kingdom', in Frowein and Stein (eds), *Legal Position of Aliens*, pp. 1675–1721, at p. 1707; and Frowein, 'Concluding Report', in ibid., pp. 2069–2090, at p. 2088.

[28] See, e.g., Evans, *'Ordre Public* in French Immigration Law', *Public Law* (1980), 132–149, at 136. Administrative practice, nevertheless, is becoming more liberal in this area. According to a decision taken by the French *Conseil d'Etat* 'comportement politique n'est pas à lui seul de nature à justifier légalement l'expulsion d'un étranger' (*Conseil d'Etat*, Mai 13, 1977, *Perregaux*). See, however, also Requêtes No. 15773/89 and 15774/89, *Dorothée Piermont contre France*.

[29] See Art. 21 of the German Constitution, Art. 4 of the French Constitution, Art. 6 of the Spanish Constitution, Art. 29 of the Greek Constitution, Art. 49 of the Italian Constitution and Arts 10, 40, 51, 117 and 154 of the Portuguese Constitution.

[30] Silveira, 'Le régime juridique', p. 1284.

[31] See, e.g., Art. 38.1 of the German Constitution and Art. 2 of the *Parteiengesetz*, according to which a political organization ceases to be a party within the meaning of the law if a majority of its members, or if its leaders, are non-nationals.

formal restrictions whatsoever as regards the possibilities of non-nationals forming or joining political parties.[32]

Where the legal system contains no rules on aliens and political parties, each political party remains free to decide whether to accept non-nationals as members or not. Generally speaking, alien participation in political parties has been fairly uncommon even in systems which entertain no formal restrictions in this respect. The low level of participation is, however, not surprising, given the fact that political parties in general are created with the express intention of influencing the formation of the political will at the national level;[33] a process from which aliens, in any case, are excluded. The fact that political parties also tend to dominate the electoral process at other levels, including the European and municipal levels might, on the other hand, create problems for non-nationals who are entitled to participate at these levels. In some cases political parties are entitled to special privileges, such as financial support for arranging their electoral campaign and/or free access to media during the campaign (for example, in Germany and Spain).[34] Moreover, the right to nominate candidates for elections is in some cases a privilege of political parties, either *de jure* or *de facto*.[35]

To conclude, it is clear that some of the existing differences in treatment between nationals and non-nationals as regards their political freedoms could complicate the exercise of the new participatory rights of Union citizens set out in Article 8b TEU. The mere fact that non-nationals still run the risk of being subjected to limitations, or ultimately of being expelled, for example, when engaging in politically sensitive issues may prevent them from participating fully in the electoral process. More importantly, however, taking into consideration the

---

[32] Belgium, France, Greece, Luxembourg, The Netherlands and the UK (see Herdegen, 'Political Rights and Other Aspects of Resident Status', in Frowein and Stein (eds), *Legal Position of Aliens*, pp. 2003–2018, at p. 2008.

[33] See, e.g., Tsatsos, 'Europäische politische Parteien? Erste Überlegungen zur Auslegung des Parteienartikels des Maastrichter Vertrages — Art. 138a EGV', 21 Eu GRZ (1994), 45–53, at 45.

[34] See *The Funding of Political Parties in European Community Member States* (European Parliament, Directorate General for Research, Political Series 12, 2nd edn, 1991).

[35] As far as elections to the European Parliament are concerned, Denmark, Greece, Germany and The Netherlands restrict the right to nominate candidates to political parties or equivalent organizations (see *Les lois electorales pour les elections européenes*, Parlement Européen, 1994). In Germany the right to nominate candidates for elections in general tends, *de facto*, to be restricted exclusively to political parties (see, e.g., Stoklossa, *Der Zugang zu den politischen Parteien im Spannungsfeld zwischen Vereinsautonomie und Parteienstaat* (1989), p. 33).

prominent role that political parties tend to play in the electoral process in some Member States, is it possible to talk about an effective right to stand as a candidate under the same conditions as nationals if the possibilities of non-nationals to join and form political parties are not guaranteed?

In the following I intend to examine to what extent Community law can be seen as providing Union citizens with the protection needed to secure the effective exercise of the new electoral rights granted under Article 8b TEU.

4 THE PROTECTION OF FUNDAMENTAL RIGHTS IN THE EUROPEAN UNION

In view of the prominent role played by both Member State constitutional traditions and the ECHR within the EU legal order, one might ask in what way the Union could be expected to augment the level of protection for the political freedoms of non-nationals. According to Article F.2 TEU, the Union has a duty to respect fundamental rights, as guaranteed by the 1950 ECHR and as they result from the constitutional traditions common to the Member States, as general principles of Community law. The concrete legal implications of this commitment, nevertheless, remain somewhat uncertain, as Article F.2 was left outside the jurisdiction of the Court of Justice of the European Communities (ECJ).[36]

However, as long as the Union has not acceded to the ECHR it is clear that the provisions of the ECHR do not as such enjoy the status of directly applicable law within the Union Member States. The fundamental rights recognized by the ECJ are not absolute as they may be balanced against other interests and objectives set out by the Union, such as the organization and functioning of a Common Market.[37] Hence, the interpretation of the ECHR provisions within the Union

---

[36] See Art. L TEU. Moreover, as the Union is not a party to the ECHR, the control organs set up by the Convention will be unable to rule on the compatibility of actions taken by the Union with the rights set out in the ECHR (see, e.g., Application No. 8030/77, *Confédération Française Démocratique du Travail* v *The European Communities*, Decisions and Reports 13, 231).

[37] See, e.g., Cases 5/88, *Huber Wachauf* v *Federal Republic of Germany*, [1989] ECR 2609, para. 18; and C-159/90, *Society for the Protection of Unborn Children Ireland Ltd (S.P.U.C.)* v *Stephen Grogan and Others*, [1991] ECR I-4685. According to the ECJ, the objectives of the EC Treaty, none the less, may justify limiting human rights only in so far as the substance of the rights is not affected (see Case 4/73 *J. Nold, Kohlen- und Baustoffgrosshandlung* v *Commission of the European Communities* [1974] ECR 491). See also, e.g., Coppel and O'Neill, 'The European Court of Justice: Taking Rights Seriously?', 29 CML Rev. (1992), 669–692.

framework may differ from that given by the Strasbourg organs.[38]

As far as the fundamental political freedoms are concerned the ECJ has affirmed that freedom of expression, as embodied in Article 10 ECHR, should be seen as a general principle of law the observance of which is ensured by the ECJ.[39] The ECJ has also affirmed that although Member States in principle are free to determine the requirements of public policy in the light of national needs, the concept of public policy, when used to derogate from the fundamental Community principles of equality of treatment and freedom of movement, should be interpreted strictly. Any limitations placed by Community law as regards the control of aliens should be seen as:[40]

> a specific manifestation of the more general principle, enshrined in Articles 8, 9, 10 and 11 ECHR, which provide that no restrictions in the interest of national security or public safety shall be placed on the above-quoted articles other than such as are necessary for the protection of those interests 'in a democratic society'.

Practice has shown that the margin of appreciation left to Member States with regard to derogations on grounds of public policy tends to be interpreted more narrowly within the Community system than in the ECHR system.[41] It has repeatedly been contended that the Community, because of the far-reaching legal implications its activities have on individuals, should not settle for the minimum level of protection offered by the ECHR.[42] The European Parliament, in particular, has strongly advocated the adoption of a specific Community catalogue of funda-

---

[38] See, e.g., Joined Cases 46/87 and 227/88, *Hoechst AG v Commission of the European Communities*, [1989] ECR 2859, at paras 17 and 18 and Case 85/87, *Dow Benelux NV v Commission of the European Communities*, [1989] ECR 3137, paras 28 and 29, where the ECJ of Justice asserts that the fundamental right to inviolability of the home set out in Art. 8(1) ECHR only applies to private dwellings of natural persons within the Community legal order.

[39] See Case C-260/89, *Elliniki Radiophonia Tileorassi AE v Dimotiki Etairia Pliroforissis and Sotirios Kouvelas*, [1991] ECR I-2925. See also, e.g, Case C-23/93, *TV10 SA v Commissariaat voor de Media*, Les activités de la cour et du tribunal de première instance des communautés européennes, No. 27/94, 32–34.

[40] Case 36/75, *Roland Rutili v Minister for the Interior*, [1975] ECR 1219. See, in particular, paras 26–32 of the judgment.

[41] For a detailed comparison of the jurisprudence of the Courts in Luxembourg and Strasbourg, see Hall, 'The European Convention on Human Rights and Public Policy Exceptions to the Free Movement of Workers under the EEC Treaty', 16 EL Rev. (1991), 466–488.

[42] For a discussion on this, see, e.g., Lenaerts, 'Fundamental Rights to be Included in a Community Catalogue', 16 EL Rev. (1991), 367–390.

mental rights, going beyond the level of protection offered by the ECHR.[43]

Bearing in mind that it is the principles rather than the provisions of the Convention that form part of the general principles of Community law, there seems to be no compelling reason why the restrictions laid down by Article 16 ECHR should affect Member State nationals in the same way as they do with respect to third-country nationals.[44] Recent events, such as the creation of a European Union and a Union citizenship, arguably reinforce the basic Community idea of making clear distinctions between the rights of Member State nationals and other third-country nationals.

5   THE POLITICAL STATUS OF UNION CITIZENS

The idea of creating a kind of 'European' or 'Community citizenship',[45] by affording nationals of the Member States certain rights as Community nationals, dates back to the early 1970s and has ever since been closely linked to the idea of creating a closer political union between the Community Member States.[46] It gained renewed momentum in the late 1980s during the preparations for the intergovernmental conferences on political and economic and monetary union. In this context it was argued that a genuine European citizenship would entail, *inter alia*, the right to participate in the political life of the Member States of residence, beginning with the *full recognition of freedom of expression,*

---

[43] See, in particular, the Resolution of the European Parliament of 12 April 1989 adopting a Declaration on Fundamental Rights and Freedoms (O.J. 1989, C 120/52).

[44] See, e.g., Evans, 'Nationality Law and European Integration', 16 EL Rev. (1991), 190–215, at 207.

[45] The discussion concerning European citizenship and the possible rights of European citizens has been dealt with in detail elsewhere. See, e.g., Evans, 'European Citizenship', 45 MLR (1982), 497–515; and Magiera, 'Politische Rechte im Europa der Bürger', 20 *Zeitschrift für Rechtspolitik* (1987), 331–337. See also, in general, *Citizens' Europe: Action taken by the European Parliament to Create a European Community to Serve its Citizens* (European Parliament, Citizens' Europe Series E1, 1992).

[46] See, e.g., the Tindemans Report on European Union (Supplement 1/76 – Bull. EC), *Proceedings of the Round Table on Special Rights and a Charter of the Rights of the Citizens of the European Community and Related Documents*, European Parliament (1978), the Addonino Report 'A People's Europe' (Supplement 7/85 – Bull. EC). See also the Commission draft proposal for a Council directive on voting rights for Community nationals in local elections in their Member States of residence (COM (88) 371 final 11.07.1988)

association and assembly.[47] The idea of extending certain civil and political rights of Member State nationals was supported by the Commission, which, *inter alia*, advocating the inclusion into the Treaty of a right to be a member of a political association or group, saw European citizenship as an important means of countering the democratic deficit and strengthening the democratic legitimacy of the Community.[48] The citizenship idea was also supported by the European Parliament, where, nevertheless, it was argued that a European citizenship had to based on a general extension and improvement of the protection of fundamental rights, rather than on simply affording Member State nationals certain 'special rights'.[49] Only some of these expectations were met in the final version of the TEU, signed in February 1992.

According to Article B of the Common Provisions of the TEU, one of the objectives of the Union is 'to strengthen the protection of the rights and interests of the nationals of its Member States through the introduction of a citizenship of the Union'. This citizenship, which is created by Articles 8–8e of the TEU, is, however, of a complementary nature. It does not replace the citizenship of Member States.[50] The Union citizenship is conferred exclusively on persons holding the nationality of a Member State.[51]

Whereas the essence of 'national citizenship' lies in the exercise of state sovereignty through political participation, the core and the origin of Union citizenship is the right to free movement.[52] The primary objective of the rights set out by Article 8b TEU is not to achieve an overall approximation of the Member States' electoral laws, but to

---

[47] See 'European Citizenship. Towards a Citizens' Europe', Memorandum submitted by the Spanish Government, published, e.g., in (1990) *Europe*, No. 5252, 3.

[48] Supplement 2/91 – Bull. EC.

[49] Bindi Report on Union Citizenship, EP Doc. A3–0139/91, 23 May 1991.

[50] See, e.g., the Declaration of the European Council in Birmingham, 16 Oct. 1992 SN 343/1/1992, 4; and COM (90) 600 final.

[51] The question of who is a national of the Union is ultimately to be decided by the Member States themselves. See the Declaration on Nationality of a Member State annexed to the TEU. See, however, also Case C-369/90, *Mario Vincente Micheletti and Others* v *Delegación del Gobierno en Cantabria*, [1992] ECR I-4239; and d'Oliveira, Annotation of Case C-369/90, *M.V. Micheletti and Others* v *Delegación del Gobierno en Cantabria*, [1992] ECR I-4239, 30 CML Rev. (1993), 623–637.

[52] d'Oliveira, 'European Citizenship: its Meaning, its Potential', in Monar, Ungerer and Wessels (eds), *The Maastricht Treaty on European Union—Legal Complexity and Political Dynamic* (1993), pp. 81–106, at p. 88.

promote and facilitate the free movement of Union citizens.[53] National regulations concerning participation in referendums, elections at the regional and national levels are unaffected by the TEU provisions. Moreover, the existing restrictions as regards, for example, access to public office and the exercise of official authority remain in force.[54] Thus, the provisions on Union citizenship do not guarantee the full civil and political rights protection conveyed by the citizenship of a Member State. The TEU does not establish a new federal state. Nor does it create a new political subject.[55]

Having said this, it must, however, also be noted that the European Community can no longer be considered as an exclusively economic device. The fact that nationals of the Member States are now entitled to certain political rights as citizens of the Union certainly constitutes a step towards a closer political union.

6   THE *EFFET UTILE* OF THE RIGHTS SET OUT IN ARTICLE 8B TEU AND THE PRINCIPLE OF EQUAL TREATMENT

In view of the principle of subsidiarity which permeates the TEU, any regulation at the Union level must be confined to what is strictly necessary to achieve the objectives set out by the Treaty.[56] According to the Commission, Article 8b concerns only 'the conditions to be met in order to be entitled to vote or stand as a candidate, such as those relating to citizenship, minimum age and disqualification, and the conditions to be met for a voter or a person entitled to stand as a candidate to be able *effectively* to exercise his right in a particular election'.[57] It is submitted that the use of the adverb 'effectively' in this context is of pivotal importance. The ambition to secure the effective exercise of all Treaty-based rights has been one of the main objectives of the activities of the ECJ. Resorting to teleological interpretations of Treaty provisions, the ECJ has gone beyond strict, literal interpretations

---

[53] The rights set out in Art. 8b shall also be exercised without prejudice to Art. 138(3) concerning the right of the European Parliament to draw up proposals for elections by universal suffrage in accordance with a uniform procedure in all Member States.

[54] See Arts 8, 48(3) and 55 EC Treaty.

[55] O'Keeffe, 'Union Citizenship', in O'Keeffe and Twomey (eds), *Legal Issues of the Maastricht Treaty* (1994), pp. 87–107, at p. 91.

[56] See Chapter 3.

[57] COM (93) 534 final, 9 (emphasis added).

in order to promote the objectives set out by the Treaty.[58] The ECJ has even been prepared to grant individual rights which have no explicit legal basis in the Treaty itself. It may, for example, consider such 'accessory rights' as 'indispensable' in order to secure the full effectiveness (*effet utile*) of a Treaty-based right.[59] The basis for this doctrine was sketched out in the *van Gend & Loos* judgment, where the ECJ declared that Community law confers rights upon individuals independently of the legislation of Member States and that these rights arise, '*not only where they are expressly granted by the Treaty, but also by reason of obligations which the Treaty imposes in a clearly defined way* upon individuals as well as upon the Member States and the institutions of the Community'.[60]

Concrete examples of situations where the ECJ has provided protection for 'accessory, indispensable rights' are found, for example, in the area of free movement of persons. In *Heylens* the ECJ held that since free access to employment is a fundamental right which the Treaty confers individually on each worker of the Community, the existence of a remedy of a judicial nature against any decision of a national authority denying the benefit of this right was essential in order to secure the individual an effective protection of this right.[61] In *Cowan* the ECJ considered the right to protection of the physical integrity of the person, in this case the right to compensation by the state for physical injury caused by an assault, as a corollary to the right of free movement of recipients of services, in this case a British national holidaying as a tourist in France.[62]

Furthermore, the rights set out in Article 8b TEU are to be exercised '*under the same conditions as nationals*'. Generally speaking, Article 8b thus amounts to what the ECJ has referred to as 'a specific

---

[58] See, e.g., Pescatore, 'Les objectifs de la Communauté européenne comme principes d'interprétation dans la jurisprudence de la cour de justice', in *Miscellanea W.J. Ganshof van der Mersch*, Tome deuxieme (1972), pp. 325–363; and Schermers and Waelbroek, *Judicial Protection in the European Communities* (1992), p. 21.

[59] See Fallon, 'Les droits accessoires à l'exercice des droits economiques de la personne dans la Communauté', 2 *Annales de Droit de Louvain* (1993), 235–255.

[60] See Case 26/62, *N.V. Algemene Transport— en Expeditie Onderneming Van Gend & Loos v Nederlandse administratie der belastingen [Netherlands Inland Revenue Administration]*, [1963] ECR 1, 12 (emphasis added).

[61] Case 222/86, *Union nationale des entraîneurs et Cadres techniques professionels du football (Unectef) v Georges Heylens and Others*, [1987] ECR 4097, para. 14 of the judgment. For a similar line of reasoning in the field of fundamental human rights, see Eur. Court H. R., *Airey* judgment of 9 Oct. 1979, Series A no. 32.

[62] See Case 186/87, *Ian William Cowan v Trésor public*, [1989] ECR 195.

enunciation of the general principle of equality, which is one of the fundamental principles of the Community'.[63] According to the Commission, the general principle of equal treatment, in the case of Article 8b, means 'that identical or similar situations are to be treated in the same way and that situations can be treated differently only if they are dissimilar' and that 'no special requirements are to be imposed on non-nationals unless there is a difficulty specific to non-nationals which justifies a difference in treatment.' This rather formal and abstract definition of what is meant by the phrase 'under the same conditions as nationals' is of limited use. It could be argued that specific restrictions are acceptable in the case of non-nationals because there are difficulties specific to them. On the other hand, it could be contended that specific protective measures, going beyond formal equal treatment, are needed in the case of non-nationals, precisely because in practice they are in a situation which differs in many respects from that of nationals. Is the Commission talking about so-called formal or substantive equality?

More information about the concrete functioning and interpretation of the principle of equality of treatment set out in Article 8b TEU can again be obtained by comparison with other fundamental rights provisions of Community law. With the free movement of persons, the principle of equal treatment or non-discrimination on grounds of nationality has undergone a process of significant widening, both as regards its scope of application *ratione personae* and *ratione materiae*.[64] Contrary to initial interpretations of the original EEC Treaty provisions, this principle is no longer strictly confined to rights directly derived from the actual exercise of an economic activity. In *Commission* v *Italy* the ECJ, for example, held that the fundamental right to equal treatment set out in Articles 52 and 58 EEC Treaty had been violated because a national of a Member State who wished to pursue an activity as a self-employed person in another Member State could not obtain housing in conditions equivalent to those enjoyed by his competitors who were

---

[63] See, e.g., Joined Cases 117/76 and 16/77, *Albert Ruckdeschel & Co. and Hansa-Lagerhaus Ströh & Co.* v *Hauptzollamt Hamburg-St. Annen; Diamalt AG* v *Hauptzollamt Hzehoe*, [1977] ECR 1753, para. 7; or Joined Cases 124/76, *SA Moulins et Huileries Pont-à-Mousson* v *Office National Interprofessionnel des Céréales; Société Coopérative 'Providence Agricole de la Champagne'* v *Office National Interprofessionnel des Céréales*, [1977] ECR 1795, paras 16–17. See also Advocate General Lagrange's opinion in Case 13/63, *Government of the Italian Republic* v *Commission of the European Economic Community*, [1963] ECR 165; see, in particular, 189–192.

[64] See Arts 48(2), 52 and 59 EC Treaty. For a detailed analysis of this evolution see, e.g., Arnull, *The General Principles of EEC Law and the Individual* (1990), pp. 25–69.

nationals of the latter Member State.[65] Moreover, as regards the social advantages of migrant workers, the principle of equal treatment has been interpreted very extensively.[66] In *Mutsch* the ECJ, for example, concluded that workers who are nationals of one Member State and resident in another are entitled to require that criminal proceedings against them take place in a language other than the language normally used in proceedings before the court which tries them if workers who are nationals of the host Member State have that right under the same circumstances.[67]

We are well aware of the fact that the guarantees set out in Article 8b do not concern economic, but political, activities instead. It is, nevertheless, submitted that the examples provided tell us something about the way in which fundamental rights set out by the basic Community Treaties are protected. First, the ECJ is prepared to go beyond the text of the Treaty in order to secure the full effectiveness of a Treaty-based fundamental right. Secondly, the ECJ is clearly willing to interpret the principle of equal treatment widely in order to promote such a right.[68] On a more general level, Article 6 TEU, which prohibits any discrimination on grounds of nationality falling within the scope of application of the Treaty, requires that persons *in a situation governed by Community law* must be placed *on equal footing with nationals of the Member State.*[69]

In view of these examples, it is argued that any situation, such as, for example, differences in the protection of political freedoms, obstructing the effective exercise of the electoral rights set out in Article 8b is likely to be corrected by the ECJ. Consider, for instance, the situation of a Danish national residing in Germany, wishing to exercise his right to stand as a candidate in elections to the European Parliament

---

[65] Case 63/86, *Commission of the European Communities* v *Italian Republic,* [1988] ECR 29, para. 16

[66] See Art. 7 of Council Regulation 1612/68 (O.J. Sp. Ed., 1968 (II), 475).

[67] See 137/84, *Ministère public* v *Robert Heinrich Maria Mutsch,* [1985] ECR 2681, para. 18.

[68] The guarantees on free movement of persons do, however, not appear to allow for discrimination in favour of the weak, that is affirmative action (see Mancini, 'The Free Movement of Workers in the Case-Law of the European Court of Justice', in Curtin and O' Keeffe (eds), *Constitutional Adjudication in European Community and National Law, Essays for the Hon. Justice O'Higgins* (1992), pp. 67–77, at p. 72).

[69] See Joined Cases C-92/92 and C-326/92, *Phil Collins* v *Imtrat Handelsgesellschaft mbh; Patricia Im- and Export Verwaltungsgesellschaft GmbH* v *EMI Electrola GmbH,* [1993] ECR I-5145. See also, e.g., Case 186/87, *Ian William Cowan* v *Trésor public,* [1989] ECR 195, para. 10.

in Germany in accordance with Article 8b TEU and secondary legisla-tion.[70] Bearing in mind that the possibilities of non-nationals to form political parties and to join, and to exercise substantial influence within, a political party, are restricted by law, is it possible for him or her to exercise effectively a right to stand as a candidate under the same conditions as nationals, if political parties, in practice, control the nomination of candidates and enjoy a privileged position with respect to financial support and access to media during the electoral campaign? Even if other political groups, theoretically and formally speaking, have an equal right to nominate candidates, it is submitted that they are unable to do so on equal terms with groups enjoying the legal status of a political party. It is, furthermore, worth pointing out that Union citizens of foreign nationality who reside, and wish to stand as a candidate in elections to the European Parliament, in Portugal, may be faced with similar problems, given the fact that non-nationals are excluded both from forming and joining political parties.

One might perhaps argue that these kinds of situations are covered by the Treaty provisions, since Article 8b allows for derogations 'where warranted by problems specific to a Member State'. A closer exam-ination of all the relevant provisions, however, indicates that this possibility of derogating will probably be of rather limited relevance.

7   DEROGATIONS FROM THE RIGHTS SET OUT IN ARTICLE 8B TEU

In the human rights context the possibilities of derogating from funda-mental rights are strictly limited. The term 'derogation' is normally used only in situations involving a public emergency.[71] In the Commu-nity legal framework this term appears to be used in a slightly different, more flexible way. According to the ECJ, derogations from the fundamental right set out by the basic Community Treaties are, nevertheless, to be interpreted narrowly. Thus, the ECJ has, for instance, indicated that the right to equal treatment is a fundamental right within the framework of the free movement of persons and that any deroga-

---

[70] See Council Directive 93/109; and Europawahlordnung, 27 July 1988, with subsequent amendments, notably, Zweite Verordnung zur Änderung der Europawahlordnung, 15 March 1994; and Berichtigung der Neufassung des Europawahlgesetzes, Bundesgesetzblatt, No. 17 1994, 19 March 1994, 544 and 555. See also Borchmann, 'Änderungen im deutschen Europawahlrecht', (1994) NJW, Heft 23, 1522–1523.

[71] See, e.g., Article 15 ECHR and Article 4 CCPR. See also Rosas, 'Emergency Regimes: A Comparison', in Gomien (ed.), *Broadening the Frontiers of Human Rights. Essays in Honour of Asbjørn Eide* (1993), pp. 165–199.

tions from this right on grounds of public policy[72] must be interpreted restrictively.[73] Only activities which amount to a 'genuine and sufficiently serious' threat to public policy and which affect one of the 'fundamental interests of the society' fall within the scope of application of the derogation clauses provided for by the Treaty. Derogation clauses cannot, for instance, be used by a Member State to justify the expulsion of a national of another Member State by reason of conduct which, when attributable to the former state's own nationals, would not give rise to repressive measures or other genuine and effective measures intended to counter such conduct.[74]

The possibilities of making derogations from the principle of equal treatment set out by Article 8b seem to be even more limited. To begin with, derogations are allowed only from the detailed arrangements, not from the Treaty-based guarantees as such.[75] According to secondary legislation, the possibility of derogating arises only where more than 20 per cent of the residents entitled to vote and stand as a candidate in a Member State are nationals of other Member States of the Union.[76] Thus, a Member State which fulfils the above-mentioned condition regarding the size of its foreign population, may restrict the right to vote in elections to the European Parliament to those non-national Community voters who have been residents in that state for a minimum period, which may not exceed five years. In the case of the right to stand as a candidate the minimum period may not exceed ten years.[77] In addition to this, Member States may take 'appropriate

---

[72] See in particular Arts 48(2) and 56 EC Treaty, which allow for restrictions on the rights of free movement and equal treatment on grounds of public policy, public security and public health. See also Council Directive 64/221 (25 Feb. 1964, O.J. Sp. Ed., 1963–64, 117).

[73] See, e.g., Cases 41/74, *Yvonne van Duyn v Home Office*, [1974] ECR 1337; 67/74, *Carmelo Angelo Bonsignore v Oberstadtdirektor der Stadt Köln*, [1975] ECR 297; 36/75, Case 36/75, *Rutili*, see note 40; *Concetta Sagulo, Gennaro Brenca and Addelmadjid Bakhouche*, [1977] ECR 1495; 30/77, *Regina v Pierre Bouchereau*, [1977] ECR 1999.

[74] Joined Cases 115 and 116/81, *Rezguia Adoui v Belgian State and City of Liège; Dominique Cornuaille v Belgian State*, [1982] ECR 1665, 1708.

[75] See COM (93) 534, at 19–20; and Council Directive 109/93, O.J. 1993, L 329/37. See also COM (94) 38 final, 14.

[76] See Art. 14 of Council Directive 109/93. See also Art. 12 of the Commission draft proposal for detailed arrangements as regards participation in municipal elections, COM (94) 38 final 23.02.1994.

[77] According to the Commission draft proposal concerning municipal elections the equivalent minimum periods may not be longer than the term for which the representative council of the municipality is elected in the case of voting and twice this term as regards eligibility (see COM (94) 38 final, 36).

measures' with regard to the composition of lists of candidates, which are intended, in particular, to 'encourage the integration of non-national citizens of the Union'.[78] The term 'appropriate measures' is not defined, but this provision seems to indicate that nationals from other Member States may be prevented from setting up separate lists of candidates in elections to the European Parliament.

The above-mentioned possibilities of limiting the rights set out by Article 8b TEU have been criticized within the European Parliament,[79] where it has been argued, *inter alia*, that they might result in discrimination on grounds of nationality contrary to the Treaty since they will affect mainly voters of certain Member States. The practical effects of any derogations will, nevertheless, remain limited in practice as only one Member State, namely Luxembourg, may avail itself of this possibility.

8   POLITICAL PRIORITIES AT THE EUROPEAN LEVEL?

Article 8(2) TEU stipulates that: 'Citizens of the Union shall enjoy the rights conferred by this Treaty and shall be subject to the duties imposed hereby'.[80] Hence, the question arises whether there are other provisions of the TEU which advocate equal protection of the freedom of expression, assembly and association of Union citizens.

Whereas Article 138 TEU, which states that appropriate provisions shall be adopted to secure elections of the European Parliament by direct suffrage in accordance with a *uniform procedure* in all Member States, is only of indirect relevance in this context, the new Article 138a TEU is quite interesting. Article 138a provides, *inter alia*, that political parties at the European level contribute to forming a European awareness and expressing the political will of the citizens of the Union. This provision was originally placed among the citizenship provisions, but was moved to the section concerning the European Parliament in the chapter on the institutions of the Community in the final version of

---

[78] Equivalent provisions are set out in the Commission draft proposal concerning the detailed arrangements for the right to vote and stand as a candidate in municipal elections (COM (94) 38 final, Art. 12).

[79] See, e.g., the draft Report of the Committee on Institutional Affairs on the Commission proposal to Parliament and the Council for a directive on laying down detailed arrangements for the exercise of the right to vote and to stand as a candidate in municipal elections by citizens of the Union resident in a Member State of which they are not nationals, EP 207.471, 11.

[80] For a discussion on the interpretation of this provision, see Chapter 4.

the text.[81] The concrete legal effects of this article in its present form and context are, so far, unclear. It has, however, been contended that the intended purpose of this provision was to provide a framework for future legislation in the area, not to grant Union citizens a directly effective right.[82] On a general level, Articles 138 and 138a TEU none the less imply that equal opportunities to participate in elections and to organize politically, even on a transnational basis, are essential elements of political participation at the 'European level'. In view of this, it appears questionable whether a Member State may entertain rules restricting or impeding the formation of transnational parties at the European level.

9 CONCLUSION

It has been the purpose of this chapter to demonstrate that the electoral rights granted by Article 8b TEU might be impeded without adequate protection for certain 'indispensable or accessory' fundamental rights, such as freedom of expression, assembly and association. It has been submitted that the Court of Justice of the European Communities has demonstrated a willingness to 'read an unwritten bill of rights into Community law'[83] in order to secure the effectiveness of Community law and to promote objectives set out by the basic Treaties, such as the emergence of 'an ever closer union among the peoples of Europe'. This must be taken into account when discussing the practical implications of any fundamental right set out by the Treaty. Thus, if, for instance, a Union citizen's possibility of joining or exercising influence within a political party is restricted in a situation where political parties tend to dominate the nomination of candidates, and/or enjoy financial or other privileges during the electoral campaign, a violation of his or her rights set out in Article 8b may occur. Should such a situation occur, it has been submitted here that the ECJ would be inclined to protect the 'accessory, indispensable' right of Union citizens to associate freely for political purposes, taking into account the principles of equality of treatment and *'effet utile'*.

It could certainly be argued that the freedoms of expression,

---

[81] See Nickel, 'Le traité de Maastricht et le parlement européen; Le noveau paysage politique et la procédure de l'article 189 B', in Monar et al. (eds), *The Maastricht Treaty*, pp. 117–125, at p. 118.

[82] See Tsatsos, 'Europäische politische Parteien?'.

[83] See, e.g., Mancin, 'The Making of a Constitution for Europe', 26 CML Rev. (1989), 595–614, at 611.

assembly and association of Union citizens only apply as far as activities relating to elections in the municipal and European levels are concerned, since Article 8b TEU only relates to these two levels. In practice, however, it might be extremely difficult to draw a distinguishing line between political activities involving only the municipal and European levels as opposed to activities involving only the national level.[84] So far there are very few, if any, political parties which restrict their activity to the national or to the municipal/European levels.

In the absence of an explicit legal basis and in the light of the strong political considerations involved, the ECJ, nevertheless, might be somewhat cautious as regards extending the protection afforded by Article 8b to political freedoms. The adoption of explicit guarantees for the freedoms of expression, assembly and association of Union citizens at the Union level would certainly be a more effective means of doing away with the prevailing legal uncertainty and of guaranteeing *all Union citizens* the right to vote and to stand as a candidate for elections at the municipal and European levels under the same conditions as nationals. Such measures could perhaps be taken even before 1996, as the TEU, in fact, already provides the necessary legal basis. For Article 8e TEU provides that the Council unanimously and without prejudice to other provisions of the Treaty may adopt provisions to strengthen or to add to citizenship rights. Should the request for unanimity create problems, resort to Article 6 TEU, which covers any discrimination on grounds of nationality occurring in situations governed by Community law, might provide an alternative basis.[85]

---

[84] The same conclusion is reached in the explanatory report on the Council of Europe Convention on Participation of Foreigners in Public Life at Local Level (1993), 9.

[85] This article can provide a basis for legislation aiming to eliminate discrimination on grounds of nationality within the framework of Community law, without prejudice to the specific provisions on discrimination contained in the Treaty (see in particular Case C-295/90, *European Parliament* v *Council*, [1992] 3 CMLR 281, judgment of 7 July 1992, not yet reported).

7 UNION CITIZENSHIP AND NATIONAL ELECTIONS

Allan Rosas

1 INTRODUCTION

The concept of Union citizenship as spelled out in Article 8–8e EC Treaty includes the right to vote and to stand as a candidate at *municipal* and *European* elections in the country of residence rather than the country of nationality. This right of Union citizens does *not* cover national parliamentary elections, 'regional' elections in autonomous areas or states composing federal states, or referendums and plebiscites.

This exclusion of national and similar elections is often regarded as self-evident.[1] According to a widely held view, only the citizens of a state constitute the people which should be allowed to exercise political power in accordance with the principle of popular sovereignty.

The present chapter will question this basic assumption and place the question of voting rights in the European Union in the broader framework of both constitutional and human rights developments and discussions. Included in the discussion will be the concepts of nation-state, sovereignty, nationality and citizenship. I shall also give an account of a previous Nordic discussion on a 'Nordic citizenship' and specific voting rights in this sub-regional context.

It is submitted that such a broader framework may contribute to an understanding of the political dimension of a 'citizens' Europe' and the European Union itself, whatever view one takes on the specific relationship between Union citizenship and national elections and decision-making. In any case, this chapter should be seen mainly as a future-oriented *de lege ferenda* point of view rather than a statement of the law as it stands.

---

[1] See, e.g., a report from the Commission to the European Parliament on voting rights in local elections for Community nationals, Supplement based on COM (86) 487 final, to be discussed below, at note 69.

2 VOTING RIGHTS AND THE NATION-STATE

The emergence and development of modern political democracy and political rights, based on notions of universal suffrage and the principle of equality, were inextricably linked to the sovereign and independent nation-state of the nineteenth and early twentieth centuries. The outcome of the American and French Revolutions did not extend beyond granting voting rights to a minority of male property-owners. It was only gradually, and with various steps back and forth, that the ideas of popular sovereignty, universal suffrage, and equal political right, gained ground.

In line with the conservative restorations that took place during the nineteenth century, there was a tendency in many countries to deny the status of political rights *qua* fundamental (constitutional) rights.[2] Even the Finnish Constitution Act of 1919, which was enacted against the background of the first European electoral reform which involved universal suffrage and eligibility and a unicameral parliament (1906), does not list the right to vote and to be elected among the fundamental rights of citizens recognized in chapter II of the Constitution Act. Instead, these rights are spelled out in a separate Parliament Act of 1928. Only in a current Government Bill for a new chapter II of the Finnish Constitution Act have the right to vote and be elected been included in the constitutional Bill of Rights itself.[3]

When governing elites in Europe and elsewhere have conceded electoral reforms, this has usually been seen as a *concession* rather than acknowledging an entitlement and a human right. This explains why there was reluctance in the late 1940s to include the right of political participation[4] in the Universal Declaration of Human Rights and the Convention for the Protection of Human Rights and Fundamental Freedoms (European Convention on Human Rights; ECHR).[5] After some discussions, this right was included in Article 21 of the Universal Declaration and subsequently in Article 25 of the International

---

[2] Nowak, *Politische Grundrechte* (1988), p. 39 et seq.

[3] Government Bill No. 309/1993, submitted to Parliament on 17 Dec. 1993. At the time of writing, this Bill is still pending before Parliament. The new Bill of Rights is expected to be finally adopted only after the general elections of March 1995.

[4] Steiner, 'Political Participation as a Human Right', 1 *Harvard Human Rights Yearbook* (1988), 77–134.

[5] See Rosas, 'Democracy and Human Rights', in Rosas and Helgesen (eds), *Human Rights in a Changing East-West Perspective* (1990), pp. 17–57, at pp. 23–26; Rosas, 'Article 21', in Eide et al. (eds), *The Universal Declaration of Human Rights: A Commentary* (1992), pp. 299–317, at pp. 301–305.

Covenant on Civil and Political Rights (CCPR) of 1966. It was left out of the ECHR in its original version but included as a somewhat more limited requirement of free and periodic elections in Article 3 of Protocol No. 1 (1950).[6]

Article 21 of the Universal Declaration also contains a flicker of popular sovereignty as a collective right in referring to 'the will of the people' which 'shall be the basis of the authority of government'. Article 1 common to the two International Covenants of 1966 on the right of self-determination of peoples can be read in the same light ('internal self-determination'), although this is a more controversial point.[7]

The special nature of the right of political participation is to be seen in its relation to citizenship. Article 21 of the Universal Declaration is not entirely clear in speaking of the right of 'everyone' to take part in the government 'of his country', while Article 3 of Protocol No. 1 to the ECHR merely refers to 'the opinion of the people' without further specification. Article 25 of the Civil and Political Covenant, however, explicitly limits the subject of the right to 'every citizen',[8] a limitation not to be found in the other provisions of the Covenant, which refer to 'every human being', 'everyone', 'all persons' or the like.[9]

It is obvious also that the drafters of the Universal Declaration and of Protocol No. 1 to the ECHR, in referring to 'his country' and 'the people', respectively, had in mind the people of a given nation-state, meaning as a general rule the citizens of that state as recognized under its domestic laws.[10] There is a link to the concept of sovereignty, which under general international law has referred to more or less absolute state power over a given territory and to the constitutional indepen-

---

[6] See also Art. 23 of the American Convention on Human Rights and the survey of other human rights provisions relating to political participation in Rosas, 'Democracy and Human Rights', pp. 29–39.

[7] Rosas, 'Internal Self-Determination', in Tomuschat (ed.), *Modern Law of Self-Determination* (1993), pp. 225–252; Salmon, 'Internal Aspects of the Right to Self-Determination: Towards a Democratic Legitimacy Principle', in ibid., pp. 253–282.

[8] The same limitation is contained in Art. 23 of the American Convention on Human Rights.

[9] But see Art. 13 of the Covenant on the rights of aliens. See also General Comment No. 15, adopted by the Human Rights Committee in 1986, on the position of aliens under the Covenant (para. 2), 1 IHRR (1994), No. 2, 16.

[10] With respect to Art. 3 of Protocol No. 1 to the ECHR, see van Dijk and van Hoof, *Theory and Practice of the European Convention on Human Rights* (1990, 2nd edn), pp. 483–484, 560, who, on the other hand, argue that the reference in the wording of the provision to the 'people' does not necessarily settle the question.

dence of this territorial state.[11] In so far as there has been constitutional recognition of the notion of popular sovereignty,[12] this has referred to the authority of the people of a given sovereign state ('the nation' and its nationals).[13]

3   CITIZENS V ALIENS AS SUBJECTS OF POLITICAL RIGHTS

The traditional approach in constitutional Bills of Rights has been to limit the rights catalogues to the citizens (nationals) of the state concerned.[14] At the same time, questions of nationality and citizenship have been deemed to fall under the competence of each state.[15] The present century has implied a gradual loosening of this linkage between sovereignty, nationality and citizenship, and fundamental rights.

First of all, constitutional and other laws have increasingly granted rights to persons other than citizens. One can roughly distinguish between the following 'stages' in this process:[16]

— civil rights, the rule of law
— economic and social rights
— political freedoms (freedom of expression, freedom of assembly, etc.)
— political rights in the strict sense (voting and similar rights)

---

[11] Rosas, 'The Decline of Sovereignty: Legal Perspectives', in Iivonen (ed.), *The Future of the Nation State in Europe* (1993), pp. 130–158, at pp. 131–135.

[12] Cf. Suksi, *Bringing in the People: A Comparison of Constitutional Forms and Practices of the Referendum* (1993), pp. 16–24, who (from a constitutional point of view) distinguishes between popular sovereignty, national sovereignty and state sovereignty as three rough categories of internal sovereignty and models of national decision-making.

[13] See also Neuman, '"We are the People": Alien Suffrage in German and American Perspective', 13 *Michigan Journal of International Law* (1991), 259–335.

[14] For instance, the Finnish constitutional Bill of Rights referred to above (see note 3) is limited to Finnish citizens. Only in a pending Government Bill has the Bill of Rights been extended, in principle, to everyone.

[15] See, e.g., Donner, *The Regulation of Nationality in International Law* (1983); Rosas, 'Nationality and Citizenship in a Changing European and World Order', in Suksi (ed.), *Law under Exogenous Influences* (1994), pp. 30–59, at pp. 30, 34. According to the opening sentence of Art. 1 of the Hague Convention on Certain Questions Relating to the Conflict of Nationality Laws of 1930, 'it is for each State to determine under its own law who are its nationals.'

[16] Cf. Rosas, 'Medborgarskap och rösträtt' [Citizenship and Voting Rights], *Forhandlingene ved det 30. nordiske juristmøtet*, Oslo, 15–17 august 1984, vol. I (1984), pp. 225–244, at p. 228.

— access to posts involving national security

Generally speaking, aliens on a temporary visit enjoy rule of law-related civil rights. Economic and social rights are often subject to residence but not necessarily to citizenship (citizenship may even be barred as a formal criterion within special communities of states, such as the European Union or the Nordic sub-region).

The question of political rights and freedoms poses more difficulties, as 'citizens are the persons entitled to form the political subject, different from those who enjoy protection and/or rights granted by the State (i.e. social rights as well as human rights)'.[17] As already indicated above, there is a direct linkage between citizenship, people, the nation-state and sovereignty.[18] However, the political freedoms such as freedom of assembly, association and expression are increasingly being granted to aliens,[19] a development which is also called for by the International Covenant on Civil and Political Rights.[20] This question, on the other hand, is far from settled (even in the context of the European Union[21]).

With respect to voting and similar political rights, a distinction is often made between local and national elections. As will be elaborated below, the Nordic states detached voting rights in municipal elections from national citizenship in the late 1970s. In the European Communities, discussions on voting rights for aliens began in the early 1960s but then with respect to elections for the European Parliament. The local level was brought more fully into the picture during the 1970s.[22]

---

[17] Closa, 'The Concept of Citizenship in the Treaty on European Union', 29 CML Rev. (1992), 1137–1169, at 1138.

[18] This has been particularly obvious in countries such as France, see Peuchot, 'Droit de vote et condition de nationalité', 1 *Revue du droit public et de la science politique en France et à l'étranger* (1991), 481–524, and Germany, see below.

[19] See, e.g., Özsunay, 'The Participation of the Alien in Public Affairs (Political and Associative Life)', in Council of Europe, *Human Rights of Aliens in Europe* (1985), pp. 197–254, at pp. 199–214; Herdegen, 'Politische Rechte und sonstiger Status von Ausländern', in Frowein and Stein (eds), *Die Rechtsstellung von Ausländern nach staatlichem Recht und Völkerrecht* (1987), pp. 1985–2002, at pp. 1988–1991.

[20] But see Art. 16 ECHR, according to which 'nothing in Articles 10, 11 and 14 shall be regarded as preventing the High Contracting Parties from imposing restrictions on the political activity of aliens', see, e.g., van Dijk and van Hoof, *Theory and Practice*, pp. 560–562.

[21] See Chapter 6.

[22] See, e.g., van den Berghe, *Political Rights for European Citizens* (1982), pp. 46 et seq., 186 et seq.; Nickel, 'Kommunalpolitische Partizipation—Erfordernisse im "Europa der Bürger"', in Sieveking et al. (eds), *Das Kommunalwahlrecht für Ausländer* (1989), pp. 91–111, at p. 93.

The actual extension of voting rights in local and/or European elections started in some of the Member States[23] but was implemented at the European level only with the coming into force of the Treaty on European Union (TEU). In 1992, the Council of Europe opened for signature a Convention on the Participation of Foreigners in Public Life at Local Level (which has not yet come into force).[24] Some non-Union and non-Nordic states nowadays grant foreigners voting rights in local elections.[25]

As to national elections in Europe, only Ireland and the United Kingdom have, on a reciprocal basis, granted voting rights to residents who are citizens of the other country.[26] This special regime is, of course, explained by the historical ties of the two countries and is to be seen against the background that the United Kingdom grants voting rights to all British subjects, including Commonwealth citizens.[27] In Ireland, this extension of the national franchise required a constitutional amendment, as the Supreme Court had held that the existing constitution did not allow the extension of electoral rights to non-nationals.[28]

Public posts involving national security responsibilities, often perceived as the core of sovereignty, will for the foreseeable future be reserved for citizens, and in some instances, citizens meeting certain additional conditions, such as being citizens by birth.[29]

---

[23] See, e.g., d'Oliveira, 'Electoral Rights for Non-Nationals', 31 NILR (1984), 59–72, at 60–65; Magiera, 'Politische Rechte im Europa der Bürger', 20 ZRP (1987), 331–337, at 332; Closa, 'The Concept of Citizenship', 1149.

[24] Convention No. 144. As of 19 May 1994, there were five signatory states and only two states (Norway and Sweden) which had ratified the Convention (according to Art. 12, four ratifications are required for it to come into force). Chart showing signature and ratifications of conventions and agreements concluded within the Council of Europe, signatures and ratifications between 1 Jan. 1989 and 19 May 1994.

[25] See, e.g., Section 70, para. 3, of the Hungarian Constitution, as amended in 1989, and the Estonian Act on the Elections of Local Government Councils of 19 May 1993.

[26] In Ireland, the Electoral (Amendment) Act, No. 12/1985 provides that the Minister may by order declare that citizens of other Union Member States than the United Kingdom are given the right to vote in Irish national elections, on conditions of reciprocity. See also Art. 16 of the Irish Constitution, as amended in the ninth amendment, 14/6/1984.

[27] This principle, embodied in the Representation of the People Act of 1983, has a common law background, see Blackburn, 'The Right to Vote', in Blackburn (ed.), *Rights of Citizenship* (1993), pp. 75–98, at pp. 79–80.

[28] *In the Matter of Article 16 of the Constitution and the Electoral (Amendment) Bill*, 1983, [1984] I.L.R.M. 539.

[29] For a survey of the right to access to civil services in Council of Europe Member States see Özsunay, 'Participation of the Alien', pp. 225–237.

The importance of restrictions on the political and other rights of aliens should, of course, not be separated from the concepts of nationality and citizenship and the conditions that states follow in their national legislation on granting nationality and citizenship by way of naturalization. If these conditions are very liberal, political rights may easily be obtained by way of naturalization.

Generally speaking, states—including Member States of the European Union among themselves—still insist on requiring periods of residence of several years (in most cases ranging from five to fifteen years).[30] A number of other conditions may be imposed as well, including the requirement that the person to be naturalized will lose his or her previous nationality. Prohibitions of dual nationality may raise the threshold for applying for naturalization, as persons residing in other countries than their own often do not wish to cut their bonds to the state of origin.[31]

As was noted above, international law has left decisions on nationality and citizenship largely to the sovereign states. In the interest of some minimum order, states' freedom of action has probably never been unlimited, however.[32] The *Nottebohm* case before the International Court of Justice underlined that third states do not have to recognize determinations of nationality under the municipal law of a state, if there is no genuine connection between the individual and the state that has granted her or him its nationality.[33] This case concerned nationality rather than citizenship, in so far as nationality is linked to external relations (diplomatic protection), while citizenship can be

---

[30] Closa, 'Citizenship of the Union and Nationality of Member States', in O'Keeffe and Twomey (eds), *Legal Issues of the Maastricht Treaty* (1994), pp. 109–119, at p. 117. According to Closa, only Italy has lowered the qualifying period of residence for European Community nationals. The Nordic states follow shorter periods of residence with respect to Nordic nationals; Rosas, 'Medborgarskap', p. 233.

[31] O'Leary, 'Nationality Law and Community Citizenship: A Tale of Two Uneasy Bedfellows', 12 YEL (1992), 353–384, at 366, notes that 'one of the standard reasons for low naturalization figures is the deterrent factor involved in the loss of previous nationality.'

[32] In the *Tunis and Morocco Nationality Decrees*, P.C.I.J. Ser. B, Advisory Opinion No. 4 (1923), p. 24, the Permanent Court of International Justice noted that the question whether a matter such as nationality is or is not solely within the jurisdiction of a state 'is an essentially relative question' and 'depends upon the development of international relations'. The second sentence of Art. 1 of the Hague Convention on Certain Questions relating to the Conflict of Nationality Laws of 1930 provides that a municipal nationality law must be recognized by other states 'only in so far as it is consistent with international conventions, international custom, and the principles of law generally recognised with regard to nationality'.

[33] *Nottebohm case (second phase)*, I.C.J. Reports 1955, p. 4, at p. 23.

perceived as a bundle of political and other rights under the domestic constitutional and legal system.[34]

While the Nottebohm principle may serve to limit the effects of states' decisions to grant nationality, modern human rights law may work in another direction by limiting states' freedom of action in refusing nationality to a given person. According to Article 15 of the Universal Declaration of Human Rights, 'everyone has the right to a nationality' and 'no one shall be arbitrarily deprived of his nationality nor denied the right to change his nationality'. Not only may the Universal Declaration contain principles which may have become binding under customary law,[35] but it has also been supplemented by a number of provisions relating to nationality in binding human rights conventions.[36] In an advisory opinion of 1984, the Inter-American Court of Human Rights observed that 'the manners in which states regulate matters bearing on nationality cannot today be deemed within their sole jurisdiction; those powers of the state are also circumscribed by their obligations to ensure the full protection of human rights'.[37] The Inter-American Court in its reasoning alluded, *inter alia*, to the fact that nationality is 'the basic requirement for the exercise of political rights'.

This is not to say that the international minimum standards on nationality are clear or that states do not continue to have a wide margin of appreciation. A special illustration of the problems at hand is offered by the controversy surrounding the status of the Russian-speaking populations of Estonia and Latvia, who in large numbers have found themselves in an intermediate status of statelessness, devoid of

---

[34] The distinction between nationality and citizenship is not clear-cut and domestic legal systems apply varying terminology; Closa, 'Citizenship of the Union', p. 113.

[35] See, e.g., Eide and Alfredsson, 'Introduction', in Eide et al. (eds), *The Universal Declaration of Human Rights: A Commentary* (1992), pp. 5–16, at pp. 6–7.

[36] Arts 1(3) and 5 of the International Convention on the Elimination of All Forms of Racial Discrimination of 1965; Art. 24(3) of the International Covenant on Civil and Political Rights of 1966; Art. 20 of the American Convention on Human Rights; Art. 9 of the Convention on the Elimination of Discrimination against Women of 1979; Art. 7 of the Convention on the Rights of the Child of 1989. See also the Convention relating to the Status of Stateless Persons of 1954, the Convention on the Nationality of Married Women of 1957 and the Convention on the Reduction of Statelessness of 1961.

[37] *Proposed Amendments to the Naturalization Provisions of the Constitution of Costa Rica*, I/A Court H. R., Advisory Opinion OC-4/84 of 19 Jan. 1984. Series A No. 4, at pp. 93–94 (para. 32).

the right to vote and be elected in national elections.[38] The situation in EC law is somewhat confusing,[39] with Article 8 EC Treaty restricting Union citizenship to persons 'holding the nationality of a Member State' and accompanying political declarations stressing the competences of the Member States,[40] while two cases decided by the Court of Justice of the European Communities may contain the seeds of a Community law approach.[41] Moreover, the question of the harmonization of nationality laws is becoming an issue for discussion at the Community level.[42]

This is not the place to analyse further these intricate problems of nationality and citizenship. I merely wish to remind the reader of the inescapable link which exists between political rights on the one hand and decisions on nationality and citizenship on the other. The human rights dimension, including the notion of political rights *qua* human rights, also points to the interrelation between 'nationality' as an international law concept and 'citizenship' as a constitutional concept.[43]

In so far as the concept of Union citizenship will erode Member States' freedom of action with respect to nationality 'for Union citizenship purposes', this will not necessarily 'solve' the problem of voting rights in national elections, assuming that national elections will stay outside the ambit of Union citizenship for the foreseeable future. If this is so, it becomes even more important to place questions of nationality and citizenship in the broader framework of international law and international human rights law outlined above.

---

[38] But in Estonia voting rights in local elections do not require Estonian citizenship, see note 25 above. On the nationality and citizenship *problematique* of the Baltic Republics see Öst, 'Who is Citizen in Estonia, Latvia and Lithuania?', in Dahlgren (ed.), *Human Rights in the Baltic States* (1993), pp. 43–86.

[39] See, in particular, O'Leary, 'Nationality Law and Community Citizenship'; Rosas, 'Nationality and Citizenship', pp. 43–50.

[40] Declaration No. 2 on Nationality appended to the Final Act of the Treaty on European Union; European Council in Edinburgh, 11–12 Dec. 1992, Conclusions of the Presidency, Part B. Denmark and the TEU, Annex 1, O.J. 1992, C 348/2.

[41] Case 21/74, *Jeanne Airola* v *Commission of the European Communities*, [1975] ECR 221; Case C-369/90, *Mario Vincente Micheletti and Others* v *Delegación del Gobierno en Cantabria*, [1992] ECR I-4239. For a comparison between these two cases, see Rosas, 'Nationality and Citizenship', pp. 47–49.

[42] Rosas, ibid., p. 50.

[43] See also note 34 above.

4 THE NORDIC EXPERIENCE

As early as the 1960s, the question of the political rights of immigrants, notably the possibility of their taking part in local and regional elections, was taken up in Denmark and Sweden. In Sweden, this was against the background of a considerable influx of Finnish and southern European immigrants. In Finland, as well, this matter came up as a question of protecting the civil and political rights of Finns in Sweden while preserving their Finnish citizenship.[44]

In the early 1970s, by a Finnish initiative the matter was placed on the agenda of the Nordic Council, which in 1973 asked the Nordic Council of Ministers to conduct a study on extending the right of Nordic citizens to vote and to stand as a candidate in local elections in another Nordic country. This study was presented in 1975 and concluded that a Nordic system of voting rights in municipal elections could be accomplished and that a period of residence of around three years would be appropriate.[45] In Sweden, the matter had already been the subject of an independent national study, which led to a Government Bill by the end of 1975 proposing voting rights not only in local but also in regional and local church elections and not only for Nordic citizens but for all foreigners who had resided in Sweden for a minimum period of around three years.[46] Swedish regional self-government and the local self-government of the Swedish Lutheran Church were thought to be comparable to local government. The decision to grant voting rights to all foreigners residing in Sweden and not only to citizens of other Nordic countries was explained as a measure to prevent some immigrant groups (meaning non-Nordic citizens) from finding themselves in an inferior position, which would 'hardly be acceptable'.[47]

The other Nordic countries, however, originally followed the Nordic model and restricted their reforms to Nordic citizens.[48] In Finland, this even required a constitutional amendment, as the reference in the Constitution Act to the local self-government of 'citizens' was in-

---

[44] Rosas, 'Medborgarskap'.

[45] Nordisk kommunal rösträtt och valbarhet, *Nordisk utredningsserie* NU 1975:4.

[46] *Regeringens proposition* 1975/76:23 om kommunal rösträtt för invandrare (23 Oct. 1975). See also Kommunal rösträtt för invandrare. Betänkande av rösträttsutredningen. *Statens offentliga utredningar* SOU 1975:15.

[47] SOU 1975:15, p. 117. See also the Government Bill 1975/76:23, p. 92.

[48] Rosas, 'Medborgarskap', p. 234.

terpreted to mean Finnish citizens only.[49] Denmark was the first to reconsider. The Danish Government in a Bill in 1980 explained that the restriction to Nordic citizens made three years earlier had been partly because of on-going discussions in the European Communities on voting rights for EC nationals. As these discussions had encountered difficulties, it was thought feasible not to await further EC consideration of the matter but to follow the Swedish model of granting voting rights to all foreign immigrants on an equal basis.[50] Norway followed suit in 1984. In a Government Bill it was noted that Nordic and non-Nordic citizens generally have the same duties when residing in Norway and that it was thus fair to treat them in the same way as far as the right to vote and to be elected was concerned.[51] In this context, reference was also made to the idea of extending voting rights to foreigners for national elections but this idea was dismissed because foreigners would then come to influence national politics, in particular foreign and security policy.

Finland was more reluctant to adhere to the 'Swedish model'. In 1991, however, a Government Report proposed a similar reform as there 'did not seem to be reasons' to continue making a distinction between citizens of the Nordic countries and other foreigners, taking into account the recent enlargement of the political freedoms (freedom of association, assembly and expression) of foreigners in Finland, as well as international developments, including the reforms in Sweden, Denmark and Norway and current plans in the Council of Europe and the European Communities.[52]

The idea was to follow the other Nordic countries, too, in setting the same period of residence (around three years) for Nordic and non-Nordic citizens as a requirement of electoral rights in local elections and advisory local referendums (but not in regional elections, as there has been no regional self-government of the Swedish, Danish or Norwegian

---

[49] Art. 51, para. 2, of the Constitution Act (amended by Act No. 334/1976).

[50] Intervention by the Danish Minister of the Interior in the Danish Parliament on 11 Dec. 1980, 37th meeting, Government Bill No. L 100 (Forslag til lov om aendring af lov om kommunale valg). See also the report by a Government Commission, Betænkning nr. 903 (1980).

[51] Ot. prp. nr. 22 (1982–1983), p. 17. See also a private initiative by a Member of Parliament submitted in 1979 and a report by the Foreign and Constitutional Committee of Parliament, Innst. O. nr. 29 (1978–1979), a Government Report to Parliament on immigration policies St. meld. nr. 74 (1979–1980) and a report by a Government Commission in Norsk offentlige utredninger NOU 1982:6.

[52] Komiteanmietintö–Kommittébetänkande KM 1991:1, 17.

type in Finland). However, when the Government Bill[53] came up for consideration in Parliament, it was held that foreigners other than Nordic citizens come from such a variety of different countries, the legal culture of which may differ significantly from the Finnish one, that it was preferable to set a longer period of residence as a condition for their electoral rights. Parliament accordingly amended the Bill so that the period for non-Nordic foreigners will be around five (instead of three) years (Act No. 1718/1991).

This amendment caused a lively discussion in Parliament. The longer period for non-Nordic citizens was generally supported by the Rightist parties (which in this case voted against the proposal by their own conservative government), while the Left-wing parties and the Greens supported the Government's Bill.[54] Among the arguments advanced in favour of the amendment was that human rights and political rights for foreigners were two entirely different matters. The arguments put forward in favour of retaining the government's proposal and thus equating Nordic and non-Nordic citizens were based on political and ideological considerations rather than any legal discussion on the principle of non-discrimination.[55]

While the above developments have concerned municipal (and in Denmark, Norway and Sweden also regional) elections, the question of voting rights in national elections has not led to legislative reforms. This possibility has not gone unnoticed, however. In Sweden the reform concerning municipal and regional elections was followed by a series of private bills by Left-wing Members of Parliament on extending voting rights to foreigners taking part in national elections as well.[56] While these proposals were turned down by the Rightist majority of the then Parliament, foreigners who had voting rights in local elections were granted the right to participate in the consultative national referendum on the use of nuclear power energy.[57] And, after the return of the Swedish Labour Party to government in 1982, a study was initiated on voting rights in the national elections. In 1984, a Government Commission proposed by a narrow Left majority the granting of

---

[53] Regeringens proposition RP 78/1991.

[54] The Constitutional Committee of Parliament approved the idea of distinguishing between Nordic and non-Nordic nationals by a vote of 8–5, GrUB 6/1991, pp. 3–4, the plenary of Parliament by a vote of 97 votes for, 84 votes against, two abstentions and with 16 MPs absent, Valtiopäivät 1991, Pöytäkirjat, vol. 3, 3316.

[55] Valtiopäivät 1991, Pöytäkirjat, vol. 3, 3285–3296.

[56] These private bills are listed by Rosas, 'Medborgarskap', p. 236 (n. 30).

[57] Act of 17 Jan. 1980 (1980:7) and Suksi, *Bringing in the People*, p. 227.

the right to vote—but not the right to stand as a candidate—for Nordic citizens who qualified for voting rights in municipal election.[58]

In February 1983 the Finnish Prime Minister, in a speech before the Nordic Council, had proposed a follow-up to the municipal election reforms of the 1970s amounting to granting voting rights to Nordic citizens in national elections.[59] This would have been restricted to the right to vote for Nordic citizens residing in another Nordic country, while the right to stand as a candidate would have required national citizenship. In 1984, I was commissioned by the Finnish Ministry of Justice to conduct a study on this question, taking into account the possibility of a bilateral arrangement between Finland and Sweden. The discussions held on this question at the thirtieth Nordic Lawyers' meeting in Oslo in August 1984,[60] as well as the municipal election reforms in Denmark and Norway mentioned above, had indicated that the idea of including foreigners in national elections would encounter even more opposition in these countries than in Sweden. The difficulties in amending the Danish Constitution, because of the requirement of a decisive referendum, were also taken into account.

In Sweden, the possibility of a minority (1/3) in Parliament initiating a referendum on constitutional reform—combined with the wide criticism that the above-mentioned proposal to grant Nordic citizens voting rights in national elections had caused in Sweden—led the Swedish Labour Government to abstain from pursuing the matter and Finno-Swedish discussions did not lead to any concrete results. Since 1984, the question has not been visible on the political agenda. During the spring of 1994, there was some discussion in Sweden on whether to follow the pattern of the 1980 referendum in the coming referendum on joining the European Union and thus also granting foreign nationals residing in Sweden voting rights, but this idea was abandoned, because of the perceived constitutional character of the referendum.[61]

The following general observations can be made on these Nordic discussions and developments:

---

[58] Statens offentliga utredningar SOU 1984:11.

[59] Speech by Kalevi Sorsa, Prime Minister of Finland, Nordiska rådet, 31:a sessionen 1983, Protokoll från 2:a mötet, 22 Feb. 1983, 24–25.

[60] *Forhandlingene ved det 30. nordiske juristmøtet*, Oslo 15–17 august 1984, Vol. II, pp. 409–439.

[61] The referendum was held on 13 Nov. 1994. The majority approved Swedish membership of the European Union.

1 The question of voting rights for foreigners has been a politically controversial issue, with a clear Left–Right dimension.

2 The municipal and regional levels were less controversial, as matters decided by local and regional councils concern fairly concrete questions of education, health care, physical planning, culture, etc.

3 On the other hand, the opponents of the municipal and regional election reforms of the 1970s stressed that it was difficult to draw a line between national and local government; after these reforms, however, some of them have started to emphasize the differences and the 'political' nature of national elections, as opposed to the municipal and regional levels.

4 Regional elections were in Denmark, Norway and Sweden equated with local elections, as the regional councils in these countries, which are unitary states, are not constituent states of a federal state but rather larger areas of local self-government.

5 The large number of foreign residents in a given country became an argument for, rather than against, an electoral reform. Sweden, with the largest number of immigrants and refugees, took a leading role in being first to implement the municipal election reform and extending it from the very start to all foreigners, while Finland and Iceland, being more on the outskirts of the Nordic sub-region and with smaller immigrant communities, have been much more hesitant to grant voting rights to non-Nordic citizens (in Finland, a longer period of residence is required for this category while Iceland has not given non-Nordic citizens any voting rights).

6 The discussions on national elections of the early 1980s gained more momentum than had been imaginable in an EC context.

7 There seem to have been no serious opinions claiming that international human rights law required voting rights for foreigners; the discussions on avoiding making a distinction between Nordic and non-Nordic citizens (at the municipal election level) may have been influenced by a general idea of non-discrimination but was, then, hardly based on any express legal reasoning.

5 NATIONAL ELECTIONS: A SPECIAL CASE?

Especially in relation to the discussions on Union citizenship, it seems to have been taken almost for granted that voting rights on the basis of residence, in regard to municipal and European elections under Article 8b EC Treaty, cannot be extended to national and regional elections and referendums. The United Kingdom policy of granting voting rights to Commonwealth citizens, the special arrangement between Ireland and the United Kingdom, the potential Irish extension, on the basis of reciprocity, of electoral rights in national elections to nationals of other Member States and the Nordic and Finno-Swedish discussions of 1983–1985 indicate that this basic assumption could be questioned. At least it is worthwhile to take a closer look at the systemic considerations and arguments which arise in this context.

First, a reversed experience should be noted: in international human rights law, the discussion on formulating political rights in the strict sense (voting rights and other similar elements of what has been called a right of political participation) has centred on national rather than local elections. The clearest example is Article 3 of Protocol No. 1 to the ECHR, which refers to the 'choice of the legislature'. The European supervisory bodies have included in this concept the constituent states of federal states and regional councils with legislative functions, whereas there has been a tendency in the case law of the Commission to exclude regional councils without constitutionally anchored legislative powers or local government authorities competent to adopt by-laws only.[62] Elections to the European Parliament also seem to be included, at least with the TEU.[63] The wording of Article 25 CCPR is more flexible and can be interpreted as covering regional and local self-government councils as well.[64] On the other hand, a Soviet proposal to provide for a right of citizens to vote and to be elected 'to all organs of authority' was rejected in the preparation of the Covenant.[65]

This brief look at international human rights law brings out two considerations: first of all, the emphasis has been on national elections, in contrast to the emphasis on local and European elections in EC law.

---

[62] Eur. Court H. R., case of *Mathieu-Mohin and Clerfayt*, judgment of 2 March 1987, Series A no. 113, p. 23 (para. 53). For the case law of the Commission see *Digest of Strasbourg Case-Law*, vol. V, pp. 864–865; van Dijk and van Hoof, *Theory and Practice*, pp. 485–487; De Meyer, 'Electoral Rights', in Macdonald, Matscher and Petzold (eds), *The European System for the Protection of Human Rights* (1993), pp. 553–569, at 553–555. van Dijk and van Hoof, *Theory and Practice* (p. 486) note that the Court in the above-mentioned judgment did not mention the criterion of autonomous legislative powers based directly on the constitution, which seems to come out of the case law of the Commission.

[63] For the case law preceding the Maastricht Treaty, see De Meyer, 'Electoral Rights', p. 554. According to Art. 189, para. 1, as amended by the TEU, the law-makers with respect to secondary legislation are 'the European Parliament acting jointly with the Council, the Council and the Commission'.

[64] Rosas, 'Democracy and Human Rights', p. 47.

[65] Bossuyt, *Guide to the 'Travaux Préparatoires' of the International Covenant on Civil and Political Rights* (1987), p. 474.

This difference is easy to explain. In human rights law, the focus is on enforcing the principles of democracy and popular sovereignty through individual political rights for the people of a nation-state, usually defined as the totality of its nationals (citizens). In EC law, again, the focus is on expanding the rights of non-nationals (albeit the citizens of a broader political union). Secondly, international human rights law illustrates the difficulties in making a clear-cut distinction between national and other elections. While Article 8b EC Treaty, as supplemented by existing and emerging secondary legislation,[66] is fairly clear in its delimitation of the elections covered, these difficulties are of interest for a discussion *de lege ferenda*.

In the discussions of a 'people's Europe', later to be rephrased as a 'citizens' Europe', which started in 1974, it was often assumed that the granting of voting rights on the basis of residence—also taking into account Article 138 EC Treaty—should start with European elections and then eventually be followed by the 'Europeanization' of local elections. The Commission proposal for a Council Directive on voting rights in local elections in 1988,[67] legally based on Articles 235 and 236 EC Treaty, became quite controversial, and this not merely for reasons *de lege lata*.[68]

Against the background of these political problems, it is understandable that the Commission did not dare to step into the minefield of national elections but rather distanced itself from this level of decision-making. In its report on local elections submitted to the European Parliament in 1986, the Commission had this to say on national elections:[69]

---

[66] Council Directive 93/109/EC of 6 Dec. 1993 laying down detailed arrangements for the exercise of the right to vote and stand as a candidate in elections to the European Parliament for citizens of the Union residing in a Member State of which they are not nationals, O.J. 1993, L 329/34; Commission proposal for a Council Directive laying down detailed arrangements for the exercise of the right to vote and to stand as a candidate in municipal elections by citizens of the Union residing in a Member State of which they are not nationals, COM (94) 38 final 23.02.1994.

[67] COM (1988) 371 final 11.07.1988, O.J. 1988, C 246/3.

[68] See, e.g., Closa, 'The Concept of Citizenship', 1147–1149.

[69] Voting rights in local elections for Community nationals, Report from the Commission to the European Parliament transmitted for information to the Council in Oct. 1986, Supplement based on COM (86) 487 final, at p. 9. On earlier pronouncements on local voting rights in the Tindemans, Macchiochi and Addonino Reports, see O'Keeffe, 'Union Citizenship', in O'Keeffe and Twomey (eds), *Legal Issues of the Maastricht Treaty* (1994), pp. 87–107, at p. 96.

The same case cannot be made for 'political' elections (parliamentary and presidential elections, referenda) since these play a part in determining national sovereignty. The national aspect of these elections is clearly incompatible with the participation of non-nationals, even nationals of other Community countries, since the Community is not intended to impinge on national sovereignty, or replace States or nations. That would come from a federalist process which is not provided for in the existing Treaties. There is no contradiction, therefore, in considering the possibility of broadening the electorate for local elections but not for other elections.

That the Commission proposal for voting rights in local elections was not free from problems is further illustrated by the fact that such a reform was considered to require constitutional amendments in several Member States,[70] an observation confirmed by subsequent developments relating to the ratification of the TEU.[71] Germany provides a special case, as local election reforms in Schleswig-Holstein and Hamburg were declared unconstitutional by the Constitutional Court in judgments of 31 October 1990, because foreigners could not be included in the concept of people contained in Article 20 of the Basic Law, which, through Article 28, was held to be applicable to local elections as well.[72] An amendment to Article 28 of the German Constitution paved the way for ratification of the Maastricht Treaty, a measure accepted by the Constitutional Court in its judgment of 12 October 1993 on the relation between the German Basic Law and the Maastricht Treaty.[73]

The political and legal problems surrounding the granting of electoral rights to non-nationals in municipal elections are further illustrated by the possibility provided in Article 8b itself for 'deroga-

---

[70] The Commission in its 1986 report named Greece, Italy, Luxembourg, Belgium, Germany and France, ibid., p. 5.

[71] See, generally, Rideau, 'The Constitutional Adaptation of the Member States to Maastricht', Paper submitted to the Norsk Forum for Europa Forskening Conference in Oslo on 26–27 Jan. 1994. On the national constitutional aspects of ratification of the Maastricht Treaty see also Herdegen, 'Die Belastbarkeit des Verfassungsgefüges auf dem Weg zur Europäischen Union', 19 Eu GRZ (1992), 589–594; López Castillo and Polakiewicz, 'Verfassung und Gemenscheiftsrecht in Spanien—Zur Maastricht-Erklärung des spanischen Verfassungsgericht', 20 Eu GRZ (1993), 277–285; Walter, 'Die drei Entscheidungen des französischen Verfassungsrat zum Vertrag von Maastricht über die Europäische Union', 20 Eu GRZ (1993), 183–187. In addition to Belgium, France and Germany, a constitutional revision had to be undertaken in Spain, too, concerning the non-citizens' right to be elected in local elections, whereas this could be avoided in Greece and Italy.

[72] BVerfGE 83, 37; BVerfGE 83, 60. See, e.g., Neuman, '"We are the People"', 283–291.

[73] 2 BvR 2134/92; 2 BvR 2159/92. Text also in 20 Eu GRZ (1993), 429–446.

tions where warranted by problems specific to a Member State'.[74] The Commission has also proposed to grant Member States the right to provide under national law that only their own nationals may hold the office of elected head or member of the executive of a basic local government unit, as the mayors and similar officials may participate in the exercise of official authority and the safeguarding of the general interest.[75]

These examples point to the links which exist between local government and the democratic order of the nation-state and the popular sovereignty of its people. As was noted above, this was one of the arguments advanced against the local election reforms carried out in the Nordic countries in the 1970s. If this is so, it can be asked whether there is such a big step from local voting rights based on residence rather than nationality to adopting the same principle for national elections. The difficulties there may be in making a distinction between area and regional councils belonging to the concept of local government and regional bodies exercising state powers[76] underlines the significance of this question. And if one stresses the idea of equal rights for European Union citizens, it is possible to observe, as Evans has done, that 'from the point of view of the development of Community citizenship . . . participation at the national level might be thought to be more important than participation at the local level.'[77] This might be a significant step towards the effective integration of Union citizens who are not nationals of the host country.[78] It would also lower the threshold of exercising freedom of movement.[79]

---

[74] This reservation has led the Commission to propose that derogations can be applied in Member States where the proportion of Union citizens of voting age who are residents but not nationals exceeds 20 per cent of the total number of Union citizens of voting age residing there, Art. 12, para. 1, of the Proposal for a Council Directive mentioned above, note 66. This possibility, in practice, applies to Luxembourg only.

[75] See Art. 5, para. 3, of the Proposal for a Council Directive mentioned above, in note 66, and the preceding Explanatory Memorandum, p. 24.

[76] See the definition of 'basic local government unit' in the Annex to the proposed Council Directive COM (94) 38 final 23.02.1994 mentioned in note 66 above, the discussion above on Art. 3 of Protocol No. 1 to the ECHR and Art. 13 of the European Charter of Local Self-Government of 1985 (on this Convention see note 79 below).

[77] Evans, 'Nationality Law and European Integration', 16 EL Rev. (1991), 190–215, at 210.

[78] Cf. the objective of integrating third-country nationals 'into society', discussed, e.g., in Joined Cases 181, 283 to 285 and 287/85, *Federal Republic of Germany and Others* v *Commission of the European Communities*, [1987] ECR 3203.

[79] In this respect, it is significant that the Court of Justice of the European Communities has considered even a bar to compensation under a national scheme for compensating victims of crime as an impediment to freedom of movement and thus as falling under the

If one further takes the approach—as I tend to do—that we are at least in Europe (but perhaps in the long run also at the world-wide level) moving towards a system of several 'layers' of public decision-making, where the nation-state will be seen more as one among many layers rather than as the dominating, 'sovereign' hub of the whole system,[80] then it becomes all the more questionable to have differently defined electorates for, on the one hand, local and European elections and, on the other hand, national and regional elections. In this context, it is noteworthy that there is a Council of Europe sponsored European Charter of Local Self-Government of 1985, which among the Contracting Parties[81] makes the status of local self-government a matter of international concern, characterizes local self-government as including 'the right and the ability of local authorities, within the limits of law, to regulate and manage a substantial share of public affairs under their own responsibility and in the interests of the local population'. With a perception of many more or less equal 'layers' of decision-making (European, national, regional and local levels), it would be natural to base electoral rights on residence rather than nationality. Dual or multiple nationality would not solve the problem, as one would in any case have to decide in which state electoral rights could be exercised (to avoid double voting).

From a more practical point of view, it can be asked to what extent the distinction between national elections as 'political' and local elections as 'non-political' holds true. There is a trend in many states to transfer more powers to local and regional government. And, apart from the specific powers of local governments, local elections are often perceived as important political signals, for instance, in assessing the political support of the government in power.

What has been said so far is not to deny the formidable political threshold which, especially in the context of the European Union, seems to exist with respect to extending the principle of voting rights based on residence rather than nationality to the level of national parliaments, referendums and the like. There is in some Member States a strong insistence on national independence and sovereignty. The 'people', who

---

prohibition of discrimination on grounds of nationality, Case 186/87, *Ian William Cowan* v *Trésor public*, [1989] ECR 195.

[80] Rosas, 'The Decline of Sovereignty', pp. 151–153.

[81] As of 19 May 1994, there were twelve Contracting Parties, including four Member States of the European Union (Greece, Italy, The Netherlands, Portugal) and three candidate members (Finland, Norway, Sweden); Chart showing signature and ratifications of conventions and agreements concluded within the Council of Europe between 1 Jan. 1989 and 1 May 1994.

may be required to take up arms in defence of their country, are not too keen on enlarging the electorate to 'foreigners'. In support of exclusion, they can point to Article F(1) TEU, which requests the Union to 'respect the national identities of its Member States'.

In such an ideological setting, it would be difficult indeed to use Article 8e(2) EC Treaty, which gives the Council, acting unanimously on a proposal from the Commission and after consulting the European Parliament, the right to adopt provisions 'to strengthen or to add to the rights laid down in this Part, which it shall recommend to the Member States for adoption in accordance with their respective constitutional requirements'. Some might even question the right to resort to Article 8e as a means for extending electoral rights to national elections. And one wonders whether such extension, irrespective of the legal method adopted, would be accepted by national constitutional courts, in particular the German Constitutional Court. Thus, it is understandable that the federalist Draft Constitution of the European Union, considered by Parliament in February 1994,[82] is rather cautious on electoral rights, providing explicitly for municipal and European elections only but, on the other hand, stating that 'the electoral rights of citizens may be extended by a constitutional law' (Article 4).[83]

There seem to be two reasons why the question, perhaps paradoxically, is particularly difficult to approach in the European Union. An obvious reason is the Community law principle of freedom of movement and its—at least symbolic—development by the Maastricht version of Article 8a EC Treaty. Under general international law, states can, even with a system of voting rights based on residence, control the scope of the electorate by controlling the influx and right of residence of aliens, while this is not possible under Community law. Another more general reason (which is certainly related to the former) can be found in the political and psychological intricacies of political union and the fight between federalists and confederalists. In this sometimes heated atmosphere of suspicions and fears, any move affecting the holy triad of nationality, nation and sovereignty is viewed with hostility in some quarters.

It may be advisable, then, to place such discussions on the 'structure' of the democratic system in a wider context than Community law and the European Union. International human rights law, treaty law

---

[82] European Parliament 1993–1994 Session, Extract of the minutes of the meeting of 10 Feb. 1994. Parliament merely decided to note with satisfaction the work of the Committee on Institutional Affairs, which has resulted in a draft Constitution, and called upon Parliament to be elected in June 1994 to continue that work.

[83] Cf. the judgment of the German Constitutional Court mentioned above, note 73.

and standards created by the Council of Europe and the experiences of the British Commonwealth and Ireland may offer more relaxed settings. Maybe it is also time to revitalize the discussions among and within the Nordic countries of the 1970s and 1980s. It has been the main purpose of this chapter to bring out such broader contexts and perspectives, rather than advocate this or that solution.

8 THE SOCIAL DIMENSION OF COMMUNITY CITIZENSHIP

Siofra O'Leary

1 INTRODUCTION

The scope of Community law as regards the free movement of persons has generally been determined in accordance with (a) possession of Member State nationality; and (b) whether or not the Member State national in question performs, or is involved in the performance of, an economic activity. The status of Union citizen in Article 8 EC Treaty now rests solely on the possession of Member State nationality. It appears that Member State nationals need no longer demonstrate their economic contribution to the Community's integration process as workers, self-employed persons, or as providers or recipients of services, to enjoy the status of Union citizenship and the rights which it entails. Numerous commentaries have been made on the personal scope and substantive content of the citizenship rights in Article 8 EC Treaty.[1] Most commentators agree that Article 8 EC Treaty has succeeded mainly in constitutionalizing rights which already existed in Community law, or which had already been proposed on the basis of the free movement provisions. They emphasize the symbolic nature of the status as it stands, but discuss the prospects for its future development.[2] Indeed, the Commission has stated that 'the rights flowing from citizenship of the Union are in effect granted constitutional status by

---

[1] See, for example, Closa, 'The Concept of Citizenship in the Treaty on European Union', 29 CML Rev. (1992), 1137–1170; d'Oliveira, 'European Citizenship: Its Meaning, its Potential', in Monar, Ungerer and Wessels (eds), *The Maastricht Treaty on European Union* (1993), pp. 126–146; Garrone, 'Les droits du citoyen européen: l'acquis communautaire et l'apport de traité de Maastricht', 3 *Revue Suisse de Droit International et Européen* (1993), 251–271; Kovar and Simon, 'La citoyenneté européenne' (1993) CDE, 283–315; O'Keeffe, 'Citizenship of the Union', 2 *Actualités du Droit* (1994), 227–248; O'Keeffe, 'Union Citizenship', in O'Keeffe and Twomey (eds), *Legal Issues of the Maastricht Treaty* (1993), pp. 87–107; O'Leary, *The Evolving Concept of Community Citizenship—from the Free Movement of Persons to Union Citizenship* (forthcoming); and Verhoeven, 'Les citoyens de l'Europe', 2 *Annales de Droit de Louvain* (1993), 165–191.

[2] See, e.g., Verhoeven, 'Les citoyens de l'Europe', 288.

being enshrined in the Treaties themselves' and that 'the provisions of Part II of the EC Treaty are not static'.[3]

Article 8 EC Treaty does not explicitly provide for the enjoyment of any social rights by Union citizens, nor does it indicate that Union citizenship involves any social dimension for that matter. However, the scope of Union citizenship need not be limited to the provisions of Article 8 EC Treaty, since Article 8(2) EC Treaty expressly provides that 'Citizens of the Union shall enjoy the rights conferred by this Treaty ...'. This provision invites us to delve beyond the underambitious content of the citizenship package in the Treaty on European Union (TEU) to discover whether Community or Union citizenship can boast an effective social dimension and whether it might entail the effective exercise of social rights by Member State nationals detached from the exercise of an economic activity. This chapter thus seeks to establish whether the constitutionalized status of Union citizen might move Member State nationals beyond market or consumer citizenship towards a more-rounded political and social as well as economic citizen, participating in the development of European integration in a Union of Member States.

This chapter briefly refers to the provisions on the free movement of persons in Community law and comments on their dependence on the performance of an economic activity (Section 2.1). Thereafter, it details the relationship which inevitably developed between the regulation of free movement and the enjoyment by Member State nationals of certain limited rights in the social field (Section 2.2). Having outlined this development of limited socio-economic rights on the basis of the free movement provisions, the chapter sketches the evolution of Community social policy generally, discussing the controversy which surrounds any assertion of supranational Community competence and the troubled question of a suitable legal basis for a Community social policy. Both issues have hampered progress at Community level (Sections 3.1 and 3.2). Section 3 concludes with a brief reference to the adoption of the Agreement on Social Policy by eleven Member States which is annexed to the Maastricht Treaty in the form of a special protocol (Section 3.3).

In Sections 4.1 and 4.2, with specific reference to the free movement of Member State nationals who wish to pursue educational activities in another Member State, the weak social content of Community or Union citizenship is analysed. The discussion in Section 4 focuses on the interpretation already conceded by the Court of Justice of the European

---

[3] See *Report from the Commission on the Citizenship of the Union*, COM (93) 702 final, 2.

Communities (ECJ) of the principle of equal treatment in Article 6 EC Treaty (previously Article 7) and the apparent reticence of the ECJ and Community legislature to apply this broad interpretation equally to social welfare type rights and benefits. The application of a broad interpretation of equal treatment would expand the substantive content of Community or Union citizenship considerably. However, policy rather than legal principle appears to take precedence with respect to aspects of Community citizenship which would involve a greater financial burden with respect to resident Community citizens than would otherwise have fallen on the host Member States.

This discussion of the social rights of Member State students highlights two extremely important issues in the context of the possible emergence of a new civic order in the Community on the basis of the TEU: the future scope of the principle of equal treatment, which can be regarded as fundamental to the status of citizenship, and the role which the principle of subsidiarity may play in the legal and political relationship between the Member States and the Community and in the development of Union citizenship.[4] The chapter concludes the discussion of social policy and citizenship by referring to the broader and more controversial consequences of any extension of Community competence in the social field. It discusses some of the political, economic, structural and even ideological obstacles which hamper an increase in the Community's competence and suggests some of the direct consequences of these obstacles for the development of an effective and full-blooded concept of Community or Union citizenship.

2 FREE MOVEMENT IN THE EUROPEAN COMMUNITIES AND ECONOMIC ACTIVITY

2.1 Free movement and the relevance of economic activities

The concept of 'worker' in Article 48 EC Treaty and the related concept of 'activities of an employed person' in Article 1(1) of Regulation 1612/68[5] are not defined anywhere in the Treaties. The ECJ has come to assess the legal status of Member State nationals under the free movement provisions according to (a) the existence of the elements of a classic employment relationship (service, direction, remuneration);

---

[4] See Chapter 3.

[5] O.J. 1968, 1257/2.

and (b) whether the activity in question is 'genuine and effective'.[6] 'Stagiaires' (interns),[7] part-time workers,[8] persons no longer in an existing employment relationship[9] and jobseekers[10] have all been brought, on an *ad hoc* judicial basis, within the scope of Article 48 EC Treaty. However, the primary purpose and function of Community law in the field of free movement was to regulate economic activity. Thus, 'the provisions of the Treaty relating to free movement are intended to facilitate the pursuit by Community citizens of occupational activities of all kinds throughout the Community, and preclude measures which might place Community citizens at a disadvantage when they wish to pursue an economic activity in the territory of another Member State.'[11]

These primarily economic objectives limited the Community's power of action with respect to Member State nationals and the scope of its substantive provisions in the field of free movement. The definitions delivered by the ECJ of concepts like economic activity, remuneration, workers etc., were fundamental to the determination of whether or not Community law, and therefore Article 6 EC Treaty, could be said to apply.[12] Unless Member State nationals were involved in some sort of cross-border economic activity they did not come within

---

[6] See Cases 66/85, *Deborah Lawrie-Blum* v *Land Baden-Württemberg*, [1986] ECR 2121; and 53/81, *D.M. Levin* v *Staatssecretaris van Justitie*, [1982] ECR 1035.

[7] Case 66/85, *Lawrie-Blum*, see note 6; Case C-27/91 *Union de Recouvrement des Cotisations de Sécurité Sociale et d'Allocations Familiales de la Savoie (URSSAF)* v *Hostellerie Le Manoir S.à.r.l.*, judgment of 21 Nov. 1991, [1991] ECR I-5538; and Case C-3/90, *M.J.E. Bernini* v *Minister van Onderwijs en Wetenschappen*, [1992] ECR I-1071.

[8] Case 53/81, *Levin*, see note 6; Case 139/85, *R.H. Kempf* v *Staatssecretaris van Justitie*, [1986] ECR 1741; and Case C-357/89, *V.J.M. Raulin* v *Minister van Onderwijs en Wetenschappen*, [1992] ECR I-1027.

[9] Case 39/86, *Sylvie Lair* v *Universität Hannover*, [1988] ECR 3161.

[10] Case C-292/89, *The Queen* v *The Immigration Appeal Tribunal, ex parte Gustaff Desiderius Antonissen*, [1991] ECR I-745.

[11] See Case 143/87, *Christopher Stanton and SA Belge d'assurances L'Étoile 1905* v *Inasti (Institute national d'assurances sociales pour travailleurs indépendents)*, [1988] ECR 3877, at para. 14. See also Case 36/74, *B.N.O. Walrave and L.J.N. Koch* v *Association Union Cycliste Internationale, Koninklijke Nederlandsche Wielren Unie and Federacion Española Ciclismo*, [1974] ECR 1405; Case 13/76, *Gaetano Donà* v *Mario Mantero*, [1976] ECR 1333; and Mattera, 'La libre circulation des travailleurs a l'interieur de la CE', (1993) *Revue du marché commun européen*, 47–108, at 58 et seq.

[12] Art. 6 EC Treaty applies 'within the scope of application of this Treaty ...'. Note that the extent of entitlements to social benefits differed once the status of worker had been established, cf. Case 53/81, *Levin*, see note 6; Case 66/85, *Lawrie-Blum*, see note 6; and Case 344/87, *I. Bettray* v *Staatssecretaris van Justitie*, [1989] ECR 1621.

the scope of Community law and their situation was purely internal to the Member State. The object of the free movement rules, namely the establishment of a Common Market and the unification of economic systems, thus limited the Community's abolition of restrictions on free movement to circumstances which promoted, in the main, trading activities.[13] Insistence on an economic element in a transaction or activity similarly applies in the area of services and establishment,[14] although the ECJ's definition of what constitutes a service has been widened considerably in recent years to activities in which the economic element seems slight or incidental. Thus tourists, students and medical patients, who are all recipients of services,[15] and members of religious sects,[16] all come within the scope of the provisions on services. Like the Treaty provisions on the free movement of workers, however, Articles 52 and 59 EC Treaty were primarily aimed at the liberation of *factors of production* within the Common Market and to facilitate the creation of similar competitive conditions between the Member States.

2.2 Free movement and the adoption of Community measures in the social field

Despite the fundamentally economic rationale for the original Treaty provisions on free movement, the status of worker, self-employed person or provider/receiver of a service also conferred a variety of social rights. Indeed, secondary legislation reflected the idea, even to a limited extent, that free movement was also a means to enable Community nationals 'to pursue the activity of their choice within the Community'.[17] From this perspective, economic integration was a possible vehicle for further social and political integration. Thus, by aggregating all previous periods of insurance and employment within the Member State as regards social security rights, exporting these benefits to ensure that a worker does not suffer any loss by taking up residence in another Member State and by generally treating workers

---

[13] See Chapter 5.

[14] See Case C-159/90, *Society for the Protection of Unborn Children Ireland Ltd. (S.P.U.C.)* v *Stephen Grogan and Others*, [1991] CMLR 849; and Case 263/86, *Belgian State* v *René Humbel and Marie-Thérèse Humbel née Edel*, [1988] ECR 5365.

[15] Joined Cases 286/82 and 26/83, *Graziana Luisi and Giuseppe Carbone* v *Ministero del Tesoro*, [1984] ECR 377; Case 186/87, *Ian William Cowan* v *Trésor public* [1989] ECR 195.

[16] Case 196/87, *Udo Steymann* v *Staatssecretaris van Justitie*, [1988] ECR 6159.

[17] See the third recital of the preamble to Regulation 1612/68, O.J. 1968, L 257/2; and generally Shockweiler, 'La dimension humaine et sociale de la Communauté Européenne', (1993) *Revue du marché commun européen*, 11–45.

equally as regards the benefits and allowances granted under national social security legislation, Article 51 EC Treaty and Regulation 1408/71, which was adopted to give it effect, served to 'abolish(ing) as far as possible the territorial limitations on the application of the different social security schemes'.[18] Although the concept of social security pursuant to Article 51 EC Treaty was broadly interpreted, Community legislation was limited to measures to facilitate free movement of workers and their dependants and was only in later years extended to self-employed persons.[19]

Regulation 1612/68 also amplifies the benefits available to Community workers and their dependants. Article 7(2), for example, provides that they shall enjoy 'the same social and tax advantages as national workers'. Pursuant to this provision, the ECJ has extended the principle of equal treatment to, *inter alia*, the right to be joined by one's unmarried partner,[20] education scholarships to facilitate study in another Member State,[21] child-birth loans[22] and the use of one's own language in judicial proceedings.[23] Members of a worker's family also enjoy equal treatment in this respect on the basis of their relationship with the worker[24] and the benefits which come within the scope of Article 7(2) have clearly not been confined to employment-related benefits. The distinction in Community and national law between social security and social assistance was originally quite straightforward, the former being paid on the basis of insurance or employment, the latter being determined on the basis of discretionary decisions generally related to need and are generally independent of the exercise of an economic activity. Social assistance did not originally come within the scope of Article 51 EC Treaty and Regulation 1408/71, but many

---

[18] See Case 44/65, *Hessiche Knappschaft* v *Maison Singer et Fils*, [1965] ECR 965. A proposal to amend Art. 51 EC Treaty and introduce qualified majority voting was rejected during the negotiation of the Maastricht Treaty, see *Agence Europe*, 5 July 1991; and generally Laske, 'The Impact of the Single European Market on Social Protection for Migrant Workers', 30 CML Rev. (1993), 515–539; and Meehan, 'European Citizenship and Social Policies', in Vogel and Moran (eds), *The Frontiers of Citizenship* (1991), pp. 125–154.

[19] See the consolidated text in O.J. 1983, L 230/8.

[20] Case 59/85, *State of The Netherlands* v *Ann Florence Reed*, [1986] ECR 1283.

[21] Case 235/87, *Annunziata Matteucci* v *Communauté Française of Belgium and Commissariat Général aux relations internationales of the Communauté Française of Belgium*, [1988] ECR 5589.

[22] Case 65/81, *Francesco Reina and Letizia Reina* v *Landeskreditbank Baden-Württemberg*, [1982] ECR 33.

[23] Case 137/84, *Ministère public* v *Robert Heinrich Maria Mutsch*, [1985] ECR 2681.

[24] See, e.g., Case 316/85, *Centre public d'aide sociale de Courcelles* v *Marie-Christine Lebon*, [1987] ECR 2811.

measures which amount to social assistance at national level have been brought by the ECJ within the scope of the concept of social advantages or social security.[25] Regulation 1247/92[26] has recently inserted a new paragraph in Regulation 1408/71 to deal with the Member States' difficulties with the ECJ's expansive interpretations of social security.

The ECJ has, as a result of this jurisprudence, been hailed for its 'human' approach to the ancillary social issues which have arisen in the course of the Community's regulation of free movement and its decisions are said to go far beyond the original economic foundations of the Community's integration process.[27] No matter how progressive and human the ECJ's approach to the socio-economic rights of Community nationals may have been, their enjoyment of these rights has generally been linked to their status as workers, to their performance of an economic activity, or to their dependency on a worker and the extension of the rights in question is due to the application of the principle of equal treatment on a reciprocal basis. As one commentator has argued:[28]

> the Court was never interested in social policy as such, for example, in transforming individual rights to labour market participation into collective rights to individual or social citizenship; instead, it used international commitments to open up national labour markets as a wedge to insert transnational individual civil rights into European legal systems, trying to move as far as possible beyond the sphere of work and employment. Rather than equalizing protection *across* national regimes, the Court removed discrimination *within* them, and to this extent at least

---

[25] See Case 63/76, *Vito Inzirillo* v *Caisse d'Allocations Familiales de l'Arrondissement de Lyon,* [1976] ECR 2057; and generally O'Keeffe, 'Equal Rights for Migrants: the Concept of Social Advantages in Article 7(2) Regulation 1612/68', 5 YEL (1985), 93–123. On the issue of social security see Cousins, 'Social Security and Social Assistance—the Final Round?', 18 EL Rev. (1993), 533–539, at 534, who notes that the distinction between social security and social assistance has become increasingly blurred with the increase in non-contributory benefits and the development of statutory entitlement to many social assistance payments; and Laske, 'Impact of the Single European Market', 528.

[26] O.J. 1992, L 136/1.

[27] See generally Mancini, 'The Free Movement of Workers in the Case-Law of the Court of Justice', in O'Keeffe and Curtin (eds), *Constitutional Adjudication in European Community and National Law, Essays in Honour of Mr Justice T.F. O'Higgins* (1992), pp. 67–77; and O'Keeffe, 'Trends in the Free Movement of Persons within the European Communities', in O'Reilly (ed.), *Human Rights and Constitutional Law. Essays in Honour of Brian Walsh* (1992), pp. 263–291, at p. 267 et seq.

[28] See Streeck, 'From Market-making to State-building? Reflections on the Political Economy of European Social Policy', DOC. IUE 76/94 (col. 27) *European Law in Context: Constitutional Dimensions of European Economic Integration*, EUI Florence, 14–15 April 1994.

it remained well within the limits of intergovernmental commitments to joint market-making.

This limited market citizenship, based as it was on reciprocal equal treatment in situations where the provisions of Community law have been activated by, for example, a Member State national who enters another Member State seeking access to employment there, could not have served on its own to develop the type of 'citizen identity' to which Tiilikainen refers.[29] Indeed, even this concession of social rights in the context of free movement has proved limited. Jobseekers, for example, are excluded from the scope of Article 7(2) of Regulation 1612/68.[30] This limitation of the scope of the principle of equal treatment is largely based on fear of 'social dumping', the fear that extending social and tax advantages to jobseekers could mean that their free movement would lead to a shift of 'dependent or "high risk" groups' towards more generous Member States.[31] Member State nationals who enjoy rights of residence, limited political rights and other citizenship-like rights under Article 8 EC Treaty are also excluded from this limited but developing category of social rights, as no equivalent of Regulation 1612/68 yet applies in their respect. This survival of the criterion of economic activity to establish entitlement to equal treatment with respect to social benefits could mean that the free movement of persons under Community law and Union citizenship legally and substantively evolve along different lines and that the rights and duties which are contingent on the latter will differ from the legal rights and legal protection afforded the Community's economic agents under the existing free movement regime.[32]

3   THE DEVELOPMENT OF COMMUNITY SOCIAL POLICY

Social policy is generally taken to refer to measures in the field of social insurance, public assistance, health and welfare services, and housing. In the specific case of the European Communities it is said that:[33]

---

[29] See Chapter 2.

[30] Case 316/85, *Lebon*, see note 24.

[31] See Keithley, 'Social Security in a Single European Market', in Room (ed.), *Towards a European Welfare State* (1991), pp. 72–89, at pp. 79–80.

[32] See Section 4.2 below for further discussion of this two-speed citizenship.

[33] See Majone, 'The EC between Social Policy and Social Regulation', 31 JCMS (1993), 153–170, at 154; and Beaumont and Weatherill, *European Community Law* (1993), p. 541.

to the framers of the Treaty 'social policy' included not only social security and interpersonal distribution of income, at least for certain groups of workers, but also interregional distribution, elements of industrial and labour market policy (vocational training, measures to improve labour mobility) and social regulation (primarily occupational health and safety and equal treatment for men and women).

The rights referred to in Section 2.2 above are enjoyed on the basis of an economic cross-border activity. In contrast, the provisions of Title III of the EC Treaty on social policy refer to the rights of Community workers generally, regardless of the existence of a cross-border element.

It is a fundamental principle of Community law that the Community institutions can only legislate within the sphere of their express or implied powers and that all Community legislation must be based on a specific legal basis.[34] Article 117 EC Treaty refers to the need for Member States to promote improved working conditions and improved standards of living for workers. However, no express legislative power is granted therein. Instead, the attainment of these objectives is regarded as flowing generally 'not only from the functioning of the Common Market, which is to favour the harmonisation of social systems but also from the procedures provided for by the Treaty and from the approximation of national legislation'.[35] With this in mind, Article 118 EC Treaty assigns to the Commission the task of 'promoting close cooperation between Member States in the social field'. The ECJ has held that since Article 118 EC Treaty confers a specific task on the Commission, it must also have conferred on it the powers to carry out that task and therefore to adopt binding decisions *vis-à-vis* the Member State establishing communication and consultation procedures. Nevertheless, in *Commission* v *Germany*, the Commission's actions were held to be *ultra vires* to the extent that they imposed a precise obligation on Member States and attempted to exclude them from adopting national measures considered by the Commission not to be in conformity with the Community's policies.[36] Article 119 EC Treaty enshrines the principle of equal pay for equal work, but again does not specify a Community power to legislate.

---

[34] See the duty to state reasons under Art. 90 EC Treaty; Arts 11 and 14 of the Rules of the Procedure of the Council, O.J. 1979, L 268/1; Case 45/86, *Re Generalised Tariff Preferences: E.C. Commission* v *E.C. Council*, [1988] 2 CMLR 131; and generally, Bradley, 'The European Court and the Legal Basis of Community Legislation', 13 EL Rev. (1988), 379–402.

[35] See Joined Cases 281, 283–285 and 287/85, *Federal Republic of Germany and Others* v *Commission of the European Communities*, [1987] ECR 3203, at para. 12.

[36] Ibid., at paras 28–35.

Given this paucity of firm legal bases, it seems unlikely, at first sight, that the Community legislature could facilitate direct Community involvement in a legislative domain, such as social policy, which previously belonged exclusively to the Member States. Social policy clearly ranked amongst the Community's broad programmatic objectives but power to legislate with respect to it did not clearly figure in the specific provisions of the Treaty:[37]

> [Community social policy] is not a generalized scheme for the provision of social welfare. Nor is it designed as a means of harmonizing social security systems or levelling out social security burdens between the states by a set deadline ... Rather, it was initially tailored to the precise and immediate concerns of the three communities [viz. market integration] and focused, from the outset, on employment.

As we shall see, Community legislative activity in this domain has been slow to develop and has been fiercely contested, not least because the enjoyment of social rights at national level has generally been based on claims of access due to 'traditional Community ties of autonomy and obligation'.[38] An immediate difference is evident as regards social policy in the European Communities. The provisions of Title III, with the exception of Article 119 EC Treaty, which addresses equal pay for men and women, refers to the Member States not Community citizens and the subordination of social policy issues to the achievement of the economic objectives of the Community is evident.[39]

3.1 Controversial aspects of social policy in the European Communities

In the *Defrenne* case the ECJ referred to Community objectives in the field of social policy beyond the mere liberalization of factors of production. Thus, Article 119 EC Treaty, it was said:[40]

> forms part of the social objectives of the Community, which is not merely an economic union, but is at the same time intended, by common action, to ensure social progress and seek the constant improvement of the living and working conditions of their peoples ....

---

[37] See Lodge, *The European Community and the Challenge of the Future* (1989), at p. 309; and Joined Cases 281/85, 283–285, 287/85, see note 35, at para. 14.

[38] See Culpitt, *Welfare and Citizenship. Beyond the Crisis of the Welfare State?* (1992), p. 1.

[39] See also the treatment of the issues of social policy in Case 244/87, *Bettray*, see note 12, at paras 17–20.

[40] Case 43/75, *Gabrielle Defrenne* v *Société Anonyme Belge de Navigation Aérienne Sabena*, [1976] ECR 455, at para. 10.

However, controversy about the scope and content of Community social policy is fuelled principally by the vast political, legal and economic differences between the various Member States in the social field. For example, the levels and terms of coverage of social security and assistance differ from one Member State to the next. Tax and social security systems are integrated in some Member States but not in others. In addition, Member States use their social welfare systems to fulfil different economic, fiscal and social policies, reflecting different traditions and ideologies:[41]

> The 'big trade-off' between economic efficiency and a more equal distribution of income and wealth has confronted every democracy since the dawn of industrialization ... the delicate value judgements about the appropriate balance of efficiency and equity, which social policies express, can only be made legitimately and efficiently within homogeneous communities.

The Community does not deny these fundamental differences between the Member States' social welfare systems.[42] Thus, Regulation 1408/71 does not seek to harmonize national social security systems, rather it attempts to coordinate how Member States regulate social security so that obstacles to the free movement of persons are abolished or minimized. However, the legal ambiguity in the Treaty provisions on the extent of Community competence in this field,[43] coupled with the political reticence of Member States to concede more significant and far-reaching powers of action to the Community institutions, have marked the development of social policy from the birth of the Community. Thus, although Article 2 EC Treaty referred to 'an accelerated raising of the standard of living and closer relations between the States', which seemed to indicate common action in the social sphere, overall competence in this field is effectively seen as belonging to the Member

---

[41] Majone, 'The EC between Social Policy and Social Regulations', 167.

[42] See the *Commission Action Programme on the Implementation of the Community Charter of Basic Social Rights*, 8–9/12/1989: 'because of great variations in nature from one Member State of the Community to another which reflect the history, traditions and social and cultural practices characteristic of each Member State and which cannot be called into question, there can be no harmonising systems of social policy.'

[43] See, e.g., Art. 118 EC Treaty which involves the *promotion of close cooperation* in certain fields (emphasis added); and generally Betten (ed.), *The Future of European Social Policy* (1991).

States.[44] The Community was caught between being committed to promoting social progress and being denied the legislative power to adopt its own independent policies.

3.2 Legal bases for Community action in the social sphere

During the 1970s it was increasingly argued that the Community integration process would increasingly be faced with problems resulting from the lack of social cohesion between the Member States and that action was thus necessary in the social field, if only as a by-product of the market integration in process. This shift in favour of a clearer social dimension to the free movement of persons at Community level was also encouraged by the end of the economic boom, a consequent rise in unemployment and a general shift to the left in Member State governments.[45] In the absence of clearer legislative authority in Title III of the Treaty on social policy, the Community institutions were forced to look elsewhere for appropriate legal bases on which to propose and adopt social legislation.

To adopt legislation, Community institutions are obliged to locate their legal competence within a specific legal basis. Article 100 EC Treaty is geared to the adoption of harmonizing legislation which ensures the effective functioning of the Common Market. In the 1970s it was increasingly used to adopt legislation more incidentally linked to the Common Market, including social legislation, consumer rights and environmental protection. The use of this general legal basis to harmonize laws means that the legislation in question has to be linked to the attainment of the Common Market and has to be geared towards attaining competitive equality rather than social goals in themselves.

Article 235 EC Treaty also allows the Council to act when the 'necessary powers' are not provided elsewhere in the Treaty. Reliance on Article 235 EC Treaty can be an important legal and political step forward since that provision can be used to indicate that social legislation is an appropriate concern of the Community as an objective in itself and the legislation in question need not be so closely linked to economic rationales or other justifications related to the attainment of

---

[44] See Joined Cases 281, 283–285 and 287/85, see note 35, at para. 14; Case C-113/89, *Rush Portuguesa Lda* v *Office national d'immigration*, [1990] ECR 1417, at para. 45; and Vogel-Polsky and Vogel, *L'Europe Sociale 1993: illusion, alibi ou realité?* (1991).

[45] See Keithley, 'Social Security', p. 75; and Goebel, 'Employee Rights in the EC: A Panorama from the 1974 Social Action Program to the Social Charter of 1989', 17 *Hastings International and Comparative Law Review* (1993), 1–95, at 14–15.

the Common Market as is the case under Article 100.[46] However, Articles 100 and 235 EC Treaty require a unanimous vote in Council, which enables Member States opposed to Community social legislation to block its passage. The provisions of Title III have sometimes successfully been used to adopt legislation.[47] In general, however, Commission initiatives have, if successful, been reduced to a minimum.[48]

It has been argued, however, that the Treaties were not as lacking in the necessary powers to act in the social field as first appeared, but that the Community institutions under-used the powers available to them, essentially for political reasons.[49] Nobody has brought the Council to Court, for example, for failing to fulfil its mandate under Article 117 EC Treaty. In contrast, in the field of education, no explicit Community competence could have been said to exist, but the Commission has established the far-reaching ERASMUS programme designed to increase significantly the mobility of university students and to promote greater cooperation between universities.[50] It did so on the basis of Article 128 EC Treaty, despite the fact that the general principles criterion in that provision would appear to have considerably limited the scope of substantive measures which it was able to adopt in the field of vocational training.[51] However, legislative inertia aside, the need to rely on Article 100 EC Treaty for most social measures enabled reluctant Member States to block the passage of legislation to which they were opposed. Proposals on social policy were also significantly absent from the concerns listed in the Commission's White Paper in 1985, emphasizing the weak 'social dimension' of the internal market.

---

[46] See, for example, Directive 76/207, O.J. 1976, L 39/40, on the principle of equal treatment for men and women as regards access to employment, vocational training and promotion and working conditions; and generally, Daubler, 'The Rationale and Substance of a European Fundamental Rights Act', in Daubler (ed.), *Market and Social Justice in the European Communities—the Other Side of the Internal Market. Strategies and Options for the Future of Europe*, Basic Findings 3 (1991), p. 87.

[47] See, for example, Directive 89/391 for the improvement of the health and safety of workers, O.J. 1989, L 183/1.

[48] See Joined Cases 281, 283–285 and 287/85, see note 35.

[49] Daubler, 'European Fundamental Rights Act', p. 92.

[50] ERASMUS Decision 87/327/EEC, O.J. 1987, L 166/20.

[51] See Lenaerts, 'ERASMUS: Legal Basis and Implementation', in De Witte (ed.), *European Community Law of Education* (1989), pp. 113–125, at p. 121; and Daubler, 'European Fundamental Rights Act', p. 92.

One of the SEA's most important breakthroughs was the introduction of a general provision permitting the adoption of legislation to
achieve the internal market on the basis of a qualified majority. In
conjunction with the cooperation procedure under Article 149 EC
Treaty, Article 100a heralded a new age for the adoption of internal
market legislation. However, legislation relating to the free movement
of persons and 'the rights and interests of employed persons' were
explicitly excluded from its scope (Article 100a(2)). The political and
legal difficulties in securing an appropriate legal basis to legislate in the
social field may, however, have diminished in the light of the *Titanium
Dioxide* decision on the use of Article 100a generally.[52] The titanium
dioxide Directive[53] pursued the dual objectives of protecting the
environment on the one hand and improving competitive conditions on
the other. The ECJ held that it was not possible in such circumstances
to have recourse to both Article 130s and Article 100a and that the latter
was the appropriate legal basis. Why, we may ask, when there was a
specific legal basis available which addressed environmental protection
did the ECJ opt for the application of a general basis? First of all, it will
be recalled that the ECJ in this case opted for very clear support of the
cooperation and qualified majority voting procedures on which Article
100a is based. Its preference of Article 100a EC Treaty over Article 130s
EC Treaty was based on an endorsement of democratic principles and
the European Parliament's fundamental role as the Community's
representative assembly.[54] In addition, however, the ECJ argued that
the protection of the environment might effectively be pursued by
means of harmonization measures laid down on the basis of Article
100a.[55] This decision has been seen as an endorsement by the ECJ of
a very wide interpretation of the internal market and as implying
that:[56]

---

[52] Case C-300/89, *Commission of the European Communities* v *Council of the European
Communities,* [1991] ECR 2867.

[53] Council Directive 89/428/EEC of 24 June 1989, O.J. 1989, L 201/56.

[54] See the annotation by Barnard, 'Where Politicians Fear to Tread?', 17 EL Rev. (1992),
127–133.

[55] Ibid., at para. 23.

[56] See Barents, 'The Internal Market Unlimited: Some Observations on the Legal Basis
of Community Legislation', 30 CML Rev. (1993), 85–109, at 87; Streit and Mussler, 'The
Economic Constitution of the European Community—from Rome to "Maastricht"', DOC.
IUE 72/94 (Col. 23), *European Law in Context: Constitutional Dimensions of European Economic
Integration,* EUI Florence, 14–15 April 1994; Cf. Weiler, 'Journey to an Unknown Destination:
A Retrospective and Prospective of the European Court of Justice in the Arena of Political
Integration', 31 JCMS (1993), 417–446, at 439.

the scope of the Communities' powers to harmonise national legislation has become so vast that this provision [100(A)] can no longer be seen as the attribution of a specific power, but that it amounts to a general authority for the Community to legislate in nearly all the areas which directly or indirectly concern the internal market.

By simply referring to social legislation in terms of the achievement of the internal market and the creation or protection of more competitive and economic conditions (often referred to as the 'level playing field') Article 100a could thus be used to adopt Community social legislation.[57]

If only to a limited extent, the SEA also specifically extended the scope for Community action in the social field. Article 118a, for example, provides for the adoption of legislation by qualified majority and applies to situations beyond the traditional workplace to the 'working environment'. Nevertheless, the Community's limited legal competence in the social field to date is undeniable, as are the legal and political difficulties surrounding an assertion by it of more far-reaching competence on the grounds of these general legal bases. These difficulties are further reflected in the legal form and content of one of its primary attempts to act in this field, the Community Charter of the Fundamental Social Rights of Workers. The Charter was signed by only eleven Member States, it does not amount to Community legislation, is not therefore justiciable and its vague and aspirational content has been further emphasized by the lack of concrete action with respect to the Commission's action programme which followed from it.[58] Indeed, the Charter is careful to remind the Community to stay 'within the limits of its powers' and provide that the rights thereunder are to be enforced 'in accordance with arrangements applying in each country' or with 'national practice'.

3.3 The TEU and social policy—a sui generis *protocol and agreement*

Controversy and disagreement over competence as regards social policy continued during the course of the intergovernmental negotiations. The Member States did not unanimously agree to extend their commitment to the adoption of measures in the field of social policy. Only a slight

---

[57] See, however, the subsequent decision of the ECJ in Case C-155/91, *Commission* v *Council*, 17 March 1993, where, in contrast to Case C-300/89, it held that the appropriate legal basis for a directive on the prevention or reduction of waste and the establishment of treatment facilities was Art. 130s and not Art. 100a.

[58] COM (89) 568.

amendment was made to the existing *acquis communautaire* to deal with the consequences of the *Barber* decision.[59] Provisions relating to social protection, working conditions and the promotion of dialogue between management and labour were adopted by eleven of the Member States in the form of a Protocol annexed to the Treaty. Community institutions, procedures and mechanisms are to be used to achieve the objectives of the Protocol as elaborated in the Agreement on Social Policy, but acts adopted thereunder do not bind the twelfth Member State—the United Kingdom. The provisions relating to social policy in the EC Treaty still constitute an integral part of the *acquis communautaire* which binds all Member States, the Protocol and the Agreement annexed to the Treaty do not. 'If only at the symbolic level, it [this two-speed social policy] seems inconsistent with the notion of citizenship of the Union'.[60] The amended Article 2 EC Treaty now commits the Community to 'striving towards a higher level of employment and of social protection, and the raising of the standard of living and the quality of life and economic and social cohesion and solidarity among Member States'. The scope of Community action in the social sphere is broadened in Article 1 of the Agreement on Social Policy. However, the Community still shares competence with the Member States and the measures implemented, while maintaining the competitiveness of the Community economy, must take account of national practice. Article 2 provides for the formation of regulations, directives, recommendations with a view to achieving the objectives of Article 1. Article 3, which indicates how the objectives in Article 2 are to be achieved, identifies the formulation of 'a policy in the social sphere'. This reflects further realization that legislative action at Community level in the social sphere is an essential aspect of forming 'an ever closer union'. However, the relegation of amendments in this sphere to a protocol and agreement binding only eleven Member States indicates the continued lack of consensus among the Community partners on the future scope of Community social policy and the strength of national political and ideological differences with respect to this field of policy-making.[61]

---

[59] See Curtin, 'The Constitutional Structure of the Union: A Europe of Bits and Pieces', 30 CML Rev. (1993), 17–69.

[60] See Beaumont and Weatherill, *European Community Law*, p. 571.

[61] See generally, Whiteford, 'Social Policy after Maastricht', 18 EL Rev. (1993), 202–222, at 206–207 for more detail; Watson, 'Social Policy after Maastricht', 30 CML Rev. (1993), 481–513; and Blanpain, *Labour Law and Industrial Relations of the EEC. Maastricht and Beyond: From a Community to a Union* (1992), p. 31 et seq.

4   THE SOCIAL CONTENT OF COMMUNITY CITIZENSHIP

One of the objectives of the TEU is 'to strengthen the protection of the rights and interests of the nationals of the Member States through the introduction of a citizenship of the Union' (Article B). Having outlined the development of Community social policy, we now turn to the question posed earlier, namely, whether Union citizenship affects any changes in the Community's regulation of the free movement of persons and the rights which Member State nationals can enjoy thereunder, or whether the rights and benefits of free movement are distinct from those extended to Member State nationals on the basis of Union citizenship? Most importantly, for our purposes, does Union citizenship increase the social content of the rights which Member State nationals derive from Community law, or do its provisions point to the possibility of such an extension in the future?

4.1 Social rights independent of the exercise of an economic activity?

Article 8 EC Treaty does not provide explicitly for any social rights, but the content of Union citizenship is not necessarily limited to that provision. As Section 2.1 outlined, the initial attempt by the Treaty authors to create an integrated labour market focused on Community nationals as economically active agents and Member State nationals thus enjoyed the right to enter and reside in another Member State to pursue the economic objectives envisaged in the Treaty and secondary legislation. The establishment of a general right of residence independent of the exercise of an economic activity has always been regarded as an essential component of a citizens' Europe and was listed among the 'special rights' agenda first proposed at the Paris Summit in December 1974.[62] The Commission presented its initial proposal for a directive on residence, which it based on Article 235 EC Treaty, in 1979.[63] Thirteen years passed before agreement could finally be reached in Council on three separate residence directives which addressed the right of residence of economically inactive persons, retired persons and

---

[62] See Bull. EC 12–1974. Thereafter see the Tindemans Report which contains a special chapter entitled 'Towards a Europe of Citizens', Bull. EC (8) 1975 II no. 7/8; the Scelba Report, EP Working Documents 1977–78, 25/10/1977, Doc. 346/77, 10; and EP Resolution O.J. 1977, C 279/25. See also the Reports from the Round Table Conference in the EUI Florence on 'Special Rights and a Charter of the Rights of the Citizens of the EC' 26–28 Oct. 1978.

[63] See O.J. 1979, C 207/14.

students.[64] This legislative position is reflected in Article 8a(1) EC Treaty, which provides that Union citizens shall 'have the right to move and reside freely within the territory of the Member States ...'.

Does this provision effectively detach residence from the exercise of an economic activity so that a Member State national can reside in another Member State and enjoy the benefits which that Member State extends to its own nationals on an equal treatment basis? In other words, does Article 8a EC Treaty imply that Union citizens may enjoy a right of residence regardless of their economic status and that when doing so they are entitled to equal treatment with respect to rights which facilitate the exercise of the principal right (i.e. residence), such as access to social assistance and medical care while resident in those Member States? The answer, at first sight, appears to be no. Article 8a(1) EC Treaty also provides that the right of residence of Union citizens is 'subject to the limitations and conditions laid down in this Treaty and by the measures adopted to give it effect'. The traditional Article 48(3) EC Treaty limitations on free movement—public policy, security, and health—will thus continue to apply.[65] Further limitations, or rather conditions, are to be found in the three 1990 Directives which all stipulate that the right of residence depends on the possession of sufficient resources and medical insurance. Article 1 of Directives 90/364 and 365 provides with respect to the residence applicant that:

> they themselves and the members of their families ... [must be] ... covered by sickness insurance in respect of all risks in the host Member State and have sufficient resources to avoid becoming a burden on the social assistance of the host Member State during their period of residence.

In the case of students, the requirement is limited to medical insurance coverage and to the applicant presenting proof that he or she possesses sufficient resources.[66]

What does this legislative framework supplementing the constitutional provision in Article 8a EC Treaty of a general right of residence tell us about the present or future social content of Community or

---

[64] See Directives 90/364, 365, 366, respectively, O.J. 1990, L 180/26–30. The Directives were all based on Art. 235 EC Treaty, but following a successful request for the annulment of Directive 90/366 by the European Parliament, the legal basis of the Students' Directive was amended to Art. 6 EC Treaty, Case C-295/90, *Re Students' Rights: European Parliament v E.C. Council*, [1992] CMLR 281.

[65] See in this respect Demaret, 'L'égalité de traitement', 2 *Actualités du Droit* (1994), 165–208.

[66] See Art. 1 Directive 90/366, and Art. 1, paras 2 and 3, for a definition of sufficient resources.

Union citizenship? Free movement and residence are after all the foundations of Union citizenship and almost the only instance when the 'privileged' status of Member State nationals can be clearly seen. This issue is debated in more detail in the following section with specific reference to the Directive on the right of residence for students and the social welfare type rights which students can claim on the basis of Articles B TEU and Articles 6 and 8(a) EC Treaty as amended.

4.2 A focused analysis of the social deficit of Community citizenship

Is it legally and politically possible to make the right of residence of Union citizens depend on the fulfilment of these two criteria, namely, the possession of sufficient resources and coverage by medical insurance against all risks? Equal treatment in relation to conditions of access to vocational training apply not only to conditions imposed by educational establishments, but also to any measure liable to hinder the exercise of that right.[67] The ECJ has held that to deny students a right of residence is to deny them the very right to attend vocational courses on an equal basis and the principle of non-discrimination thus requires that a national of a Member State admitted to a vocational training course in another Member State automatically enjoys a right to reside there for the duration of the course.[68] Article 6(1) EC Treaty only applies 'within the scope of application of this Treaty' and 'without prejudice to any special provisions' contained therein. Nevertheless, it is fair to say that the scope of application of the Treaty and, consequently, the scope of application of Article 6 EC Treaty have proved far from static and the ECJ has been said to be 'ready surreptiously to extend the *acquis communautaire* through a broad interpretation of this phrase'.[69] One need only refer to the *Matteucci* case, where equal treatment was extended to an educational grant under a bilateral cultural agreement which itself fell outside the scope of Community law, to support this submission.[70] Similarly, in the *Cowan* case, the principle of equal treatment was extended to persons 'in a situation

---

[67] Case 293/83, *Françoise Gravier* v *City of Liège*, [1985] ECR 593; and for a detailed commentary on the development of the role of Community law in the field of education see Lenaerts, 'Education in European Community Law after "Maastricht"', 31 CML Rev. (1994), 7–41.

[68] Case C-357/89, *Raulin*, see note 8; and Case C-295/90, *European Parliament* v *Council*, see note 64.

[69] See Weatherill, 'The Scope of Article 7 EEC', 15 EL Rev. (1990), 334–341, at 340; see also De Moor, 'Article 7 of the Treaty of Rome Bites', 48 MLR (1985), 452–459, at 458–459.

[70] See Case 235/87, *Matteucci*, see note 21.

governed by Community law' so that a discriminatory criminal injuries compensation scheme, which on its own clearly fell outside the scope of Community law, was held to fall foul of Article 6, since it obstructed free movement.[71] Furthermore, in the students' Directive case, the ECJ very broadly held that acts adopted pursuant to Article 6(2) EC Treaty need not necessarily be limited to regulating rights which derive from Article 6(1) EC Treaty and can cater for what rights appear to be necessary to ensure the effective exercise of those rights.[72] Thus, students can be joined by their spouse and dependent children in order to facilitate the effective exercise of their right of residence and right of access to education. This interpretation of the scope of Article 6 EC Treaty is another aspect of the ECJ's general insistence on the principle of the effectiveness of Community law and the effective protection of the rights which it entails for Community nationals.[73]

The inclusion of the condition on sufficient means of support and health insurance is said to protect the 'legitimate interests' of the Member States.[74] However, in the light of the ECJ's established case law, it is difficult to accept the exclusion of the principle of equal treatment with respect to these conditions, or to reconcile this exclusion with the spirit of a legal instrument such as Directive 90/365 (which is actually based on the Community principle of equal treatment) or with the afore-mentioned objective of the TEU with respect to the rights and interests of Member State nationals (Article B). Furthermore, Article 8a(1) EC Treaty is said to 'build(s) on the fundamental ban on discrimination on grounds of nationality', and the status of the right of residence, like the other rights of citizenship, is said to be 'fundamentally altered' and on a par with other rights central to Community law.[75] These legislative conditions and this reference to 'legitimate interests' in the ECJ's decision in *Raulin* and the Advocate General's Opinion in Case C-295/90 reflect a policy decision to prevent economically inactive Union citizens from becoming a financial burden on the

---

[71] See Case 186/87, *Cowan*, see note 15; O'Keeffe, 'Free Movement of Persons', p. 270 et seq.; and Shockweiler, 'La portée du principe de non-discrimination de l'article 7 du traité CEE', (1991) *Rivista di Diritto Europeo*, 3–24.

[72] Case C-295/90, *European Parliament v Council*, see note 64, at para. 18.

[73] See, for example, Case 222/86, *Union nationale des entraîneurs et Cadres techniques professionels du football (Unectef) v Georges Heylens and Others*, [1987] ECR 4097.

[74] See the Opinion of Advocate General Jacobs in Case C-295/90, *European Parliament v Council*, see note 64, at para. 34.

[75] See *Report from the Commission on the Citizenship of the Union*, COM (93) 702 final, 3.

host Member States.[76] Admittedly, Article 6 EC Treaty applies without prejudice to special provisions contained in the Treaty, but the ECJ has not yet identified specific Treaty provisions justifying the exclusion of medical and maintenance expenses from the scope of the principle of non-discrimination and has not sufficiently explained the legitimate interests of Member States in imposing such limitations as prior conditions of residence. Article 4(4) Regulation 1408/71 specifically excludes social and medical assistance from its scope[77] since the latter were thought to relate to the social and economic situation specific to each Member State and there was thus thought to be no justification for their exportation. But Article 8a(1) EC Treaty does not refer to the exportation of social benefits, but is instead concerned with the effective exercise by Union citizens of their constitutional right to reside in another Member State on an equal treatment basis.

If the content of Article 8 EC Treaty is not static, as the Commission suggests, the essential question is whether the Community institutions and, in the short term, the ECJ, are willing to apply a broad interpretation of the principle of equal treatment in this context. To date the ECJ has not brought its interpretation of the principle of equal treatment—that Article 6(2) EC Treaty is not limited to the rights in para. 1, but should also cater for ancillary rights necessary to allow those rights to operate effectively[78]—to its logical conclusion. To argue that medical coverage and sufficient resources are not conditions of access is unacceptable—without that medical coverage, for example, there is no right of residence[79] and, by the ECJ's own admission, without a right of residence there is no access to vocational training.[80] After all, there seems to be no real difference between extending the principle of equal treatment to the residence of a student's spouse and children and extending him or her maintenance grants on an equal basis as the host Member State's nationals, at least as far as facilitating his or her exercise of the right of equal access to vocational training is concerned.

---

[76] See also Lenaerts, 'Education in European Community Law', 16.

[77] O.J. 1971, L 149/2.

[78] See also Joined Cases 154–155/87, *Rijksinstituut voor de Sociale Verzekering der Zelfstandigen (RSVZ) v Heinrich Wolf and NV Microtherm Europe and Others*, [1988] ECR 3897.

[79] Art. 4 Directive 90/365.

[80] Case C-295/90, *European Parliament v Council*, Judgment of 7 July 1992, annotations by O'Leary, 30 CML Rev. (1993), 639–651.

4.3 Social rights as fundamental rights in the context of Community citizenship

The supremacy of Community law depends on the Community limiting itself to areas in which it is competent to act.[81] If the ECJ extended equal treatment with respect to maintenance grants and access to other social services to resident Member State nationals it would most probably be charged with disrespecting the limits on the competence of the Community judiciary and legislature on which supremacy is based. However, one of the objectives of the Union is to strengthen the rights and interests of Community citizens who, on the basis of Article 8 EC Treaty, enjoy a new constitutional status and a constitutional right of residence. The ECJ has often reasoned according to the method of the 'effect of necessity' whereby it 'takes the goals of the Treaty as a first premise in order to deduct the content and the application of the obligation in question'.[82] With reference to 'an ever closer union' and the status of Union citizenship, the ECJ may be obliged in future to interpret the scope of Article 8 EC Treaty in a broader manner than expected by Member States and to apply Article 6 EC Treaty in conformity with how it has previously been interpreted in other cases. There thus seems no reason to exclude the possibility of the scenario outlined above unravelling in a case before the ECJ. Indeed, take the specific case of a Member State national who is admitted to an educational course in another Member State and proves that he (or she) is in possession of sufficient resources and is adequately covered by medical insurance. Having fulfilled the conditions laid down by Directive 90/366, a residence permit is awarded. During the course, through no fault of his own, it transpires that the student can no longer support himself. On the basis of Article 4 Directive 90/366, his right to reside thereby comes to an end and consequently, as the ECJ itself has conceded, he will no longer have access to the education course in question.

It is well established that fundamental rights form an integral part of the general principles of law which the ECJ is bound to observe[83] and that national constitutional provisions and international treaties may supply guidelines which the ECJ should follow in the protection

---

[81] See De Witte, 'Fundamental Rights in Community Law and National Constitutional Values', (1992) LIEI, 1–22, at 3: 'only Community acts adopted within the sphere of Community competences can prevail over national law.'

[82] See Berlin, 'Interactions between the Lawmaker and the Judiciary within the EC', (1992) LIEI, 17–48, at 23.

[83] See Case 26/69, *Erich Stauder* v *City of Ulm, Sozialamt*, [1969] ECR 419.

of fundamental rights within the framework of the structure and objectives of the Community.[84] Various national constitutions provide for a right to education.[85] In addition, a basic right to education and non-discriminatory access figures in a number of international conventions of which some, if not all, Member States, are contracting parties.[86] Socio-economic rights do not simply demand, however, that states desist from certain activities, but usually require some sort of positive legislative and financial commitment on their part. Given this commitment, it is difficult to establish these rights as fundamental and enforceable.[87] In the *Belgian Linguistics* case, the European Court of Human Rights allowed contracting states discretion with respect to the measures they considered appropriate to support the right to education in Article 2, Protocol 1. A similar approach was adopted in the *Johnston* case. These difficulties with respect to the enforcement of socio-economic rights as fundamental rights do not mean, however, that the principle of equal treatment can be denied with respect to discriminatory conditions to establish a right of residence without which there is no access to education. With reference to the essential role which education has been assigned to achieve the objectives of the Community,[88] some sort of fundamental right of access to education on an equal treatment basis could be constructed on the basis of the aforementioned national constitutional provisions and conventions. In addition, although the responsibility of Member States with respect to the content and organization of education is recognized in the TEU, the Community is charged with promoting 'quality education' and Articles 126 and 127 EC Treaty strongly emphasize the mobility of students and teachers and the importance of educational and cultural exchanges.

---

[84] See Case 11/70, *Internationale Handelsgesellschaft mbH* v *Einfuhr- und Vorratsstelle für Getreide und Futtermittel,* [1970] ECR 1125; and Case 4/73, *J. Nold, Kohlen- und Baustoffgrosshandlung* v *Commission of the European Communities,* [1974] ECR 491.

[85] See, *inter alia,* Art. 27 of the Spanish Constitution and Arts 42.3.2 and 42.4 of the Irish Constitution.

[86] See Art. 13 of the International Covenant on Economic, Social and Cultural Rights, 1966; Art. 30 of the International Convention on the Protection of the Rights of All Migrant Workers and their Families, 1990; Art. 3 of the Convention against Discrimination in Education; and Art. 2, Protocol 1, of the European Convention on Human Rights.

[87] See, for example, Weston, 'Human Rights', in Claude and Weston (eds), *Human Rights in the World Community* (1989), pp. 12–28, at p. 23: 'the covenant [the International Covenant on Economic, Social and Cultural Rights] is essentially a "promotional convention", stipulating objectives more than standards and requiring implementation over time rather than all at once'.

[88] The Commission considers that education and training are at the heart of European integration, Supplement 2/88 – Bull. EC, 13.

5 CONCLUSION: THE UNRESOLVED ASPECTS OF COMMUNITY CITIZENSHIP

It is evident that the principle of equal treatment is being applied inconsistently with respect to the rights of Community citizens. Entitlement to social benefits still varies according to the role played by the claimant in the process of economic integration taking place in the Community, be it as a worker, a dependant, or an economically inactive individual. This two-speed aspect of Community citizenship leaves one wondering whether the effective enjoyment of meaningful social rights was really envisaged as part of the Community citizenship package. Some would argue that for the Community to attain the level of popular legitimacy necessary to forge a more political or social union, the development of an effective social policy is essential.[89] Others consider that the legitimacy of the Community's legal order stems from other sources.[90] While still others argue that the type of popular legitimacy required by previous models of state-building do not apply in the Community, where national identification and sovereignty are still very strong.[91]

If a more extensive Community social policy is to be developed, it must be remembered that this is not a politically and historically neutral area of policy-making. The development of national social policies has been a fundamental aspect of nation-building and the variety of welfare state forms in the European Communities reflect the variety of ways in which European nations have developed and the economic, historical and political context in which they have done so. Majone suggests that these differences between the traditions and background of the various Member States indicate that the Communities do not enjoy the homogeneity necessary to determine the equilibrium normally decided at state level between equity and efficiency and between the provision of goods and the redistribution of income in the determination of the content and objectives of social policy measures.[92] Furthermore, when national governments determine the standards and content of national legislative intervention in the social field, it is

---

[89] See Leidfried, 'Europe's Could-be Social State: Social Policy and Post-1992 European Integration', Contribution to a conference *Europe After 1992*, Ann Arbor MI, 6–7 Sept. 1991, p. 16.

[90] See Weiler, 'Problems of Legitimacy in Post 1992 Europe', 46 *Aussenwirtschaft* (1991), 411–437, at 183 et seq.

[91] See Streeck, 'From Market-making to State-building', 23.

[92] Majone, 'The EC between Social Policy and Social Regulation', 167.

arguable that they do so in the context of decision-making programmes which are, on the whole, democratic, legitimate and accountable. From this perspective, the democratic deficit caused at national level by the transfer of legislative competence to the supranational level and the absence of a truly representative and legislatively dynamic representative assembly in the Community undermine its role in the development of a supranational social policy.

However, although the historical and political background experienced at Member State level may be lacking for the development of a more extensive Community social policy, it must not be forgotten that the Community's objectives are not themselves ideologically neutral. Weiler notes that the culture of the market and the principles of market efficiency and competition are fundamental to the Single Market programme.[93] The economic constitution of the Union is clearly that of a liberal economic order which therefore 'gives priority to the allocation function of public policy over distributional objectives. Hence the best rationale for social initiatives at Community level is one which stresses the efficiency-improving aspects of the proposed measure.'[94] Indeed Article 3a(1) TEU provides that the economic policy adopted by the Community and Member States will be 'conducted in accordance with the principle of an open market economy with free competition'.

These economic objectives already contain the scope for left–right divisions and, in a sense, indicate the contours of the social policy which the Community would have to adopt to be consistent with its objectives. Extensive social welfare rights, which are based on need as a distributive mechanism rather than work, seem to contradict one of the fundamental freedoms of Community law—the free movement of the factors of production.[95] It is clearly difficult to develop basic social rights free from competitive pressures in the context of a legal order which specifically seeks to promote the latter. Were the Community's competence in social policy-making to be extended it would be forced to develop a clearer ideological stance on social issues which, at

---

[93] See Weiler, 'Problems of Legitimacy', 428 et seq.

[94] Majone, 'The EC between Social Policy and Social Regulation', 156.

[95] See also Freeman, 'Migration and the Political Economy of the Welfare State', 485 *The Annals of the American Academy of Political and Social Science* (1986), 51–63, at 52, who states that, 'The principle that ... governs distribution in the Welfare State is that of human need. It does not replace the market principle of distribution according to economic performance, but it significantly alters it by establishing a social minimum and broadening the sphere of collective consumption ... The Welfare State is a closed system because a Community with shared social goods requires for its moral base some aspect of kinship or fellow feeling.'

national level, have been the subject of years, if not decades, of fierce political debate and which have shaped the welfare systems which operate at Member State level today. Based as it is on respect for the rule of law, the Community's task is perhaps to render compatible the development of a liberal economic order with the general social well-being of its members, or its citizens.[96]

At present, the Community is not yet financially or politically equipped to interfere to a greater extent in the determination and regulation of the social policies applicable in the Member States, or to operate more extensive Community-wide social policies. This is evident from the disagreement among Member State governments regarding the development of Community social policy in Maastricht and thus explains the 'policy' approach of the ECJ with regard to the possible financial and social consequences of a general right of residence. Were the ECJ to go further it would provoke Member State resistance (some of which until recently denied Community competence to establish a right of residence independent of the exercise of an economic activity) to the financial obligations being thrust upon them with respect to Member State nationals. Such a scenario is dramatic indeed but it would not be the first time that the ECJ handed down a decision imposing far-reaching financial obligations on Member States. *Gravier*[97] was revolutionary precisely because of the changes which it required in the organization of education at Member State level. It is thus difficult to resolve the tension between the ECJ's propensity to interpret widely the obligations on Member States which derive from the Community's objectives and the principle of equal treatment, with its inability in other difficult cases, to dictate the logical consequences of such a wide interpretation.

---

[96] See Diaz, *Estado de Derecho y sociedad democratica* (1981), p. 83.

[97] Case 293/83, see note 67.

9 THIRD-COUNTRY NATIONALS AND EC LAW

Kay Hailbronner

1 INTRODUCTION

In its Communication on Immigration and Asylum Policies of 23 February 1994[1] the Commission reports 9.1 million third-country nationals legally resident in the EC Member States.[2] The largest part of the foreign population comes from non-EC European countries (4.1 million), followed by Africa (2.7), Asia (1.5) and America (0.8). Eurostat reports an increase in thirteen countries (especially Germany) but also shows a drop in others (France, Greece) between 1986 and 1992. The report rightly observes that this does not necessarily mean that there has been a net emigration. Most of the decrease in some countries could also be attributed to the fact that third-country nationals have obtained the nationality of their host countries. This fact should also be taken into account when comparing the proportion of third-country nationals living in the different Member States. Whereas Germany has a percentage of 6.82 of its total population, third-country nationals in Italy account for only 0.75 per cent of the total population, compared to France (4.14 per cent) and the United Kingdom (2.12 per cent). In most countries there is, however, clearly an increase in immigration, partly due to a growing number of asylum seekers. In 1992, 438,199 out of 571,718 asylum seekers in all EC States were received in Germany.

2 EC COMPETENCE WITH REGARD TO MIGRATION

2.1 Immigration

The Treaty on European Union (TEU) signed in Maastricht on 7 February 1992[3] significantly extends the powers of the Community in the fields of refugee, alien and immigration policy. Article 100c EC

---

[1] COM (94) 23 final.

[2] Annex, 21.

[3] 31 I.L.M. 246 (1992).

Treaty, as amended by the TEU, empowers the Council, acting unanimously on a proposal from the Commission and after consulting the European Parliament, 'to determine the third countries whose nationals must be in possession of a visa when crossing the external borders of the Member States'. From 1 January 1996 such decisions have to be adopted by a qualified majority (Article 100c(3) EC Treaty). However, provisions agreed upon in conventions in force between the Member States (i.e., the Schengen and Dublin agreements) will remain in force until their content has been replaced by directives or measures adopted by the Community (Article 100c(7) EC Treaty). Just how sensitively Member States can react when their national interests are concerned is made apparent by Article 100c(5) which makes Community powers contingent on 'the exercise of the responsibilities incumbent upon the Member States with regard to the maintenance of law and order and the safeguarding of internal security'.

However, an extension of Community powers into further areas has been made possible without resorting to a formal treaty amendment. By a unanimous decision of the Council, Article 100c EC Treaty may be applied to certain actions in the fields of justice and home affairs (Articles 100c(6) EC Treaty and K.9 TEU). The following areas have been declared matters of common interest (Article K.1(1)–(6) TEU):

(1) asylum policy;
(2) rules governing the crossing by persons of the external borders of the Member States and the exercise of the controls thereon;
(3) immigration policy and policy regarding nationals of third countries;
(a) condition of entry and movement by nationals of third countries on the territory of Member States;
(b) conditions of residence by nationals of third countries on the territory of Member States, including family reunion and access to employment;
(c) combating unauthorized immigration, residence and work by nationals of third countries on the territory of Member States;
(4) combating drug addiction in so far as this is not covered by 7 to 9;
(5) combating fraud on an international scale in so far as this is not covered by 7 to 9;
(6) judicial cooperation in civil matters.

Before the Community starts to act in these areas pursuant to Article 100c EC Treaty, Member States shall inform and consult one another within the Council with a view to coordinating their action (Article K.3(1) TEU). In response to an initiative of any Member State or the Commission, the Council may adopt joint positions and joint actions in so far as the objectives of the Union can be better attained by joint action than by the Member States acting individually on account of the scale or effects of the actions envisaged (principle of subsidiarity). The Council may also draw up conventions which it shall recommend to the Member States for adoption in accordance with their respective constitutional requirements (Article K.3(2) TEU).

Common action is particularly urgent in the field of asylum policy. This preoccupation of the Member States is reflected in their Declaration on Asylum, which has been annexed to the TEU:[4]

1. The Conference agrees that, in the context of the proceedings provided for in articles K.1 and K.3 of the provisions on cooperation in the fields of justice and home affairs, the Council will consider as a matter of priority questions concerning Member States' asylum policies, with the aim of adoption, by the beginning of 1993, common action to harmonise aspects of them, in the light of the work program and timetable contained in the report on asylum drawn up at the request of the European Council meeting in Luxembourg on 28–29 June 1991.

2. In this connection, the Council will consider, by the end of 1993, on the basis of a report, the possibility of applying Article K.9 to such matters.

Article K.3 shows that immigration policy as such remains within the authority of the Member States. As under the original EC Treaty, immigration of third-country nationals therefore does not fall within the powers of the EC. The authority of the Community to regulate the entry and residence of migrants from non-member countries cannot be derived from Article 48 et seq. in conjunction with Article 3(c) nor from Article 100 or 113 EC Treaty.[5] It has, however, been suggested that the creation of an internal market envisaged by Article 7a EC Treaty might lead to an extension of the powers of the Community in this field, because it will require a common policy *vis-à-vis* nationals of third states, especially in the field of visa requirements (now Article 100c)

---

[4] 31 I.L.M. 374 (1992).

[5] Hailbronner, *Möglichkeiten und Grenzen einer europäischen Koordinierung des Einreise- und Asylrechts: ihre Auswirkungen auf das Asylrecht der Bundesrepublik Deutschland* (1989), p. 194 passim; Hailbronner in Hailbronner, Klein, Magiera, and Müller-Graff (eds), *Handkommentar zum EWG-Vertrag, Art. 49/9* (1991); Hilf, 'Europäisches Gemeinschaftsrecht und Drittstaatsangehörige', in Hailbronner et al. (eds), *Staat und Völkerrechtsordnung, Festschrift für K. Doehring*, pp. 339–364; Hoogenboom, 'The Position of Those who are not Nationals of a Community Member State', in Cassese, Clapham and Weiler (eds), *Human Rights and the European Community: Methods of Protection* (1991), vol. II, pp. 351–422, at p. 394.

and employment.[6] Article 7a EC Treaty, which was introduced by the Single European Act (SEA), provides for the creation of an internal market by the end of 1992, comprising 'an area without internal frontiers in which the free movement of goods, persons, services and capital is ensured in accordance with the provisions of this Treaty'. In line with this view, the Commission envisaged in its 1985 White Book on the Completion of the Internal Market a harmonization of national legislation on asylum, entry, residence and access to employment of non-Community nationals.[7]

However, the Member States have remained reluctant to cede their sovereignty in these sensitive areas. In the General Declaration on Articles 13–19 SEA,[8] they emphasized that their right 'to take such measures as they consider necessary for the purpose of controlling immigration from third countries' should not be affected by the provisions of the SEA. Additionally, in a political declaration on the free movement of persons, the governments of the Member States affirmed that 'in order to promote the free movement of persons, the Member States shall cooperate, without prejudice to the powers of the Community, in particular as regards the entry, movement and residence of nationals of third countries.'[9] Both declarations are evidence of the intention of the Member States not to surrender their powers of controlling the migration of non-EC nationals. The mention of the powers of the Community in these declarations must be understood as referring to the powers explicitly transferred to the Community. The General Declaration constitutes an 'agreement relating to the treaty which was made between all the parties in connection with the conclusion of the treaty'[10] which has to be taken into account when

---

[6] Mattera, 'L'achèvement du marché intérieur et ses implications sur les relations extérieures', in Demaret (ed.), *Relations extérieures de la Communauté européenne et marché intérieur: aspects juridiques et fonctionnels* (1988), Colloque 1986, Collège d'Europe no. 45, pp. 217–218; Constantinesco, 'Les compétences internationales de la Communauté et des Etats membres à travers l'Acte Unique Européen', in ibid., pp. 63, 68; Ehlermann, 'L'Acte unique et les compétences externes de la Communauté: un progrès?', in ibid., pp. 79, 88; see also Lobkowicz, 'Quelle libre circulation des personnes en 1993?', (1990) *Revue du marché commun et de l'union européenne*, No. 334, 93–102, at 96–97.

[7] Commission des Communautés européennes (see also Commission of the European Communities), L'achèvement du marché intérieur, Livre blanc de la Commission à l'intention du Conseil européen (Milan, 28–29 juin 1985), COM (85) 310 final, Bruxelles 14 juin 1985, 15.

[8] 25 I.L.M. 504 (1986).

[9] 25 I.L.M. 505 (1986).

[10] Art. 31(2)(a) of the Vienna Convention on the Law of Treaties.

interpreting the relevant provisions of the SEA.[11]

So far, attempts made by the Commission to assert its authority in this field have met considerable resistance from Member States.[12] A draft for a directive to coordinate the rules governing the right of asylum circulated in 1988 was not even formally presented to the Council.[13] Member States also opposed the decision of the Commission to set up a prior communication and cooperation procedure on migration policies in relation to non-member states, which was based on Article 118 EC Treaty. In its judgment of 9 July 1987,[14] the Court of Justice of the European Communities (ECJ) did not rule directly on the scope of Article 8a (now Article 7a) EC Treaty. Nevertheless, it recognized the sole responsibility of Member States to take measures with regard to workers who are nationals of non-member countries, either by adopting national rules or by negotiating international agreements, which are based on considerations of public policy, public security and public health (para. 25). Recently, the Commission adopted a more cautious position. In its report of 16 January 1989 on the abolition of border checks on persons, while maintaining its interpretation of the amended EC Treaty, it proposed that henceforth Community legislation should only be enacted in those areas where legal certainty and the uniformity inherent in it are the best means of achieving the desired objectives.[15]

As far as the general power of regulating the legal position of nationals from third countries is concerned, it therefore seems to be appropriate to draw a distinction between the free movement of aliens already residing lawfully in the Community and the first admission of nationals from third countries to the territory of one of the Member States. With regard to the latter, the authority of the Community may

---

[11] Hailbronner, *Möglichkeiten und Grenzen*, p. 199; Herdegen, 'Auslegende Erklärungen von Gemeinschaftsorganen und Mitgliedsstaaten zu EG-Rechtsakten', 155 *Zeitschrift für das gesamte Handelsrecht und Wirtschaftsrecht* (1991), 52–67, at 59–60; Opinion of Advocate General Mancini, Joined Cases 281, 283–285/85 and 287/85, *Federal Republic of Germany and Others* v *Commission of the European Communities*, [1987] ECR 3203, 3229.

[12] E.g., the proposals of directives to combat illegal immigration and illegal employment, O.J. 1976, C 277/2 and O.J. 1978, C 97/9.

[13] Plender, 'The Circulation of Persons and Services', in Hague Academy of International Law (ed.), *The Peaceful Settlement of International Disputes in Europe: Future Prospects* (1991), pp. 69–92, pp. 77–78.

[14] Joined Cases 281, 283–285/85 and 287/85, see note 11.

[15] Kommission der Europäischen Gemeinschaften (see also Commission des Communautés européennes and Commission of the European Communities), Bericht der Kommission über die Abschaffung der Personenkontrollen an den innergemeinschaftlichen Grenzen. KOM (88) 640 endg. Brüssel 16. Januar 1989, 4.

only arise if the existence of conflicting national policies in relation to nationals of non-member countries threatens to jeopardize the free movement of persons within the internal market.[16] It is obvious that national migration policies *vis-à-vis* third-country nationals may affect the Community's social and labour market policies.[17] This potential impact of non-EC immigration was recognized by the Council as early as 1974. In its resolution of 21 January 1974 concerning a social action programme,[18] the Council acknowledged the need to promote consultation on immigration policies *vis-à-vis* non-member countries. This view has been reiterated on several occasions.[19] The contested prior communication and consultation procedure on migration policies in relation to non-member countries was finally introduced by a decision of 8 June 1988.[20] According to this decision, Member States are asked to provide in good time, and at the latest at the moment when made public, information concerning:

— draft measures which they intend to take with regard to third-country workers and members of their families, in the areas of entry, residence and employment, including illegal entry, residence and employment, as well as the realization of equality of treatment in living and working conditions, wages and economic rights, the promotion of integration into the workforce and society, and the voluntary return of such persons to their countries of origin;

— draft agreements relating to the above-mentioned matters, as well as draft cooperation agreements which they intend to negotiate or renegotiate with third countries, when these agreements involve provisions relating to the above-mentioned matters;

— draft agreements relating to conditions of residence of their nationals working in third countries and members of their families, which they intend to negotiate or renegotiate with those countries.

These developments show that national regulations concerning aliens and asylum seekers can no longer be enacted without having due regard for the common policies and actions taken at the Community

---

[16] Hilf, 'Europäisches Gemeinschaftsrecht' p. 352; Pipkorn, in von der Groeben, Thiesing and Ehlermann (eds), *Kommentar zum EWG-Vertrag* (1991), p. 199.

[17] Joined Cases 281, 283–285/85 and 287/85, see note 11, paras 16–17.

[18] O.J. 1974, C 13/1.

[19] E.g., Resolution of 9 Feb. 1976 on an action programme for migrant workers and members of their families, O.J. 1976, C 34/2; Resolution of 27 June 1980 on guidelines for a Community labour market policy, O.J. 1980, C 168/1; Resolution of 16 July 1985 on guidelines for a Community policy on migration, O.J. 1985, C 186/3.

[20] O.J. 1988, L 183/35.

level. Even in the absence of a general Community authority to regulate in these matters, Member States must cooperate with one another and the Community in order to coordinate their policies.

National migration policies of the Member States must respect their obligations under the EC Treaty, which accords priority to Community nationals with regard to access to employment and to establishment. Their position cannot be totally separated from that of non-EC nationals. Since both compete within the same labour market, the treatment accorded to migrants from third countries may have serious repercussions on the situation of nationals of other Member States.[21] Two provisions of the EC Treaty may be referred to in this respect. According to Article 5(2) EC Treaty, Member States shall refrain from any measure which could jeopardize the attainment of its objectives. Article 234(3) EC Treaty makes it clear that Member States must not extend the advantages granted to each other within the framework of this Treaty to other countries or their nationals.[22] Therefore, Member States are required to refrain from adopting measures which are likely to hinder the free movement of workers from the other Community countries or to compromise the common policy agreed upon by the Community. This view has been confirmed by the Court of Justice of the European Communities in its judgment of 9 July 1987 concerning the prior communication and consultation procedure on migration policy in relation to non-member countries.[23] There the ECJ stated:

> that the employment situation and, more generally, the improvement of living and working conditions within the Community are liable to be affected by the policy pursued by the Member States with regard to workers from non-member countries ... the Commission rightly considers that it is important to ensure that the migration policies of Member States in relation to non-member countries take into account both common policies and the actions taken at Community level, in particular within the framework of Community labour market policy, in order not to jeopardize the results. (para. 16)

Additionally, the powers of the Community may be used to harmonize certain aspects of the law concerning aliens and asylum seekers. The distinction between the powers of the Community in the area of labour

---

[21] Greenwood, 'Nationality and the Limits of the Free Movement of Persons in Community Law', 7 YEL (1987), 185–208; Hilf, 'Europäisches Gemeinschaftsrecht', pp. 339, 351; Wölker, in von der Groeben et al. (eds), *Kommentar zum EWG-Vertrag*, p. 841.

[22] Smits and Herzog (eds), *The Law of the European Economic Community. A Commentary on the EEC Treaty* (1991), 6 Vols, 234.03.

[23] Joined Cases 281, 283–285/85 and 287/85, see note 11.

market and social and migration policy, subject to intergovernmental cooperation (Article K.3 TEU), may not be easy to draw. Under Articles 49 and 7a EC Treaty, the Community claims a power of regulating access to the labour market of third-country nationals who are already residing in the territory of one of the Member States.[24] Measures concerning non-Community nationals may also be taken within the ambit of social policy (Article 117 et seq. EC Treaty). In the above-mentioned judgment of 9 July 1987, the ECJ concluded that migration policy was capable of falling within the ambit of Article 118 EC Treaty to the extent that it concerned the impact of workers from non-member countries on the employment market and on working conditions in the Community (para. 23).

2.2 Migration and Association agreements

Beyond the framework of social policy (Article 118), the ECJ has also attributed a power to the Community for regulating the legal structure of third-state nationals within the EEC under Article 238 (Association agreements with third states). In the *Demirel* case concerning the right of a Turkish worker's wife to move to Germany to join her husband, the ECJ rejected the argument that the EC Treaty does not provide for the authority to regulate the entry and stay of nationals of EC-associated states.[25] The ECJ concluded from Article 238 that an agreement of association does create a special relationship between the EC and the associated state covering all areas regulated in the EC Treaty including the freedom of movement for workers. Article 238 is, therefore, interpreted as implying the authority to extend the market freedoms to nationals of associated states as part of an association treaty. Finally, if there is agreement between all the Member States as to the necessity of a common policy, Articles 100 et seq. and 235 EC Treaty may be used to implement this policy.[26]

The provision in the Association agreement with Turkey whereby the parties agreed to be guided by Articles 48 et seq. EC Treaty for the purpose of progressively securing freedom of movement to workers between them until the end of 1986 was declared as not directly applicable within the domestic legal order of the Member States. The ECJ held that the Association agreement and an additional protocol fixing the time-limit were not sufficiently precise to grant individual rights to Turkish workers.

---

[24] Wölker, in von der Groeben et al. (eds), *Kommentar zum EWG-Vertrag*, p. 841.

[25] Case 12/86, *Meryem Demirel v Stadt Schwäbisch Gmünd*, [1987] ECR 3719.

[26] Hailbronner, *Möglichkeiten und Grenzen*, p. 201.

The Additional Protocol gives the Council of the Association power to lay down rules for the attainment of freedom of movement. Since the original assumptions of both parties concerning the economic and political assimilation of Turkey to EC standards could not be realized, the Council only reached consensus in 1976 and 1980 on the right of Turkish workers after five or four years lawful residence and employment in a Member State to enjoy free access to any paid employment of his choice in that state. Both Council decisions were clearly limited to the access to employment. Due to a stalemate in the negotiations between Turkey and the European Community no consensus could be reached on the freedom of movement. The ECJ nevertheless in a methodologically doubtful reasoning did imply a right of residence for Turkish workers from these Council decisions.[27] The ECJ's argument that, without the existence of a right of residence for Turkish workers lawfully established in a Member State, the right of access to employment would be useless, does not sufficiently take into account that within the labour market of the Member States preference is given to EC nationals. Equal access to employment, therefore, is a privilege not necessarily connected with a right of residence. The most one could have concluded from the Council's decisions was an obligation by Member States not to frustrate the right of access to employment by terminating a lawful stay of a Turkish worker exclusively based on labour market considerations.

In addition, the ECJ neglected the fact that the unpublished decisions of the Association-Council explicitly provided for further implementation by regulations of the Member States. Association law is clearly intended by the Member States to be incomplete in the sense that no individual rights could be inferred from the Council's decisions. The ECJ, brushing aside the Member States' intention, applied the same principles as in the case of EC law proper. It overlooked that there are substantial differences between EC regulations on freedom of movement and contractual obligations with third states on access to employment. The ECJ, arguing as if Turkey were already part of the European Community by applying identical rules, ignored the different concepts of a progressive and dynamic Community legal order and the limited framework of Association law. Therefore, general principles of public international law on the interpretation of treaties as well as the principle of reciprocity were disregarded by applying EC rules to Association law.

Recently, the ECJ went even further in deciding on an equal

---

[27] Case 192/89, *S.Z. Sevince* v *Staatssecretaris van Justitie*, [1990] ECR 3461, 3497.

treatment clause in the cooperation agreement between the EC and Morocco.[28] The clause, like many other provisions in cooperation agreements with the EC, provided in the field of social security for the same treatment for migrant workers and members of their families as nationals of the Member States in which they are employed. Mrs Kziber, a Moroccan national, living in Belgium, after the retirement of her father, who had been working in Belgium, applied for special unemployment benefits for school leavers, which the ECJ designated as a social benefit within the meaning of Article 7, para. 2, of Regulation 1612/68 applicable to EC migrant workers. Following the same reasoning as in the *Sevince* decision, the ECJ held that the equal treatment clause does grant individual rights in the Member States and is sufficiently precise to be applied without further implementation measures by Member States. Again, no reasons were given as to why the equal treatment clause was interpreted in the same extensive meaning as the equal treatment clauses in Community law. Originally the ECJ had justified a wide interpretation of the social benefit clause in the basic regulation 1612/68 by arguing that in order fully to complete the freedom of movement within the Community, every discrimination in social rights and benefits has to be abolished as a possible obstacle preventing EC nationals from making use of the freedom of movement. By applying the same rules to the cooperation agreement the ECJ has neglected the essential distinction between the legal status of non-EC nationals under a cooperation agreement and EC nationals relying directly on the freedom of movement guarantee as a basic individual right in the EC Treaty. There is no freedom of movement for non-EC nationals. Social rights, therefore, cannot be interpreted as auxiliary means of achieving a market freedom for non-EC nationals.

The ECJ should have interpreted the clause in the context of the cooperation agreement and based on the general principles of treaty law as laid down in Article 31 of the Vienna Convention on the Law of Treaties. As was pointed out by the French government, there was never any intention to include unemployment benefits in the cooperation agreement with Morocco as is apparent from the context of various provisions of the cooperation agreement as well as from the fact that there are no unemployment benefits in Morocco.[29]

---

[28] Case C-18/90, *Office national de l'emploi (Onem)* v *Bahia Kziber*, [1991] ECR 199, 221; cf. Alexander, 'Free Movement of Non-EC Nationals: a review of the case-law of the Court of Justice', 3 EJIL (1992), 53–64, at 62.

[29] Cf. Conclusions by Advocate General van Gerven in [1991] ECR 208, 216 et seq.

3 INTERGOVERNMENTAL COOPERATION

So far, the Member States have shown a certain preference to cooperate in this field through intergovernmental negotiation outside the framework of the Treaties. On 14 June 1985, Belgium, France, Germany, Luxembourg and The Netherlands concluded the so-called Schengen Agreement concerning the gradual abolition of controls at their common frontiers.[30] This framework agreement has been complemented by the Convention Applying the Schengen Agreement on the Gradual Abolition of Checks at their Common Borders, which was signed by the same parties on 19 June 1990.[31] Italy acceded to both the Agreement and the Convention on 17 November 1990. Portugal and Spain did so on 25 June 1991. Greece acceded to the Convention in November 1992. The Convention came into force for the five signatory states on 1 September 1993, for Spain and Portugal on 1 March 1994. To become applicable in its substantive parts the Convention prescribes a formal decision that all conditions for applying the Convention in the legal order of the Contracting States are met and that controls at the external borders are indeed carried out in accordance with the provisions of the Convention. Due to difficulties with the establishment of the Schengen Information System the Convention as yet is not fully applicable.

The Schengen Agreements are generally regarded as having a 'pilot function' with regard to future EC legislation.[32] Their main aim is the abolition of border checks on persons at the internal borders of the Member States. Uniform principles on the control of persons at external borders including airports were agreed upon in the 1990 Convention (Article 6). This Convention also envisages a common policy on the movement of persons and in particular on the arrangements for visas, in so far as these are issued on the basis of common conditions and criteria which will be determined jointly (Article 10 et seq.). The Convention aims at realizing a certain free movement of non-Community

---

[30] 30 I.L.M. 68 (1991).

[31] 30 I.L.M. 84 (1991); see, for an analysis of different aspects of this Convention, the contributions in Meijers et al. (eds), *Schengen. Internationalisation of Central Chapters of the Law on Aliens, Refugees, Security and the Police* (1991); Weichert, 'Drittausländer in der Europäischen Gemeinschaft (EG)', Informationsbrief Ausländerrecht (1990), 259 passim; Malangré, 'Entwurf eines Berichts über den freien Personenverkehr und die Sicherheit in der Europäischen Gemeinschaft, Europäisches Parlament—Ausschuß für Recht und Bürgerrechte', DOC-DE\PR\105260, 1 March 1991, 8–16.

[32] This term was used by the Commission, see *Agence Europe*, 16 Dec. 1989, 17; Hoogenboom, 'Free Movement of Non-EC Nationals, Schengen and beyond', in Meijers et al. (eds), *Schengen*, pp. 74–95, at p. 83.

nationals who have legally entered the territory of one of the Contracting States or are residing therein (Article 19 et seq.).[33] Furthermore, there are detailed provisions about the cooperation of national police authorities (Article 39 et seq.) and the installation of a joint information system (Article 92 et seq.).

As far as asylum laws are concerned, the Schengen Agreements have been complemented by the Convention Determining the State Responsible for Examining Applications for Asylum Lodged in one of the Member States of the European Communities, which was signed in Dublin on 15 June 1990.[34] This Convention has been signed by all Member States. However, neither the Dublin Convention nor the 1990 Schengen Convention have led to a harmonization in the sense of an adjustment of substantive and procedural law. It is the basic idea of both Conventions to make the examination of an application for asylum —and possibly even the execution of measures to terminate the stay—fall within a single state's jurisdiction. This state shall be determined according to objective criteria indicating the state's explicit or tacit agreement to the asylum seeker's entry to its territory. The most important among them are (in order of diminishing importance): the granting of a residence permit, the granting of a visa, illegal entry or *de facto* residence.

Both the 1990 Schengen Convention and the Dublin Convention are based on reciprocal trust in the equivalency of the different national asylum procedures. In line with this view, the Commission based its communiqué of 11 October 1991 on the principle of the mutual recognition of asylum decisions.[35] This means that Member States should no longer be allowed to fall back on the primacy of national law. Currently, however, both Conventions allow for a divergence in the applicable systems of jurisdiction.[36] It will be up to each Member State to go through asylum procedures according to its own laws, possibly even notwithstanding the completion of proceedings in other Member States.

The planned lifting of border controls within the Community by the end of 1992 also prompted negotiations on a Convention on the

---

[33] Cf. Schutte, 'Schengen: Its Meaning for the Free Movement of Persons in Europe', 28 CML Rev. (1991), 549–570, at 552–554.

[34] 30 I.L.M. 425 (1991).

[35] Communication of the Commission to the Council and the European Parliament 5 [SEC (91) 1857] final, 11 Oct. 1991, 5.

[36] Cf. Weckel, 'La Convention additionnelle à l'accord de Schengen', 95 *Revue générale de droit international public* (1991), 403–437, at 414–417.

Crossing of External Frontiers, which is to be signed by all Member States.[37] The draft agreement, which was due to be signed in June 1991 provides for uniform rules on controls at the Community's outer borders (Article 4 et seq.) and envisages a harmonization of visa regulations (Article 16 et seq.). Under the common visa policy, a list of countries subject to visa requirements and a blacklist of undesired persons will be drawn up. Non-EC nationals who are in possession of a visa issued by one Member State would be free to enter another Member State for a stay of less than three months without taking up employment (Article 17). So far, the draft Convention has not been signed because of disagreement between Spain and the United Kingdom over the question of Gibraltar.[38] The Commission, based on Article K TEU has proposed a draft version of the Convention.[39]

There is also disagreement between a majority of EC Member States and the United Kingdom on the impact of the decision to harmonize controls at external borders while abolishing national border controls. The British government has announced that it will keep border controls at all British frontiers in order to supervise nationals of third states not entitled to freedom of movement. The United Kingdom takes the view that the completion of the single market as defined in Article 8a must not result in a *de facto* extension of the principle of freedom of movement for non-Community natives resident in Member States.[40]

4   A COMMUNITY REGIME OF THIRD-COUNTRY NATIONALS

4.1 Freedom of movement for third-country nationals?

The pledge of European solidarity in dealing with refugee and immigration problems cannot hide the fact that these matters are closely connected with national perceptions. However, in recent years, Member States have increasingly become aware that issues of immigration and asylum cannot be dealt with exclusively on the national level.[41] Uncoordinated national immigration and asylum policies are no longer

---

[37] Communication of the Commission in note 35 above, 17; Plender, 'The circulation of Persons', p. 80.

[38] Cf. *Financial Times*, 12 June 1992, 2.

[39] COM (93) final; O.J. 1994, C 11/16.

[40] *Europe*, 14 June 1991, 1.

[41] Ad-hoc-Gruppe 'Einwanderung', Bericht der für Einwanderungfragen zuständigen Minister an den Europäischen Rat (Maastricht) über die Einwanderungs- und Asylpolitik, Brussels, 3 Dec. 1991, 2.

acceptable.[42] With the realization of the single market and the elimination of controls at the Community's internal borders, detrimental effects of insufficiently coordinated measures to implement migration and asylum policies are multiplied. The danger of people taking advantage of different regulations and thereby undercutting national immigration rules is growing. The achievement of the economic and political aims of the Community—free movement of persons, transparency of the labour market, and political unity—are endangered if each state sets different priorities in its policy of asylum. It is irreconcilable with the idea of a single territory offering common legal and economic conditions that aliens and refugees are accepted or rejected in the light of different procedures.

As far as a future Community regime is concerned, there is a strong tendency to grant third-country nationals who are permanently residing within the Community the same rights and benefits as are currently enjoyed by nationals of Member States.[43] As early as 1985, the European Parliament demanded that the rights enjoyed by migrant workers within the Community be extended to workers from non-Community countries (Resolutions of 9 May 1985, O.J. 1985, C 141/462). In its Resolution of 14 June 1990 on migrant workers from third countries,[44] this view was reiterated, albeit in more cautious terms:

> The European Parliament ...
> Considers that there is an urgent need to tackle the problem at Community level so as to establish a definition of Community policy on the subject and examine the possibility of gradually extending the rights evolving on EEC migrant workers, taking in particular account of the following aspects:
> — the entry and residence of workers in Community countries, including the right to reunite families, as laid down in Regulation 1612/68,
> — the free movement of persons throughout the territory of the Community,
> — access to employment and living, working and housing conditions,
> — social rights and social protection,
> — the right to education, continuing training and vocational skills,
> — social integration,
> — the position of female immigrants from third countries,

---

[42] Cf. Hailbronner, 'Wenn immer mehr kommen. Fragen einer europäischen Harmonisierung des Asylrechts', *Frankfurter Allgemeine Zeitung*, 21 April 1992, 12.

[43] See, most recently, 'Immigration and Employment', Working Document of the Commission summarized in *Agence Europe*, 15 May 1992, 11–12; Ad-hoc-Gruppe 'Einwanderung', 5.

[44] O.J. 1990, C 175/180.

— the right to vote in local elections.

In 1990, the European Parliament proposed extending the scope of application of Regulation (EEC) No. 1612/68 on freedom of movement for workers within the Community to second-generation immigrants from non-Community countries as well as to refugees and stateless persons.[45] Similar proposals have been made with regard to two of the three directives on the right of residence for persons who do not enjoy this right under other provisions of Community law.[46] The European Parliament proposed that these directives also be applied to political refugees, stateless persons and non-Community nationals who have lived on a regular basis in a Member State since before the age of six. These initiatives have, however, not succeeded. In their adopted version, both directives expressly confine the right of residence to nationals of the Member States and to members of their families.[47]

Nevertheless, in a communication to the Council and the European Parliament on immigration of 23 October 1991, the Commission reiterated its belief that, within the internal market, freedom of movement will have to be ensured for all. This does not mean, however, that non-EC nationals legally resident in one Member State will have the freedom to settle in every other Member State.[48] The criteria for entry, residence and access to employment of third-country nationals should be harmonized.[49] An additional convention may be called for in order to lay down common principles and procedures for the repatriation of immigrants in an irregular situation. Such an agreement could be supplemented by bilateral or Community agreements with non-EC countries providing for the deportation of irregular immigrants to their country of origin.[50]

It is very doubtful whether freedom of movement for non-EC nationals resident in the Community will be granted without making further progress towards a European coordination of migration policy, cooperation in police matters and at least a basic coordination of social schemes. Presently, the social systems of the EC Member States differ widely. There is consensus that harmonization cannot be achieved

---

[45] O.J. 1990, C 68/88–93.

[46] O.J. 1990, C 175/84 and 90.

[47] Cf. Art. 1 of Council Directives 90/364 and 90/365 of 28 June 1990 (O.J. 1990, L 180/26 and 28).

[48] Communication of the Commission, in note 35 above, 16.

[49] Ad-hoc-Gruppe 'Einwanderung', 5 and 25–26.

[50] Communication of the Commission in note 35 above, 22.

easily. In advocating equal treatment of non-EC nationals, one must take into account that freedom of movement for EC nationals implies not only a right of residence but also equal treatment in social rights embracing literally every social benefit granted by a Member State such as a minimum salary, financial assistance for families with children or unemployment payments or university scholarships. Social security benefits as regulated by the ordinance 1408/71 may also be transferred abroad. Family allowances, therefore, have to be paid in the same amount to EC nationals for children living in their home countries regardless of different standards of living and salaries. Recently, the ECJ has decided that the children of migrant workers may claim financial assistance to pursue their university studies even in their home country if a Member State grants financial assistance to its own nationals for university training abroad.[51] To an increasing degree, indirect social benefits, like tax reductions, dependent upon domestic situations such as the conclusion of an insurance contract, are coming under heavy attack as a disguised violation of the equal treatment clauses of EC law. The Commission wants to extend indirect benefits beyond its original territorial limits.[52]

Within the Community, Member States claim that a too extensive interpretation of the equal treatment clauses by the ECJ as part of the freedom of movement concept may put a heavy strain on the stability of the social systems of some Member States. An extended application of the freedom of movement concept by Community regulations to non-EC nationals could endanger the functioning of the system.[53] Equal treatment of non-EC nationals has to be agreed upon in bilateral agreements on the basis of the principle of reciprocity. It should be limited to particular matters like social security or employment conditions according to the different economic, social and political situation in each particular country. A global transfer of the Community's wide concept of freedom of movement to non-EC nationals risks neglecting the basic premises upon which the freedom of movement

---

[51] Case 308/89, *Carmina Di Leo* v *Land Berlin*, [1990] ECR, 4185, 4204; see also decisions of 26 Feb. 1989, Case 357/89, *V.J.M. Raulin* v *Minister van Onderwijs en Wetenschappen*, [1992] ECR I-1027; and Case 3/90, *M.J.E. Bernini* v *Minister van Onderwijs en Wetenschappen*, [1992] ECR I-1071.

[52] See, however, Decision of 28 Jan. 1992, Case 204/90, *Bachmann*, [1992] ECR 249, 276, whereby a different treatment concerning tax deductible insurance fees may exceptionally be justified by the necessity of guaranteeing the 'coherence' of the different taxation systems.

[53] For a different view see Hoogenboom, 'Symposium: The Status on Non-Community Nationals in Community Law', 3 EJIL (1992), 36–52.

and equal treatment of EC nationals within the Community rests.

For that reason, until now, initiatives at the Community level have mainly been designed to promote concerted migration policies through the Community's power to regulate the labour market.[54] The information and consultation mechanism which has been established under Article 118 EC Treaty[55] could provide a suitable framework for facilitating the integration of legal immigrants. In its Communication of 23 October 1991, the Commission emphasized that the full integration of such persons can only be achieved by strengthening their legal position. Without going so far as to call for a right of establishment which would automatically extend to the whole Community, it declared equality of treatment for aliens residing lawfully in one of the Member States to be a fundamental objective for the whole of society.[56] In the field of social security, the Commission also favours an equal treatment of workers from third countries residing lawfully in the territory of Member States.[57] At the same time, the Commission intends to propose measures to combat illegal immigration. A revised version of its proposal on the approximation of Member States' legislation in this field and the attendant question of unauthorized work may soon be submitted.[58] Such a directive might be based on Article 49 EC Treaty.[59]

4.2 The prospect of intergovernmental cooperation

However, it remains unlikely that the main areas of migration policy will be regulated by uniform Community legislation. The possibility of granting the Community regulatory powers by Article K.9 TEU without a formal amendment will most likely not be used in the near future. A meeting of EC ministers of the interior on immigration and crime, which was held in Lisbon on 11–12 June 1992, clearly confirmed the preference of Member States for intergovernmental cooperation in the

---

[54] Commission of the European Communities in note 15 above.

[55] Decision of 8 June 1988, O.J. 1988, L 183/35.

[56] Communication of the Commission in note 35 above, 24.

[57] Commission des Communautés européennes, 'L'achèvement du marché intérieur: Un espace sans frontière intérieures, Rapport sur l'état des travaux requis par l'article 8b du Traité'. COM (90) 552 final. Bruxelles 23 novembre 1990, 35; Hoogenboom, in Meijers et al. (eds), *Schengen*, p. 91.

[58] Communication of the Commission in note 35 above, 21.

[59] Wölker, in von der Groeben et al. (eds), *Kommentar zum EWG-Vertrag*, p. 842.

field of immigration and judicial policy.[60] The report of the ministers responsible for immigration and asylum policy of 3 December 1991, as well as its update of December 1993, indicate a preference for a coordination of immigration policies of the Member States in the area of control of illegal immigration, and secondly in the regulation of the legal status of nationals of third states legally resident within one Member State of the Community. It is assumed that immigration pressure into the European Union will come primarily from the Americas, Eastern Europe and other countries in Africa, Asia and other parts of the world from which either most asylum seekers come or to which some Member States have traditionally maintained a particularly close relationship. The report identifies a trend towards increased immigration to those countries in which there are already a substantial number of people of the same nationality. Special attention is to be devoted to this phenomenon.

The report envisages a coordinated (restrictive) policy on the admission of nationals of third states on the basis of demographic studies, common practices concerning the entry of spouses and children of resident workers as well as students and trainees, and, finally, the granting of residence permits for humanitarian reasons. To achieve a consensus on certain common standards on family union seems to be easier than achieving a coordination of admission on humanitarian grounds. The establishment of new legal obligations of EC Member States to admit foreigners for particular humanitarian reasons is strongly objected to by almost all EC countries. On the other hand, a common European policy in dealing with people leaving their home countries for reasons of war, civil war, famine or other compelling reasons appears to be desirable if one takes seriously political statements on European solidarity and burden sharing.

The immigration ministers' report discusses possible changes in the existing Community system on the labour market in order to improve the system's ability to react to changes in labour demands. As soon as the freedom of movement for workers is fully realized, an extension of the EC system to legally resident foreign workers from third states will be considered. This could imply, for instance, that employers have to make use of a European labour registration system before resorting to outside EC labour resources (concept of second preference).

The report generally underlines the difficulties inherent in an improvement of rights granted to nationals of third states. It is essential that possible implications of an enlargement of rights for nationals of

---

[60] *Financial Times*, 13–14 June 1992, 2; see also Commission of the European Communities in note 35 above, 7–8.

third states are worked out. All Member States will have to trust each other on their immigration policy decisions in order to stem possible adverse effects of changes on the immigration and integration policy of other states. It is, therefore, essential to make an inventory and balance sheet of possible improvements in different fields (social rights, labour market, integration programmes, education and training), and adopt a flexible approach. The fact that the ERASMUS programme is already open for nationals of third states, for instance, seems to present no major problems for the Member States. In a similar way, other EC programmes have been opened for nationals of third states legally resident in one Member State. A priority could also be established for the labour market provided that no EC citizen can be found. A programme gradually to improve the legal status of third-state nationals may also provide for different treatment according to the time spent within the EC.

Concerning the rights of foreign residents for a prolongation of their residence permits, and the termination of residence, the ministers consider a coordination of national laws as unsuitable in the short run, since the regulation of the legal status of nationals of third states is considered as being primarily a matter of national public order. The immigration ministers, however, do not ignore the implication of these issues for the achievement of the Community's aims. Different types of intra-Community migration of third-state nationals can be distinguished in this context:

1 Legal migration from one EC country to another in the framework of generally applicable national regulations for the purpose of family union. They are to be dealt with within the ambit of efforts to achieve a consensus for common criteria for admission of nationals of third states.

2 Illegal movements of third-country nationals including foreigners having entered the European Community illegally or those who move after a termination of their residence permit or who are for other reasons in another EC country illegally.

Measures against illegal immigration into the European Community are considered to be of primary importance. European coordination in controlling borders is regarded as essential, particularly in the context of the Convention on the Crossing of External Frontiers. Control of borders, however, cannot be deemed as sufficient to cope effectively with the problem of illegal immigration. Supervision of foreigners having illegally entered the European Community is also an essential element of a harmonized European immigration policy. In addition, the report rightly criticizes the policies adopted by some Member States in recent years for giving a strong incentive to further illegal immigration by repeated 'legalization programs'. Social rights granted to illegal immigrants also tend to promote illegal immigration while for humanitarian reasons exceptions will always have to be made for foreigners staying illegally within the European Community. Common European standards, however, are considered necessary to restrict illegal residence, and to prevent economic exploitation of illegal immigrants. Finally, the immigration ministers have emphasized the desirability of developing a common European policy for the return of illegal aliens including procedural standards for persons facing expulsion.

In this context also return agreements with third states are envisaged as an essential element in fighting illegal immigration. An agreement of December 1991 between Spain and Morocco on the circulation of persons, transit and readmission of illegal immigrants provides for the obligation to readmit those persons who have crossed the border illegally from one Contracting State to the other, provided certain procedural requirements are met. A similar agreement has been concluded by the Schengen States with Poland. It is expected that similar agreements will be concluded with other states.

The range of measures referred to in the immigration ministers' report of 1991 is not yet adequate to cope with all the problems arising from the abolition of border controls, and the fact that nationals of third states will be able to move freely within the European Community once internal border controls have been abolished. The very fact that administrative acts terminating an alien's right of residence are only enforceable within the country of permanent residence considerably weakens the efficacy of national alien policy. Therefore, a European recognition of the enforcement of administrative acts parallel to some asylum decisions will have to be envisaged.

4.3 Recent developments

In the priority work programme from 1994[61] the European Council has announced the following priority actions in the field of immigration:

> Adaptation to the draft Convention on the crossing of external frontiers further to the entry into force of the Treaty on European Union, signing of the draft and completion of current proceedings on application of the draft;

---

[61] DOC 10684/92 of 2 Dec. 1993.

Examination of Commission proposals on visas;
Completion of proceedings on admission (self-employed persons, employees and students);
Readmission
= Monitoring, particularly with the aid of the HCR, the return to sensitive countries of aliens who have to be expelled;
= Examination of the situation of persons who, for one reason or another, cannot be expelled;
Consultation and cooperation on the execution of expulsion measures;
Study on the improvement of Member States' methods of checking up on illegal aliens with the aim of harmonising the conditions for combating illegal immigration and illegal employment.

Other actions include the drafting of a common handbook for a check at external frontiers and possible harmonization of the position of third-country nationals established on a long-term basis on the territory of Member States.

Harmonization of certain aspects of national immigration policy has achieved some progress in the field of admission. Immigration ministers adopted a Resolution on the admission for family reunion on their meeting in Copenhagen in June 1993. The Resolution, however, does not provide for a full harmonization yet. It deals basically with the admission of spouses and children and leaves it up to the Member States to define policies on the admission of other family members. Not all of the criteria concerning the admission for family reunion have been harmonized; in some cases the Resolution contains only indications, as is, for example, the case for the maximum age limit for the admission of children.

Harmonization of policies on admission for other purposes, such as humanitarian aims and work as an employed or self-employed person, has not made a lot of progress. A first proposal submitted by the UK Presidency has not been agreed upon. The harmonization of legal provisions governing persons authorized to reside has also turned out to be difficult since no agreement as yet can be reached on the criteria under which persons should be allowed to reside permanently.

Harmonization of expulsion policy was the subject of a further recommendation by immigration ministers in June 1993 concerning checks on and expulsion of third-country nationals residing or working without authorization. The Resolution provides for measures to ensure that third-country nationals do not remain beyond the period for which they have been admitted or given permission to remain and that they do not work without authority to do so. Member States shall also examine the types of checks which it would be most appropriate to introduce with a view to detecting third-country nationals who are residing or working illegally, including those persons whose application for asylum has been rejected. In addition, the recommendation of transit for the purposes of expulsion aims for a facilitation of formalities if an expulsion via the territory of another Member State is to be carried out. The Commission in its communication of 23 February 1994 on immigration and asylum policies[62] proposes a comprehensive approach based on three elements:

(a) taking action on migration pressure;
(b) controlling migration flows;
(c) strengthening integration policies for the benefit of legal immigrants.

In the view of the Commission the three elements have to be balanced. The basic philosophy of this approach is that short-term control measures including admission measures need to be matched by long-term cooperation with countries and regions of origin, and an active policy of reinforcing the rights of those already legally residing within the Member States.[63]

As for action on migration pressure, the need for accurate information has been pointed out. A monitoring of migratory movement has already been suggested in the 1991 communication on immigration and the immigration ministers' work programme of 1991. This has led to the setting-up of the Centre for Information, Discussion and Exchange on Asylum (CIREA) and the Centre for Information, Discussion and Exchange on the Crossing of Borders and Immigration (CIREFI). Both forums are informal structures enabling experts to be brought together on an occasional basis. The Commission suggests a new institution—a 'migration observatory'—which would monitor migration flows and patterns on a comprehensive basis and from a Union-wide perspective. It is doubtful whether such a new institution is really needed. The existing institution, including Eurostat, could be developed in order to meet the needs for information.

There is general agreement on a common approach to reduce migration pressure. The Commission suggests coordination of actions in the fields of foreign policy and economic cooperation as well as in immigration and asylum policy. It is suggested that migratory movements might be slowed down by action to reduce economic disparities, by assisting developing countries with their efforts to limit

---

[62] COM (94) 23 final.

[63] Ibid., 11.

population growth and by the provision of appropriate levels of humanitarian assistance. The European Council in December 1992 on British and German initiatives agreed basically on a declaration on these external aspects of migration.

The second element, control of migration flow, is in principle based on the restrictive approach adopted by Member States towards the harmonization of admission policies. The Commission recognizes the work programme adopted by the immigration ministers in December 1991 and updated in December 1993 as the basis for future work. On the other hand, its concrete suggestions are clearly beyond the present stage of discussion between the Member States. A proposal that will certainly raise objections is that third-country nationals already legally resident in the Community should have priority over third-country nationals in access to the employment market. Some Member States insist on their sovereign power to determine the residence rights of non-EC nationals and doubt the reasoning for extending some rights of the citizens of the European Union to resident third-country nationals. The Commission's proposal in the view of the United Kingdom would have an impact on job opportunities for the resident work force and have serious implications for access to social security benefits.

As to the admission policies in respect of students, the Commission suggests that admission policies should be based upon the general principle that a migration which promotes a better understanding and an improved knowledge of each other's societies is to be welcome. It will also be important, however, to avoid policies creating a brain-drain effect on the countries of origin. Hence, according to the Commission, a policy should be developed to prevent people from staying after completion of their studies.

Family reunification is considered of primary importance to third-country nationals legally resident in the Community. Therefore, the Commission proposes a legally binding instrument, such as a convention, which would constitute a formal basis and address remaining differences in the practices of Member States in this regard. This should include waiting periods, definition of maximum age of children entitled to be admitted for a family reunification, policies on family formation as well as policies regarding the admission of unmarried partners and second-degree family members, the admission of adopted children and the legal status of admitted family members.

The third and probably most controversial element concerns integration policy. While the general intention of the Commission to pursue not only an effective immigration policy but also a policy of successfully integrating immigrants into the host society is acknowledged, there will certainly be a wide divergence of views as to what kind of measures should be taken. The report suggests that a successful integration policy must include several components: the first essential element would be the prospect and security of permanent residence status. Security of stay and permanent residence for all those satisfying stability criteria constitute the fundamental prerequisites for successful integration. Special attention has also to be given to the residence status of members of the family of legally resident immigrants. A situation in which family members continue to be dependent on the status of the immigrant, even after a long-term residence, is considered by the Commission as unsatisfactory. Similarly, foreign-born spouses of established immigrants or nationals should enjoy independent residence rights after a qualifying period.

Another equally important element would be the elimination of conditions of nationality for the exercise of certain rights. Only a first step in this respect would be—in the view of the Commission—the enabling of third-country nationals to move freely around within the Union on the basis of their residence permit, which would replace any existing visa requirements. The Commission suggests that such a right of free circulation, which the Schengen Implementation Convention already contains, should be extended to all Member States of the Union. In this respect, as far as the crossing of external frontiers is concerned, it has submitted a proposal giving residence permits of third-country nationals legally resident in one of the Member States the equivalent value of a visa. This proposal is included in a draft Council decision, already submitted to the Council, for a Convention on the crossing of external frontiers of the Member States.[64] The Commission has also announced that it will come forward with a proposal which would allow third-country nationals to enter the territory of another Member State without a visa, even in cases where the Member State concerned would otherwise require a visa for nationals of the third countries in question.

Finally, the Commission points to the different laws covering naturalization and nationality reflecting different historical and philosophical concepts of citizenship. Although the Commission recognizes that the question of nationality must be settled by reference to the laws of the Member State concerned, naturalization is considered an important legal instrument to facilitate the integration of resident immigrants and subsequent generations born in the country. The benefits of naturalization include permanent residence, freedom of movement in the Community and the enjoyment of full civil and

---

[64] COM (93) 684 final, submitted to the Council on 10 Dec. 1993.

political rights. While this idea will provoke no opposition from those Member States granting EC-access to citizenship, it will certainly give rise to a controversial discussion in those countries which are presently considering a change in their naturalization law, such as Germany.

Generally, equality of treatment for legally resident immigrants is laid down as a fundamental objective of the Commission's integration policy. Member States should review their legislation in order to remove those conditions of nationality for the exercise of rights or the granting of benefits which are no longer justified for objective reasons. While this statement will certainly be recognized in matters of remuneration, working conditions and social security for workers, some issues may arise as to equal treatment in matters of social assistance. The Commission announces that it will use the means at its disposal to monitor strict implementation of the provisions of the agreements with third countries providing for equal treatment in the light of the case law of the Court of Justice of the European Communities.

10 MECHANISMS OF PROTECTION OF UNION CITIZENS' RIGHTS

Epaminondas A. Marias

INTRODUCTION

European citizenship[1] is a dynamic institution with an evolving dimension. Introduced by the Maastricht Treaty, it is regarded as the inevitable consequence of the completion of the internal market. As the spill-over effects of economic integration reached the periphery of political integration, the establishment of a supranational European political system became essential. In the framework of this political system, the citizens of the European Union have been called upon to play an important role.

Consequently, the 'market citizen'[2] established in the framework of the European Community, was vested with basic Union rights and arrived at the centre of the political structure of the Union. Thus, the European Union is now based on two vital political cornerstones: Member States, on the one hand, and Union citizens, on the other.

European citizenship is of key importance as it forms the basis of the political union and the foundation of its democratic legitimacy. It expresses a political relation between the citizens and the Union. To this extent, the basis of the legitimation of the Union now rests upon its citizens.

Furthermore, Union citizenship contributes to the formation of a psychological *community* among the peoples of the Union and the gradual shaping of a substantive consensus between the Union and its

---

[1] Regarding European citizenship see Marias (ed.), *European Citizenship* (1994). See also O'Keeffe, 'Union Citizenship', in O'Keeffe and Twomey (eds), *Legal Issues of the Maastricht Treaty* (1994), pp. 87–107; Closa, 'Citizenship of the Union and Nationality of Member States', in ibid., pp. 109–119; Meehan, 'Citizenship and the European Community', 64 *Political Quarterly* (1993), 172–186, at 185; Closa, 'The Concept of Citizenship in the Treaty on European Union', 29 CML Rev. (1992), 1137–1170; Kovar and Simon, 'La citoyenneté européenne', (1993) CDE, 285–316; Constantinesco, 'La citoyenneté de l'Union', in Schwazze (ed.), *Vom Binnenmarkt zur Europäischen Union* (1993), pp. 25–33.

[2] See Marias, 'From Market Citizen to Union Citizen', in Marias (ed.), *European Citizenship*, pp. 1–24.

citizens. The creation among the peoples of the Union of a feeling of 'belonging to' a *Gemeinschaft* with a common destiny, common beliefs and common values is vital for the creation of real solidarity among Union citizens.

The establishment of European citizenship presupposes a third sphere of rights and duties for Union citizens.[3] These rights are additional[4] to those currently existing either in the national sphere resulting from state citizenship or in the Community sphere resulting from the Treaties of the European Communities. Union citizenship constitutes the very source of Union citizens' rights enumerated in Part Two of the European Community Treaty.

The EC Treaty establishes a catalogue of fundamental rights for Union citizens which provides, *inter alia*, for special non-judicial bodies, competent for safeguarding these rights. According to the EC Treaty, the non-judicial bodies responsible for safeguarding these rights are the Petitions Committee of the European Parliament and the European Ombudsman. These non-judicial bodies, together with the judicial system of the Community, form a broad spectrum guaranteeing the participation of the citizens in the everyday life of the Union.

The purpose of this chapter is to examine the mechanisms for protecting Union citizens' rights. The first part of the chapter will be devoted to examining the non-judicial mechanisms of protection. The second part will cover the judicial mechanisms of protection and will attempt to construct some proposals regarding the improvement of judicial protection in this respect.

---

[3] See Spanish Delegation, Intergovernmental Conference on Political Union, European Citizenship, 21 Feb. 1991, in Marias (ed.), *European Citizenship*, pp. 141–151; Marias, 'From Market Citizen to Union Citizen', p. 17.

[4] See Spanish Delegation, in Marias (ed.), *European Citizenship*, pp. 141–151; Report of the Committee of Institutional Affairs on Union Citizenship, Doc. A3–0300/91, PE 153.099/fin, 10; O'Keeffe, *Union Citizenship*, pp. 102–103; Marias, 'From Market Citizen to Union Citizen', p. 17.

PART ONE

NON-JUDICIAL MECHANISMS OF PROTECTION OF UNION CITIZENS' RIGHTS

1   HISTORICAL BACKGROUND

1.1 The tradition in the Member States of the Union

Non-judicial protection of citizens' rights is very well known in the majority of the Member States of the European Union. The models already followed comprise either Committees on Petition of the national parliaments or national ombudsmen or both. Accordingly, the functioning of the national ombudsmen does not exclude in principle the parallel functioning of the Committees on Petition of the national parliaments.

The main objective of the Committees on Petition of the national parliaments is to guarantee the extra-judicial protection of the rights of the citizens of the Member States.

In the Federal Republic of Germany, petitions committees have been established both at Federal and *Land* level.[5] The Petitions Committee of the German *Bundestag* was set up pursuant to Article 45c(1) of the German Basic Law. The right to petition the *Bundestag* is provided for in Article 17 of the German Basic Law. Pursuant to this article, everyone has the right to address written questions or complaints to the appropriate agencies and to parliamentary bodies. This right can be exercised individually or jointly with others.

When examining petitions the *Bundestag* is obliged to respect the division of powers between the *Bund* and the *Länder* provided for in the Constitution. To this extent, the *Bundestag* is empowered to examine requests concerning Federal legislation or complaints on matters falling under the jurisdiction of the Federal government or Federal agencies.

According to the case law of the Federal Constitutional Court on the right to petition parliamentary bodies or other appropriate agencies, provided for in Article 17 of the German Basic Law, the *Bundestag* is obliged:

(a)   to examine the contents of petitions as to their merits;

---

[5] Regarding the Petitions Committee of the German *Bundestag*, see Peter, 'The Committee on Petitions of the German Bundestag', in Marias (ed.), *The European Ombudsman* (1994), pp. 35–43.

(b) to take a decision on how the petition will be conclusively settled; and

(c) to inform the petitioner of the decision taken.

In the Grand Duchy of Luxembourg, the right to submit petitions is provided for in Articles 27 and 67 of the Constitution.[6] Pursuant to Article 27, everyone has the right individually or jointly with other persons to petition the public authorities of the Grand Duchy. Although Article 27 of the Constitution comes under the heading 'The Luxembourgers and their Rights', the right of petition is not a political right reserved only to the citizens of the Grand Duchy of Luxembourg, but is considered to be a natural right granted to any natural or legal person residing or having its registered office in Luxembourg.

In Belgium, unlike Luxembourg, the law does not impose any requirements as regards admissibility of petitions *ratione materiae*. Accordingly, petitioners have the right to submit requests or complaints concerning a very wide range of issues. In Portugal, it was decided to combine the establishment of the Committee on Petitions of the Portuguese Parliament with the parallel functioning of the office of the *Provedor de Justica* (Ombudsman).

The office of Ombudsman was established for the first time in Scandinavia as a means for the people to defend themselves against administrative abuses. Indeed, it was as early as 1809 that the Swedish Constitution established a justice Ombudsman responsible for supervising public officials and protecting the citizens from bureaucratic practices. In 1915, an independent military Ombudsman was established in Sweden,[7] and in 1919, Finland introduced provisions for the establishment of an Ombudsman into its new Constitution. With the introduction of a military Ombudsman in 1952 in Norway and a general Ombudsman in 1953 in Denmark,[8] Scandinavia strengthened its historical contribution to the protection of citizens' rights.

The Scandinavian experience was followed by the controversial establishment of a military Ombudsman in the Federal Republic of Germany in 1957 and the establishment of general ombudsmen in the United Kingdom in 1967, in France[9] in 1973 and later on in the other

---

[6] See Brasseur, 'La Commission des pétitions de la Chambre des Députés du Grand-duché de Luxembourg', in Marias, ibid., pp. 59–65.

[7] See Eklundh, 'The Scandinavian Model', in Marias, ibid., pp. 11–17.

[8] See Andersen, 'The Danish Ombudsman', in Marias, ibid., pp. 29–35.

[9] See Bardiaux, 'Le modèle continental', in Marias, ibid., pp. 1–11.

Member States. Sweden, Denmark, the United Kingdom and Spain[10] have demonstrated their preference for parliamentary ombudsmen. In France the *Médiateur de la République* enjoys a considerable reputation though he can be approached only through a Member of Parliament. Ombudsmen also function in The Netherlands and Ireland.[11] In Portugal the Ombudsman coexists with the Committee on Petitions of the Portuguese Parliament. In Belgium the Ombudsman[12] of the Flemish Community and the Ombudsman of the city of Antwerp function parallel to the Committee on Petitions of the Belgian Parliament. Italy, following its tradition, has introduced the institution of regional ombudsmen. There has also been a tendency over the past decade for corporations to create their own ombudsmen. Thus, General Electric[13] and Belgacom have established their own ombudsmen.

More specifically, in Sweden, the Parliamentary Ombudsman is empowered to supervise not only the administrative authorities of the state but also the courts. Supervising the courts is not only a Swedish peculiarity—the Finnish Ombudsman possesses similar powers. Moreover, the Swedish Ombudsman is authorized to supervise local government. Unlike his counterparts in Denmark and Norway, he has no authority to supervise cabinet ministers in their role as heads of ministries. The main powers of the Swedish Parliamentary Ombudsman stem from the 1974 Constitution. He also has the right to act as a prosecutor and bring charges against state officials for negligence. His main objective is to safeguard the rights and freedoms of the individual which are laid down in the laws of Sweden.

The Swedish Parliamentary Ombudsman is elected by the *Riksdag*, yet he enjoys complete independence from Parliament. Currently there are four Parliamentary Ombudsmen in Sweden, elected for a period of four years. The annual number of complaints received by the Swedish Ombudsmen amounts to 4,500.

In France, the model which was finally followed was different from that of Sweden. The *Médiateur de la République* was established pursuant to the law of 3 January 1973. He is appointed by Order in Council. He is empowered to examine instances of maladministration by the administrative authorities of the state. The *Médiateur* has the authority to propose recommendations to the relevant service, even if the case has

---

[10] See Retuerto Buades, 'Le médiateur de l'Espagne', in Marias, ibid., pp. 43–53.

[11] See Mills, 'The Irish Ombudsman', in Marias, ibid., pp. 53–59.

[12] See Goorden, 'Le service de médiation en Flandre', in Marias, ibid., pp. 23–29.

[13] See Draetta, 'Towards a New Model: Ombudsman for Multinational Companies', in Marias, ibid., pp. 17–23.

been submitted to court. The powers of the *Médiateur* were considerably extended with the enactment of the law of 24 December 1976. Introducing the notion of equity, the law empowered the *Médiateur* to recommend to the relevant administrative authority any solution which would ease in equity a plaintiff's position should he become aware that the strict application of a law results in an injustice. The *Médiateur's* term of office is six years and he receives no instructions from the government nor from the President of the Republic.

In Spain, the Ombudsman was established by the Constitution in 1978 and started functioning in 1982. He is appointed by the Spanish Parliament and is authorized to investigate complaints submitted not only by Spanish nationals but also foreigners in respect of administrative offices of the state including military and judicial ones. Hence, the Ombudsman has the right to conduct investigations in police stations, prisons and army barracks. He has the right to appear before the Constitutional Tribunal to challenge a law or to protect the freedoms of Spanish citizens. Due to the highly decentralized Spanish political system, the Spanish Ombudsman coordinates his activities with a further seven regional ombudsmen.

1.2 The tradition at the supranational level

The non-judicial protection of the nationals of the Member States was not unknown at the Community level before the adoption of the Maastricht Treaty. Indeed, nationals of the Member States have had the right to submit petitions at the supranational level since 1953 when the ECSC Assembly included petitions in its Rules of Procedure. In 1977, the European Parliament adopted a resolution demanding that the right of petition be granted to the citizens of the Community.[14] After the direct elections of its members, the European Parliament amended its own Rules of Procedure and, in May 1981, formally acknowledged the right of Community citizens to submit petitions.

In May 1981, the European Council, adopting the report of the Addonino Committee on a Citizens' Europe, acknowledged for the first time the political significance of the right of petition.[15]

In 1987, the Committee on Petitions of the European Parliament was created. According to Annex VI of the Rules of Procedure of the European Parliament, this Committee is 'responsible for matters relating to petitions, the examination thereof and the action to be taken thereon'. The details of the functioning of this Committee are provided for in

---

[14] J.O. 1977, C 299/26.

[15] Supplement 7/85 – Bull. EC.

Articles 156, 157 and 158 of the Rules of Procedure of the Parliament.

However, it was only in 1989, with the signing of the Interinstitutional Declaration by the Presidents of the Parliament, the Council and the Commission that Parliament's authority to receive and examine petitions was recognized by the other Community institutions.[16] Yet this authority was not qualified as a right deriving from Community law but as a *custom* of European citizens to petition the European Parliament.

1.3 The Intergovernmental Conference on Political Union

The historical tradition in the Member States of the Community is such that it can hardly be surprising that proposals for a European Ombudsman were submitted at the supranational level. The establishment of a European Ombudsman is closely linked to European citizenship.

The idea of introducing provisions relating to European citizenship into the Treaty on European Union (TEU) was launched by Philippe Gonzales on 4 May 1990, in a letter addressed to the other members of the European Council.[17] Following this letter, the Danish Delegation submitted on 24 September 1990, in the framework of the Intergovernmental Conference on Political Union, a note on citizenship entitled 'The Road to European Union'.[18]

According to the Spanish proposal, the adoption of a catalogue of the special rights of the citizens of the European Union should have been accompanied by establishing special bodies responsible for safeguarding these rights. Therefore, the Spanish Delegation proposed that European citizens should receive greater protection for their rights within the framework of the Union by submitting petitions or complaints to a European Ombudsman,[19] whose function would be, first, to protect the special rights of the European citizen and, secondly, to safeguard these rights. Furthermore, it was proposed that the Ombudsman for European citizens could act either through individual ombudsmen or their equivalents in the various Member States. The Spanish proposal on the European Ombudsman was further endorsed by Denmark, a Member State in which the Ombudsman has proved to be a highly successful institution.

In the Memorandum which the Danish government issued on 4

---

[16] O.J. 1989, C 120/90.

[17] See Ibáñez, 'Spain and European Political Union', in Laursen and Vanhoonacker (eds), *The Intergovernmental Conference on Political Union* (1992), pp. 99–114.

[18] Marias (ed.), *European Citizenship*, pp. 141–151.

[19] Ibid., p. 151.

October 1990,[20] it was stated that in order to strengthen the democratic basis for Community cooperation, an ombudsman system should be introduced under the aegis of the European Parliament. The institution of the European Ombudsman was approved at a political level by the European Council in Rome.

Meeting on 14 and 15 December 1990, the Heads of State or Government of the Twelve stated that consideration should be given to the possible institution of a mechanism to defend citizens' rights as regards Community matters (ombudsman).[21] In implementing such provisions, appropriate consideration should be given to the particular problems of some Member States.

A few months later, on 21 February 1991, the Spanish Delegation submitted a new and more complete proposal on European citizenship.[22] This proposal envisaged European citizenship as one of the three pillars of the European Union and the foundation of its democratic legitimacy. The proposal comprised ten Articles. While Articles 1–8 of the proposal were concerned with the substantive rights of the European citizen, Article 9 was concerned with the machinery for safeguarding these rights. It provided that in each Member State a Mediator was to be appointed to assist the citizens of the Union in the defence of their Union rights before the administrative authorities of the Union and its Member States and to invoke such rights before judicial bodies, either on the Mediator's own account or in support of the persons concerned. Furthermore, the Mediators would also have the task of making clear and complete information available to the citizens of the Union on their rights and the means of enforcing them.

At the same time, the Spanish Delegation indicated, in the form of a footnote,[23] that consideration would also be given to two other possibilities: (a) entrusting the above functions to a European Ombudsman as an independent organ of the Union or one answerable to the European Parliament; and (b) reinforcing the actions of the national Mediators with an Ombudsman acting at the European level.

A few months later, in May 1991, the European Parliament expressed its reservations about the establishment of a European Ombudsman. In the resolution on the deliberations of the Committee on Petitions during the parliamentary year 1990–1991, the European

---

[20] Laursen and Vanhoonacker (eds), *Intergovernmental Conference*, p. 297.

[21] See European Council, Rome 14–15 Dec. 1990, Presidency Conclusions, in Laursen and Vanhoonacker, ibid., p. 320.

[22] Ibid., pp. 325–328.

[23] Ibid., p. 328.

Parliament expressed its opposition to creating a European Ombudsman since this would undermine the power of Parliament and its Committees to supervise the Commission and its departments. It would amount to the creation of a new structure overlapping and detracting from existing ones such as the European Parliament's Committee on Petitions.[24]

Opposing the creation of a European Ombudsman was nothing new for the European Parliament. As early as 1985, the European Parliament had taken the view that the existing differences between national legal systems and the Community legal system made it impossible purely and simply to transpose the institution of the Ombudsman into the Community system.[25]

The same reservations were expressed not only by the European Parliament but also by the national ombudsmen and the chairmen of the national parliamentary petitions committees in a meeting held on 19 March 1991, at which the Commission presented the plans for the establishment of a European Ombudsman, discussed in the framework of the Intergovernmental Conference on Political Union.[26]

What are of importance are the European Parliament's views that the Committee on Petitions itself had the potential to develop into a kind of European Ombudsman without the drawbacks of having to set up a new body and incorporate it into the national legal system.

It is obvious from the above that the creation of the European Ombudsman had to cope with reality, that is to say, to coexist with the Committee on Petitions of the European Parliament, the national ombudsmen and the petitions committees of the national parliaments; it had to respect the functioning of these bodies and, furthermore, take care not to jeopardize them.

Accordingly, the Luxembourg Presidency issued its draft Treaty on the European Union, which can be characterized as a masterpiece of compromise. To this extent the draft Treaty provided for the first time a legal basis in Community law for the right to petition the European Parliament, which until then had been characterized as a custom.[27] At

---

[24] See the Report of the Committee on Petitions on the deliberations of the Committee on Petitions during the parliamentary year 1990–1991, Doc. A3–0122/91, PE 150.218/fin.

[25] See report of Mr Chanterie on behalf of the Committee on the Rules of Procedure and Petitions, Doc. A2–41/85, resolutions adopted on 14 June 1985, O.J. 1985, C 175/273.

[26] See the V. Reading Report on the deliberations of the Committee on Petitions during the parliamentary year 1990–1991, Doc. A3–0122/91, PE 150.218/fin, 8–19.

[27] See Interinstitutional Declaration by the Presidents of the Parliament, the Council and the Commission, O.J. 1989, C 120/90. Regarding the right to petition the European Parliament see Marias, 'The Right to Petition the European Parliament after Maastricht', 19 EL

the same time it restricted to some extent citizens' rights to petition the European Parliament by introducing a condition under which petitions to the European Parliament would not be admissible unless they directly concerned the petitioner.

On the other hand, while the draft Treaty provided for the creation of the European Ombudsman, it limited his jurisdiction only to examining instances of maladministration in the activities of the Community institutions or bodies. It also subordinated the Ombudsman to the European Parliament by providing that the latter should elect the European Ombudsman. It could hardly be argued that this compromise had failed to satisfy both Community and national actors. However, we could question whether this compromise was in the interest of the citizens of the Union, for whom, in the final analysis, the European Ombudsman was supposed to have been established.

2   THE TREATY ON EUROPEAN UNION

2.1 *The legal basis of the right to petition the European Parliament and the right to apply to the European Ombudsman*

According to Article 8d EC Treaty, every citizen of the Union has the right to address a *petition* to the European Parliament in accordance with the provisions of Article 138d EC.

Article 138d EC Treaty extends the right of petition beyond European citizens towards other categories of persons. Accordingly, any natural or legal person residing or having his or her registered office in a Member State has the right to address a petition, individually or in association with other citizens or persons, to the European Parliament on a matter which comes within the Community's fields of activity and which affects him or her directly.

Thus, it is very significant not only for the European Parliament, but also for the citizens of the European Union that the Maastricht Treaty provides for the right to submit petitions. This is because, first, petitions acquire a legal basis in the Treaties; secondly, because petitions are transformed from a Community custom to a right arising from the Treaties; and finally, because the role of the European Parliament is strengthened as it is less dependent on the Commission's willingness to cooperate since it can ask the national authorities for

---

Rev. (1994), 169–181; Pliakos, 'Les conditions d'exercice du droit de pétition', (1993) CDE, 317–350; O'Keeffe, 'Union Citizenship', pp. 100–102; Marias, 'Le droit de pétition devant le Parlement européen', in Marias (ed.), *European Citizenship*, pp. 81–101.

information directly.

The right to apply to the European Ombudsman is explicitly provided for in the Treaties establishing the European Communities, as amended by the TEU. According to Article 8d EC Treaty, every citizen of the Union may apply to the Ombudsman established in accordance with Article 138e.

Article 138e EC Treaty extends the right to apply to the European Ombudsman to other categories of persons as well as European citizens. Accordingly, the European Ombudsman is empowered to receive *complaints* from any natural or legal person residing or having his or her registered office in a Member State in respect of instances of maladministration in the Community institutions or bodies, with the exception of the Court of Justice of the European Communities (ECJ) and the Court of First Instance acting in their judicial role. Furthermore, the same rights are provided for in Article 20d of the ECSC Treaty and Article 107d of the EURATOM Treaty.

Provisions on the right to apply to the European Ombudsman may also be found in the European Parliament Decision on the regulations and general conditions governing the performance of the European Ombudsman's duties. According to the fourth paragraph of Article 138e EC Treaty, the European Parliament shall, after seeking an opinion from the Commission and with the approval of the Council acting on a qualified majority, lay down the regulations and general conditions governing the performance of the Ombudsman's duties.

On 25 October 1993, an Interinstitutional Conference took place in Luxembourg. The Conference led to the adoption of an Interinstitutional Declaration on Democracy, Transparency and Subsidiarity.[28] Furthermore, the European Parliament, the Council and the Commission, as institutions of the European Union, established in the framework of the Conference three separate Interinstitutional Agreements:

(a)   on the procedures for implementing the principle of subsidiarity;

(b)   on the arrangements for the proceedings of the Conciliation Committee under Article 189b EC Treaty;

(c)   on the draft Decision of the European Parliament laying down the regulations and general conditions governing the performance of the Ombudsman's duties.[29]

---

[28] See European Parliament, Session Documents 27 Oct. 1993, PE 164.781; and Bull. EC 10–1993, 118–119.

[29] Bull. EC 10–1993, 5–10.

Following this, the European Parliament adopted, in its November 1993 plenary session, a Resolution on the afore-mentioned Interinstitutional Agreements approving, *inter alia*, the Decision on the regulations and general conditions governing the performance of the Ombudsman's duties[30] and instructed its President to sign this Decision and to publish it in the *Official Journal of the European Communities* as soon as the Council had given its formal approval.

2.2 Admissibility of petitions and complaints

The examination of the admissibility of petitions and complaints is divided into two stages. The first stage concerns formal admissibility while the second one concerns substantive admissibility.

The examination of *formal admissibility* covers the question of whether the petitions or complaints submitted show: the name and surname, the occupation, the nationality, the permanent address of each petitioner or applicant and whether they are signed by them. In the case of legal persons, the petition or complaint must show: the title of the legal person, the activity pursued, the Member State in which its offices are registered and the address of its offices.

As regards *petitions, substantive admissibility* has three facets: (1) admissibility *ratione personae*; (2) admissibility *ratione materiae*; and (3) the *locus standi* of the petitioner.

(1) Admissibility *ratione personae*. The persons benefiting from the right of petition can be divided into the following four categories:

(a) citizens of the European Union;
(b) residents of Member States;
(c) legal persons with their registered offices in a Member State;
(d) non-resident citizens of third countries and legal persons with registered offices outside the Community.

(2) Admissibility *ratione materiae*. According to Article 138d EC Treaty, the petition submitted must come within the Community's fields of activity. The same wording was also used in Article 128(1) of the old Rules of Procedure of the European Parliament, prior to their amendment in January 1993.

On the other hand, paragraph 4 of Article 156 of the Rules of Procedure provides that the petitions entered in the register shall be forwarded by the President to the Committee responsible, which shall first ascertain whether the petitions registered fall within the sphere of

---

[30] See Doc. A3–0356/93, PE 207.045/fin, 15 Nov. 1993; and Minutes of 17 Nov. 1993, Part II, Item 5, Annex, PE 176.643, 57–63.

activities of the European Union. This difference is of great importance as the Union's fields of activity are much wider than that of the Community's.

Can we attribute this inconsistency to an accidental mistake that occurred during the legislative process? This can hardly be true as the same wording is also used in the first paragraph of Article 156 of the Rules of Procedure which provides that petitions should fall within the sphere of activities of the European Union.

The manner in which the Committee on Petitions intends to solve this problem remains to be seen. We can only speculate on the outcome, which most probably will favour the broad application of the relevant Article and will treat as admissible petitions coming within the Union's fields of activity rather than those of the Community.

(3) *Locus standi* of the petitioner. According to Article 138d EC Treaty, the matter contained in the petition addressed to the European Parliament must affect the petitioner directly. The same wording was also reproduced in the first paragraph of Article 156 of the Rules of Procedure of the European Parliament.

To this extent, the TEU has added a new requirement for the admissibility of petitions. Under what circumstances, therefore, can the matter contained in the petition affect the petitioner directly? Unfortunately, neither the TEU nor the Rules of Procedure of the European Parliament provide any indication on that. This new requirement suggests the following points:

(a) The *locus standi* of the petitioner has been restricted in comparison to that already existing before the signing of the Maastricht Treaty.

(b) As a matter that comes within the Community's fields of activity may affect more people directly, it is not necessary for the petitioner to prove exclusive interest. This is quite true of matters related to environmental pollution where many people are affected simultaneously and directly.

(c) The fears expressed in the 1990–1991 Annual Report of the Committee on Petitions have proved very real, namely that the introduction of the condition that the petitioner should be directly concerned as an individual in order to submit a petition would significantly restrict citizens' rights.[31]

(d) The Committee on Petitions has been aware of such a danger and has already advocated, in its opinion on the results of the

---

[31] Doc. A3–0122/91, PE 150.218/fin, 7.

Intergovernmental Conference and the TEU, annexed to the Martin Report, the need to interpret generously the provision in question.[32]

(e) In view of the deletion from Article 156 of the Rules of Procedure of requests as a category qualifying for petition, one could argue that petitions calling upon the European Parliament to adopt a position on a general problem which does not affect the petitioner directly might be treated as inadmissible.

(f) As the right of petition is mainly a political right ensuring that the Community operates democratically and takes into account the aspirations of the citizens, the expression in question does not mean that the petitioner should always have to prove a material or a moral personal interest in the matter contained in the petition. Such cases, even though no personal material or moral interest is involved, could affect the citizens of the Union directly: for example, petitions on organ transplants[33] or on the consequences of the civil war in Bosnia-Herzegovina,[34] or on apartheid in South Africa.[35]

(g) As petitions constitute both an indicator and a means of contributing to the democratic running of the Community, it is not to be expected that the Committee on Petitions will abide by a very narrow interpretation of the *locus standi* of petitioners.

As regards *complaints, substantive admissibility* has two facets: (1) admissibility *ratione personae;* and (2) admissibility *ratione materiae.*

As opposed to Article 138d EC Treaty regarding petitions, Article 138e EC Treaty does not provide that the complaint addressed to the European Ombudsman must affect the applicant directly. In this respect, we cannot agree with the Committee on Petitions of the European Parliament, which has stated that it is essential to require a direct interest in the matter for the submission of an application to the

---

[32] See the Opinion delivered by the Committee on Petitions for the Committee on Institutional Affairs on the results of the Intergovernmental Conference and the Treaty on European Union, PE 156.133/fin annexed to the Martin Report Doc. A3–123/92/Part II, PE 155.444/fin.

[33] See Petition No. 659/92.

[34] See Petition No. 27/93 submitted by 'Ecologic Autogestion' on ending the conflict in the former Yugoslavia.

[35] See Petition No. 424/90.

Ombudsman.[36] Therefore, any attempt to establish a third facet in the process of substantive admissibility, *inter alia*, the *locus standi* of the applicant, will amount to a restriction of the right to apply to the Ombudsman, and would be contrary to the European Community Treaties.

(1) Admissibility *ratione personae*. The persons benefiting from the right to apply to the European Ombudsman can be divided into the following three categories:

(a)   citizens of the European Union;
(b)   residents of the Member States;
(c)   legal persons with their registered offices in a Member State.

(2) Admissibility *ratione materiae*. According to Article 138e EC Treaty, complaints received by the Ombudsman must concern instances of maladministration in the activities of the Community institutions or bodies with the exception of the ECJ and the Court of First Instance acting in their judicial role.

There are three key issues regarding admissibility *ratione materiae:*

(a)   the meaning of the expression 'instances of maladministration';
(b)   the determination of the Community institutions or bodies referred to in Article 138e EC Treaty;
(c)   whether national authorities responsible for implementing Community law could be put under the surveillance of the European Ombudsman.

As there is no indication either in the EC Treaty or in the European Parliament Decision on the European Ombudsman's duties as to the possible meaning of the expression 'instances of maladministration', we might state that the term could comprise, *inter alia*, administrative irregularities; administrative omissions; abuse of power by the Community administration or its officials; administrative actions taken as a result of negligence; administrative actions based on illegal procedures; administrative actions which violate the notion of equity; malfunction, incompetence, delay or non-response of the Community administration in its relations with the citizens of the Union.

While determining the Community institutions or bodies whose activities can be scrutinized by the European Ombudsman does not pose any real problem, the question of whether national authorities implementing Community law could be placed under the surveillance

---

[36] Opinion delivered by Committee on Petitions, see note 32 above, 126.

of the European Ombudsman is more important, as there are plenty of Community powers exercised by national authorities.

According to the first paragraph of Article 2 of the European Parliament Decision on the Ombudsman's duties, no action by any authority or person not referred to in Article 138e EC Treaty may be the subject of a complaint to the Ombudsman. The same view prevails also in the framework of the Committee on Petitions which has stated, *inter alia*, that the European Ombudsman was excluded by the Treaties from investigating the actions of the national authorities even in cases where they are responsible for implementing Community law.[37]

According to Article 2(4) of the European Parliament Decision on the Ombudsman's duties, a complaint should be made *within two years* from the date on which the facts on which it is based came to the attention of the person lodging the complaint. Pursuant to Article 2(4) of the above European Parliament Decision, the complaint must be preceded by the appropriate administrative approaches to the institutions and bodies concerned. The action to be undertaken by the European Ombudsman could be limited in the following two circumstances:

(a) The Ombudsman may not question the soundness of a Court's ruling.

(b) The Ombudsman is under an obligation to declare a complaint inadmissible or terminate his consideration of it if he learns that the facts to which it refers have been subject to legal proceedings which are in progress or have been concluded.

2.3 Consideration of substance

2.3.1 Petitions

When the petition has been declared admissible it can be forwarded:

(a) to the Commission with a request for action or information;

(b) to the Parliament's services, mainly to the legal service or the Directorate-General for Research;

(c) to other Parliamentary Committees; or

(d) by the President of the Parliament to the national authorities for an *amicable solution.*

Furthermore, the Committee on Petitions, following its meeting with the national ombudsmen and the chairmen of the national parliamentary

---

[37] Opinion delivered by Committee on Petitions, see note 32 above, 125–126.

committees on petition, which took place in April 1989, advises petitioners to approach the ombudsmen or the relevant petitions committees of the countries concerned when petitions can be examined better at national level.

From the above procedures, the most interesting, from a legal point of view, is when the Committee forwards a request for action or information to the Commission. In such a case, as we have already stated, if the Commission considers that the Member State concerned has breached its Treaty obligations, it can institute proceedings under Article 169 EC Treaty against it. The action already undertaken by the Commission in recent years is very interesting.

(a) As a result of Petition No. 56/85 the Commission used Article 169 EC Treaty against The Netherlands because Dutch legislation obliged nationals of other Member States entering the country to give information regarding the purpose of their trip and the economic means for their subsistence.

(b) Furthermore, as a result of Petitions Nos. 198/86, 397/87, 270/88 and 43/89 submitted by several Belgian nationals complaining that France refused to recognize physiotherapy diplomas obtained in another Member State, the Commission instituted proceedings under Article 169 EC Treaty against France.

(c) The same legal situation arose with Greece, Italy and Spain when petitions were submitted against them complaining that nationals of other Member States were charged higher entrance fees to Greek, Italian and Spanish museums than Greek, Italian and Spanish nationals respectively.

(d) After the submission of Petition No. 686/88 expressing serious concern about the preservation of a lake in Greece, the Commission instituted proceedings under Article 169 EC Treaty against the Hellenic Republic.

(e) In Petition No. 126/89, a cultural institute in Belgium complained that the Belgian customs authorities levied charges on small packets from other Member States containing samples of non-commercial value (books and records). The Commission found that this practice was in breach of Article 5(6) of the 6th VAT Directive and commenced proceedings under Article 169 EC Treaty against Belgium.

It follows from the above that petitions constitute an essential means at the disposal of Union citizens who can address themselves to the European Parliament on issues concerning the application of Community law not only in their own Member States but also in the territory of the other Member States provided they are affected directly.

The important function of petitions as a source for tracing violations in the Member States has also recently been acknowledged by the Commission. In the 1992 Commission Report on the Monitoring of the Application of Community Law, the Commission acknowledged that petitions were the cause for the institution of proceedings under Article 169 EC Treaty in thirty-three cases.[38] At its meeting in November 1989, the Committee decided not to close consideration of petitions on the basis of which proceedings under Article 169 EC Treaty had been instituted but had not reached the point of referral to the ECJ. So while negotiations are under way between the Member State in question and the Commission, the Committee on Petitions can still intervene in favour of the petitioner. On the other hand, it was decided to close consideration of a petition once the matter was before the ECJ as it was clear that Parliament could do nothing more to assist the petitioner.

According to the Annual Reports of the Committee on Petitions of the European Parliament, the number of petitions submitted to it is continually rising. Table 1 shows the trends.[39] For the parliamentary years 1992–1993 and 1993–1994, the breakdown of petitions by petitioner's nationality and country in which the problem arose is shown in Table 2.[40]

There has been a significant increase in mass petitions. It is worth mentioning that Petition No. 280/91, submitted by the British Union for the Abolition of Vivisection, opposing the testing of cosmetic products on animals, was signed by 2,500,000 petitioners. Petition No. 250/91 regarding cruelty to animals was signed by 1,000,000 petitioners and Petition No. 322/93 on ill-treatment inflicted on animals for slaughter during transport was signed by 362,797 petitioners.

Regarding mass petitions, the total number of persons who signed them in the parliamentary year 1993–1994 amounts to 609,650, compared with 295,361 for the parliamentary year 1992–1993. The total

---

[38] See EC Commission, Tenth Annual Report on the Monitoring of the Application of Community Law, COM (93) 320 final, 28 April 1993, 147.

[39] The table is based on data taken from the R. Chanterie Report on the deliberations of the Committee on Petitions during the parliamentary year 1987–1988, Doc. A2–0044/88, PE 121.221/fin 87, 7; and the Gil Robles Gil–Delgado Report on the work of the Committee on Petitions for the parliamentary year 1992–1993, 7 April 1993, PE 204.386, 8.

[40] The table is based on data taken from the Gil Robles Gil–Delgado Report on the work of the Committee on Petitions during the parliamentary year 1992–1993, 7 April 1993, PE 204.386, 8; and the Barbara Schmidbauer Report on the work of the Committee on Petitions for the parliamentary year 1993–1994, Doc. A3–0158/94, PE 208.029, 17.

number of persons who have submitted mass petitions during the electoral term 1989–1994 exceeds 5.5 million. According to the data submitted by the Committee on Petitions during the same electoral term, the European Parliament received 4,236 petitions compared to 1,862 petitions for the previous electoral term 1984–1989.

Table 1 □ *Petitions submitted to the European Parliament, 1977–1994*

Parliamentary session	No.
1977–78	20
1979–80	57
1980–81	81
1981–82	44
1982–83	78
1983–84	100
1984–85	170
1985–86	234
1986–87	279
1987–88	487
1988–89	692
1989–90	774
1990–91	785
1991–92	694
1992–93	900
1993–94	1,083

Petitions are important for the European Parliament as they constitute a permanent link with the citizens of the Union. It is a means of contact with the Union's citizens which allows them to gain a better understanding of the institutions' roles and workings. Petitions are also a very effective means for the European Parliament to verify the application of Community law and to resolve the problems brought to light. In this respect their use strengthens the role of the European Parliament in the institutional framework and reinforces its powers to exercise control.

As a democratically elected body, Parliament uses petitions as a means of establishing a permanent dialogue with the citizens of the Union and as an opportunity for demonstrating its willingness to listen to their problems. At the same time, by submitting petitions, the citizens have a chance to participate directly in the political life of the Community.

Table 2 □ *Breakdown of petitions to the European Parliament by petitioner's nationality and country in which problem arose*

	Nationality		Country	
	1992–93	1993–94	1992–93	1993–94
Germany	195	265	111	157
Belgium	39	46	37	49
Denmark	6	5	7	8
Spain	104	127	115	135
France	104	155	97	135
Greece	58	68	59	74
Ireland	21	27	19	19
Italy	87	138	73	123
Luxembourg	6	10	2	10
The Netherlands	24	33	18	29
Portugal	117	46	117	40
UK	132	118	104	86
Various Member States	–	–	115	172
Extra-Community	–	21	66	95

As the content of petitions often points to genuine needs or expresses a general feeling of unease, the European Parliament has emphasized the need for each citizen of the Union to be made fully aware of this right and the conditions under which it can be exercised.

2.3.2 Complaints

If the complaint has been declared admissible, the European Ombudsman must, without delay, inform the person lodging the complaint in writing of the action he has taken on it.

Furthermore, according to Article 2 of the European Parliament Decision on the Ombudsman's duties, the Ombudsman must:

(a) help to uncover maladministration in the activities of the Community institutions and bodies referred to in Article 138e EC; and

(b) make recommendations with a view to putting an end to it.

In this framework the European Ombudsman has the right to conduct *enquiries* which he deems necessary to clarify the instance of maladministration which constitutes the object of the complaint.

Moreover, the Ombudsman is obliged to inform the institution or body concerned of such action. In such a case, the institution under question may submit any useful comment to the Ombudsman. It is worth mentioning at this point that the Ombudsman can also undertake the same action on his own initiative. In this instance, action on the European Ombudsman's initiative could be justified if he receives cognizance of certain instances of maladministration due to reports in the press or on television or through a European Parliament Resolution.

We could describe this first stage of action as *a preliminary investigation*. The main purpose of this stage is to gather the information required in order to draw a preliminary conclusion on whether or not the alleged instances of maladministration took place.

Community institutions and Member States are obliged to *cooperate* with the Ombudsman in order to help him in the performance of his duties. The exact scope of this duty is clarified by the Treaties and by the European Parliament Decision on the Ombudsman's duties.

The Ombudsman's powers to have access to the relevant files was an issue of disagreement between the European Parliament and the Council. The issue was finally resolved on 25 October 1993 with the signing of the Interinstitutional Agreement on the Ombudsman's duties.[41] According to Article 3 of the European Parliament Decision on the Ombudsman's duties, the Community institutions and bodies concerned are obliged to (a) supply the European Ombudsman with the requested information; and (b) to give him or the members of his secretariat access to the relevant files. It is worth mentioning that in this instance Community institutions and bodies have the right to refuse only on duly substantiated grounds of secrecy.

Moreover, they are obliged to give access to documents originating in a Member State and classed as secret by law or regulation only where that Member State has given its prior agreement. Regarding other documents originating in a Member State, Community institutions or bodies shall give access only after having informed the Member State concerned.

Determining the relations between the European Ombudsman and the authorities of the Member States was also an issue of disagreement between the European Parliament and the Council. The agreement reached on this point by Parliament and the Council is laid down in the third paragraph of Article 3 of the European Parliament Decision on the Ombudsman's duties. Pursuant to this paragraph, the Ombudsman may, via the Permanent Representations of the Member States to the

---

[41] See above, note 28.

European Communities, request from the Member States' authorities any information that may help to clarify instances of maladministration by Community institutions or bodies. In such a case the Member States' authorities are obliged to provide the information requested. They can refuse only if the information is covered by laws or regulations on secrecy or by provisions preventing its being communicated.

The main purpose of the European Ombudsman is to seek a solution with the institution concerned in order to eliminate the instance of maladministration and to satisfy the request of the person lodging the complaint. Should the Ombudsman find that there has been maladministration, he must inform the institution or body concerned and may suggest ways of remedying the matter. In this case, the institution, thus informed, is obliged to send the Ombudsman a reasoned opinion within three months.

For each case of maladministration found, the European Ombudsman must send a *report* to the European Parliament and to the institution concerned. The Ombudsman may propose solutions and measures to be taken in the future. Furthermore, the Ombudsman informs the person lodging the complaint of the outcome of the enquiries, of the opinion expressed by the institution concerned and of any recommendations made by him. At the end of each annual session the Ombudsman shall submit to the European Parliament a report on the outcome of his enquiries.

The Ombudsman and his staff are obliged not to divulge information or documents which they may obtain in the course of their enquiries. They are also obliged to treat in confidence any information which could harm the person lodging the complaint or any other person involved.

PART TWO

JUDICIAL MECHANISMS OF PROTECTION OF UNION CITIZENS' RIGHTS

1   INTRODUCTION

The judicial protection of European citizenship is essential for Union citizens. The system of the Treaty on European Union (TEU) does not provide any new judicial mechanisms in this respect. In fact, the High Contracting Parties, following the proposal of the Commission submitted in the framework of the Intergovernmental Conference on Political Union, included the relevant provisions on Union citizenship in the EC Treaty.[42]

This solution was clearly the correct one. For if the provisions on European citizenship had been included in the introductory Articles of the TEU, the relevant Union rights would have lacked any judicial enforcement at the supranational level due to Article L of the Maastricht Treaty, which provides that the ECJ has jurisdiction only regarding disputes arising under the EC, ECSC and EURATOM Treaties as well as under Article K.3(2c) and Articles L–S TEU. Consequently, provisions on the citizenship of the Union were included in Part Two of the EC Treaty even before the titles devoted to the four freedoms.

As Union citizens' rights are not set out in the Preamble or the introductory articles of the TEU, but in the EC Treaty, and more precisely under the title 'Foundations of the Community', nobody could argue that the relevant provisions on European citizenship are just declaratory clauses. On the contrary, the Articles on European citizenship constitute binding provisions which the institutions of the Union, the Member States and private individuals are obliged to respect in full. Consequently, the judicial protection afforded to Union citizens' fundamental rights, flowing from European citizenship, is the one already existing regarding all the other relevant economic or social rights guaranteed by Community primary or secondary law.

The judicial system of the Community is well known and needs no analysis in the framework of this chapter. Accordingly, the chapter will go on to examine only certain questions regarding the judicial protection of the fundamental Union citizens' rights enumerated in Article 8a–d EC Treaty, such as the direct effect of the relevant Treaty provi-

---

[42] See Commission of the EC, Union Citizenship, Supplement 2/91 – Bull. EC, 87.

sions, and the need for more strict judicial scrutiny when fundamental Union citizens' rights are at stake.

2   DIRECT EFFECT OF TREATY PROVISIONS ON EUROPEAN CITIZENSHIP

The direct effect of Treaty provisions was a popular subject among Community scholars in the 1970s. In fact, it was established as a notion by the case law of the ECJ in the 1960s. Giving its judgment in the famous *Van Gend en Loos* case, the ECJ held, *inter alia*, that Article 12 of the Treaty was capable of producing direct effects on the relationship between Member States and their subjects.

The question of whether a Treaty provision is directly effective is settled every time in an authoritative way by the ECJ itself. One need only recall that in doing so the ECJ examines:

(a)   whether the provision in question contains a clear obligation on the Member State;
(b)   whether the provision is clear and unconditional;
(c)   whether its operation is dependent on further action being taken either by Community institutions or by Member States.

Moreover, according to the case law of the ECJ, the direct effect of Treaty provisions is not limited to the relationship between private parties and Member States but also concerns the mutual relationship between private parties.[43]

To date, the ECJ has not had the chance of making any declaration on the direct effect of Treaty provisions concerning Articles 8a–8d EC. It appears from the relevant Treaty provisions that the right to vote and stand as a candidate at municipal elections and at the elections to the European Parliament are not directly effective as the operation of these rights depends on the taking of further action by Community institutions.

More precisely, with regard to the right to vote and stand as a candidate at municipal elections, Article 8b(1) EC Treaty provides that this right shall be exercised subject to the adoption of detailed arrangements before 31 December 1994 by the Council, acting on a proposal from the Commission and after consulting the European Parliament.

An analogous condition was provided by the second paragraph of

---

[43] Case 43/75, *Gabrielle Defrenne* v *Société Anonyme Belge de Navigation Aérienne Sabena*, [1976] ECR 455, at 474.

the same article regarding the right to vote and stand for election in the elections to the European Parliament. Thus, the Council, acting unanimously on a proposal from the Commission and after consulting Parliament, was obliged to adopt, before 31 December 1993, the necessary detailed arrangements for the exercise of this right. Thus, Council Directive 93/109 of 6 December 1993 was adopted.

Article 8a EC Treaty, concerning the right to move and the right to reside freely within the territory of the Member States, does seem capable of producing direct effects. The exercise of these rights is not dependent on further action being taken by Community institutions, as the second paragraph of Article 8a provides that the measures to be taken by the Council first depend on its discretion and, secondly, may be adopted with a view *to facilitating the exercise* of these rights.[44]

Of course, it is a matter for the ECJ to decide whether Article 8a is capable of producing direct effects. In doing so, the ECJ will be obliged to take into account that this Treaty provision provides that the right to move and to reside freely within the territory of the Member States is subject to the limitations and conditions laid down in the Treaty and by the measures adopted to give it effect. The right to diplomatic and consular protection is not capable of producing direct effects either as it is dependent on further action to be taken by the Member States. This action has to be taken both at the supranational and international level. Accordingly, the Member States were obliged to establish the necessary rules among themselves before 13 December 1993 and to start the international negotiations required to secure the diplomatic and consular protection of Union citizens.

3   EUROPEAN CITIZENSHIP AND THE DOUBLE STANDARD DOCTRINE

According to Article 8a EC Treaty, Union citizens' rights to move and reside freely within the territory of the Member States are subject to the limitations and conditions laid down in the Treaty and by measures adopted to give it effect. Moreover, the Council may adopt provisions with a view to facilitating the exercise of these rights.

Article 8b provides that the rights to vote and stand as a candidate both at municipal elections and in the elections to the European Parliament shall be exercised subject to the adoption of detailed arrangements

---

[44] See also Wouters, 'European Citizenship and the Case Law of the Court of Justice of the European Communities on the Free Movement of Persons', in Marias (ed.), *European Citizenship*, pp. 48–50, and the EC Commission's answer to parliamentary question No. 2958/92, O.J. 1993, C 264/4–5.

by the Council, acting unanimously on a proposal from the Commission, and after consulting the European Parliament. These arrangements may provide for derogations justified by problems specific to a Member State. Finally, the Council may adopt provisions to strengthen or to add to the enumerated Union rights (Article 8e). Hence, the role of the Council in deciding upon the strengthening of Union rights, and the conditions for limiting or derogating from them, is crucial.

What are the limits of the powers of the Council acting in this context? Can the Member States and individuals challenge the Council decisions and, if so, on what grounds? What is the margin of discretion of the Council to appreciate the political situation in the Union and in the Member States when deciding to limit Union rights or to enact measures derogating from them?

According to the case law of the ECJ, Community institutions enjoy a wide measure of discretion when evaluating a complex economic or social situation, in the light of which they have to take a binding decision.[45] This discretion is not unlimited and can be subject to judicial review. In exercising a judicial review of the legality of the exercise of such discretion the ECJ confines itself only to examining:

(a) whether the exercise of the discretion contains a manifest error; or
(b) constitutes a misuse of power; or
(c) whether the Community authority clearly did not exceed the bounds of its discretion.[46]

Contrary to what applies regarding economic and social rights, a different approach appears necessary when the fundamental Union citizens' rights enumerated in Articles 8a–8d EC Treaty are at stake. In such cases, the judicial control of the ECJ should be both stricter and more scrutinized.[47]

Limiting the discretion of Community institutions in this field is essential. The ECJ should here become the ultimate guarantor of the political rights of Union citizens. Accordingly, the ECJ should introduce a double-standard doctrine when reviewing the discretion of Commu-

---

[45] See Case 29/77, *S.A. Roquette Frères* v *French State—Administration des Douanes*, [1977] ECR 1835, at 1843.

[46] See Case 13/57, *Wirtschaftsvereinigung Eisen- und Stahlindustrie Gussstahlwerk Carl Bönnhoff, Gussstahlwerk Witten Ruhrstahl and Eisenwerk Annahütte Alfred Zeller* v *High Authority of the European Coal and Steel Community*, [1957–58] ECR 265, at 282.

[47] Regarding European citizenship and the double-standard doctrine see Marias, 'From Market Citizen to Union Citizen', pp. 19–20.

nity institutions in cases of alleged violations of the political rights of Union citizens.

The introduction of a *European-style footnote 4*[48] could mean:

(a) that the presumption of legality of Community measures is to be abandoned if the measures fall within the purview of political rights of the Union citizens;

(b) that alleged infringements of the economic and social rights of the citizens of the Union would be subjected to the minimal Court inquiry analysed above, but Community measures touching the political rights would receive a more strict juridical scrutiny;

(c) that Community legislation affecting either those political processes essential for the democratic systems of the Member States required by the TEU[49] or the legitimate and vital political interests of small Member States would also be subjected to more rigorous judicial inquiry by the ECJ than would legislation affecting economic processes;

(d) that the burden of proof should be placed on the Community institutions to show the need to take the measures in question.

---

[48] See case *United States* v *Carolene Products Co*, 304 US 144, 58 S.Ct 778,2 L.Ed. 1234 (1938) where Justice Stone, who wrote the Supreme Court's opinion, inserted a footnote to that opinion in which he stated that the standard for judicial review of legislation in respect of which a violation of civil rights had been claimed should be stricter than a judicial review of legislation in respect of which a violation of economic rights had been claimed.

[49] See Art. F(1) TEU.

INDEX